THE
DRAGON'S
PROPHECY

JONATHAN CAHN

FRONT
LINE

For more resources like this, visit MyCharismaShop.com and the author's
websites at jonathancahn.com and booksbyjonathancahn.com.

Cataloging-in-Publication Data is on file with the Library of Congress.
International Standard Book Number: 978-1-63641-399-0
E-book ISBN: 978-1-63641-400-3

2 2024
Printed in the United States of America

Most Charisma Media products are available at special quantity discounts
for bulk purchase for sales promotions, premiums, fund-raising, and
educational needs. For details, call us at (407) 333-0600 or visit our website
at www.charismamedia.com.

And another sign appeared in heaven:
behold, a great, fiery red dragon.

—Revelation 12:3

CONTENTS

PART VI: PREDATORS AND PREY

PART VII: DAY OF THE DRAGON

PART VIII: THE MYSTERY OF GAZA

PART IX: THE TRANSMISSION OF SPIRITS

PART X: THE DRAGON'S FLOOD

PART XI: THE UNHOLY DAYS

PART XII: THE END OF DAYS

PART XIII: SECRET ON THE MOUNT

PART XIV: THE OTHERS

PART XV: THE DRAGON SLAYERS

Part I

THE
MYSTERY

Chapter 1

THE MYSTERY BEHIND THE WORLD

THERE IS MORE to the world than what we see with our eyes.

———————————■■■———————————

Behind the perceivable realm lies another, beyond our ability to measure or quantify.

Behind the history of this world lies another, unrecorded, unrecited, unknown.

And behind that which moves and transforms the world lie unseen forces, causes, and agents, undying and primeval.

Could such things actually lie behind specific events of the modern world?

Have we been given warnings concerning such things in the writings of past ages, warnings of one specific force and agent?

And could that force and agent lie behind the rise of wars, evils, and calamities?

Could it have orchestrated an event that recently shocked our world, and did that event contain a mystery concerning the end of the age?

Are we all players in a mystery that began long before we were born, that has spanned the ages, and has, in modern times, threatened the future of our planet?

Was it all foretold in the words of an ancient prophecy?

Are we living in the last of days?

What does the future hold, and where does it all lead?

What is the mystery of the Dragon?

And what does all this have to do with you who are now reading these words?

———————————■■■———————————

This book will answer those questions and in the process reveal the mysteries of...

the dark resurrection,

the return of the Sea Peoples,

the revenge of the three thousand,

the black Sabbath,

the Shephelah,

the Dragon's holiday,

the secret on the mount,

the 18,263rd day,

the colors of the apocalypse,

the Beast,

the ancient vision that unlocks what is taking place in our world
and what is yet to come,

and more.

———————■■■———————

It all began on a Friday night in October.

Chapter 2

OCTOBER

THIS WAS NOT the book I had planned to write. That book was to be the sequel to *The Return of the Gods*. But what happened across the world would combine with a strong leading in my spirit that the book I was about to write was for a future time. Another mystery was now to be opened.

It was October. I was preparing the message to share at the Friday night service of the worship center I lead in Wayne, New Jersey, *Beth Israel*. I was led to speak on one of the mysteries from the previous book I had written, which had just been released a month earlier, *The Josiah Manifesto*.

The following morning, Hamas would launch a mass invasion from the Gaza Strip into the land of Israel. Israel would be taken by surprise. What happened that day would shock the sensibilities of many around the world. It would also be the manifestation of the mystery I had shared the night before.

The mystery foreshadowed a coming event:

It foretold that Israel would be attacked by its enemies.

The attack would involve a massive ground invasion, the first such invasion in half a century.

It would catch the nation by surprise.

Though there would be warnings of its coming, the warnings would not be taken seriously.

The invasion would happen on the Sabbath, the Hebrew day of rest.

It would take place on one of the sacred appointed times of God, given in the Torah.

It would lead to war.

It would happen on the first Saturday of October of 2023.

It would all come to pass the morning after I shared the mystery's foundation and parameters. In this book I will share how the mystery foreordained and foretold exactly what would take place and when.

———————■■■———————

That night and what followed would lead to the opening of a mystery that began in ancient times and lay behind the events of modern times.

Part II

THE DRAGON

Chapter 3

THE MYSTERY OF EVIL

I T IS AN ancient entity. In popular culture it is often depicted in almost cartoonish form. Because of this its existence is often dismissed. But its presence is very real, and its impact on our world, most critical. If we should dismiss or ignore it, we do so at our peril.

The Transcendent

What is evil? And how did it come into existence? It is both a mystery and a problem. The mystery *is* the problem. The problem is used in countless arguments to attempt to disprove God's existence or nature. To find the answer, we must start with the foundations.

That evil exists cannot be debated. To deny it is to deny reality. But the fact that evil exists does not disprove the existence of God. Nor does it disprove the existence of a supernatural or spiritual realm—far from it.

If there was nothing more to life or existence than the material realm or the physical universe, we could not speak of good or evil. Then war, death, murder, and destruction would not be evil or even a problem but simply the playing out of forces and the rearrangement of molecules and atoms. If there was nothing more to the universe, then we could not judge the Nazi murderer of Jewish children to be evil, or the righteous who risked their lives to save the lives of Jewish children from Nazi murderers to be good. Nor could we esteem life to be of greater value than death. As with meaning, values, and significance, good and evil require a reality beyond that of the physical. Without this all values, all moral codes, are meaningless, arbitrary, and valueless. Evil, like good, is ultimately transcendent. Its existence does not disprove that the spiritual realm exists, but proves that it does.

The Uncreated

This leads to the next question: If evil exists, then how did it come into existence? More specifically, if God is good, then how could there be evil? And if God created evil, then how could God be good? But if God did not create evil, then how could evil exist? Or how could God be God? Therein lies the problem and the mystery. But the very problem of evil contains its answer. If evil was created, it would not be a problem, nor would it be evil. Evil is a problem for the very reason that it was *not* created. It should not exist, because it was not created, and yet it does. The existence of evil defies the created order. It is not of the creation and thus exists in opposition to the created order. Evil exists in defiance of existence.

Personhood

Further, evil is not simply a force, like that of an earthquake, a hurricane, or a fire. All these bring calamity and destruction. But none would constitute true evil. Both hurricanes and serial killers bring death. But hurricanes are not evil. Serial killers are. Why? The hurricane is an impersonal force. It acts without consciousness, will, choice, volition, or intent. But the serial killer commits his acts with conscious intent, will, and volition—and so is evil. And so evil is not an impersonal force—but a personal one, requiring consciousness, volition, will, and intent. Thus in our search for an answer to evil, we are led to personhood.

The Anti-Being

What is it that makes evil *evil*? Evil is an inversion—an inversion of truth, of reality, of existence. Evil is, by nature, inverted and, by nature, inverts. It twists, bends, and turns existence in upon itself. It exists as anti-existence. Its being is anti-being, and its nature, anti-nature. It is a negation and therefore seeks to negate, a nullification that exists to nullify. It has no true, ultimate, or absolute existence and therefore acts to bring that which exists into non-existence. And so evil, by nature, seeks destruction. It opposes that which is.

Possessing no absolute or true existence of its own, evil is, as well, by nature, parasitic. Being not of the created order, it can exist only by drawing its existence from that order. Evil must use the good. And so though good can exist without evil, evil cannot exist without good. Truth can exist without falsehood, but falsehood cannot exist without truth. Laws can exist without crimes, marriage without adultery, and life without murder. But crimes cannot exist without laws, adultery without marriage, nor murder exist without life. Destruction requires structure, immorality requires morality, and sin requires the holy.

The good is primary. Evil is the parasitic inversion of the good. And so the existence of evil inadvertently testifies not against the existence of the good—but for it. It bears witness, unwillingly, to the existence of the good—the existence of God.

Origins

All this leads us to the mystery of origin. If evil is uncreated, how did it come to exist? God did not create evil, but He did create personhood, consciousness, and volition—free will. Free will is a necessity. If one does what is good

because one has no choice in doing so, then it is not good. The good must
be freely chosen and thus requires free will. And therein is the risk. To allow
the choosing of good, one must allow the choosing of its opposite. And the
opposite of good is evil. It is the allowance and risk of the good that allow
for the risk of evil.

The Inverted Angel

Let us now put together the pieces of the mystery. Evil requires personhood,
will, consciousness, and volition. Therefore, we are looking in the direction
of personhood, toward a conscious entity. It must be a created being that by
its volition turned against the created order, against existence itself, a being
that became an anti-being, an inversion.

And this is exactly what the Scriptures reveal. There are two entities with
the ability to choose good or evil: one, human, and the other, angelic. Since
evil is spiritual and beyond flesh and blood, its origin must be found beyond
flesh and blood, beyond the human, in the realm of the spiritual and the
angelic.

And it is in that realm that we find it, the entity that fulfills all the pre-
requisites—consciousness, volition, free will, and inversion and yet not of
flesh and blood—an angelic being that turned against the fabric of the created order and against existence itself. And in so turning, it, or he, became
the inversion and the one who inverts. He became the twisted reality and
the twister of reality. In his inversion he became the anti-being, the parasitic
inversion of the good, the nemesis of reality. He became the one who should
not exist and yet does.

He became the Devil.

----------■■■----------

What exactly is the Devil?

Chapter 4

THE ENEMY

H E HAS BEEN called the *Prince of Darkness, Beelzebul,* the *Father of Lies, Lucifer, Lord of the Flies,* and the *Devil.*

In popular culture he is depicted as a being of human-like form, with an angular face, two horns, a pitchfork, and a cape or wings, and in all red. Thus he is often dismissed as a figment of man's imagination. But behind the folklore, behind the portrayals and fantasies of popular imaginings, lies a very real, ancient, deadly, dark, and present danger.

The Sahtan

The English word *Satan* comes from the Hebrew *sahtan,* which can be translated as *opponent, adversary,* and *enemy.* The word goes to the heart of his essence. Satan is the one who turned away from God and thus away from existence. He became the negation, the nullification, and the one who negates and nullifies. He defies existence. He opposes that which is. He is not *an* enemy—but *the* Enemy, the one at enmity with all.

When the ancient scribes had to translate the Hebrew *sahtan* into Greek, they chose the word *Diabolos. Diabolos* means one who "throws across" or "casts through." It refers to one who casts forth accusations, slander, a divider, an accuser, an attacker—and thus the Adversary. The Enemy is the one who casts accusations against all that is, against existence. And so *Diabolos* became the Greek version of the Hebrew *sahtan*—the Enemy.

In Latin the word became *Diabolus;* in Italian, *Diavolo;* and in English—*Devil.* So the word *Devil* is the English version of a Greek translation of the Hebrew *sahtan.*

The Opposer

Both words and names match up with the mystery and essence of evil. As evil, by nature, stands in opposition to existence, so the name of the entity that personifies it means *the Opponent,* the *Opposer,* and which in Hebrew is *sahtan* or *Satan.* And as evil, by nature, stands in *enmity* with all that is, so the name of the being that embodies it is the *Enemy,* the *Adversary,* both of which are translations of *sahtan* and *diabolos, Satan* and *the Devil.*

Father of Lies

As evil is an inversion, and a lie, the inversion of truth, so of the Enemy it is written:

> He is a liar and the father of lies.[1]

And so the father of lies is the father of inversions, and as a lie exists in parasitic relationship to the truth, so the Enemy exists in relationship to God, the inversion of the good.

The Destroyer

As the Opposer of existence, the Enemy wages war against it. God *is* existence. His sacred name is *I Am*. He is the One who *is* and by whom all things come into being. So the Enemy's war centers on God. So it is written:

> I will be like the Most High.[2]

It is a vow of defiance and replacement. He wills to take the place of God and bring about His nullification. If he could destroy the Most High, he could end existence. But he cannot. Therefore, he focuses his war against the *things of* God. He attacks the will of God. He thwarts the plans and purposes of God. He wars against God's creation. He seeks to destroy God's works. He is thus the Destroyer. And so of him it is written:

> He was a murderer from the beginning.[3]

Man is the center of God's creation and bears God's image. Therefore, the Enemy especially seeks man's destruction. If he can destroy man, he can eradicate the image of God.

How would he seek to bring about that destruction? By separating man from God. If he can turn man away from God, if he can remove the creation from its Creator, then he can remove him from the purpose of his existence. And that which is removed from the purpose of its being can be nullified and brought to destruction.

Diabolical

So the work of the Enemy is to destroy the work of God. He is the creator of destruction and the destroyer of creation. His works are anti-works and so defy natural causation and rational explanation. For they have their origins in the one who should not exist but does. And so even the most secular and atheist are forced to describe such phenomena as Nazism and the Holocaust as *diabolical*, from the word *diabolos*; *demonic*, from the word *demon*; or *satanic*, from the name *Satan*, each word rooted in the realm that is beyond the natural and bearing witness to that which is beyond rational explanation.

Such evils are the manifestations of a war birthed not in the natural or the rational but in defiance of both and waged by the one who exists to end existence—the Enemy.

----■■■----

What we will see in the pages ahead is that the entity that many in the modern world would dismiss as a comical being in a red cape is not only absolutely and dangerously real but the active agent behind some of the most critical phenomena and movements of human history and specific events of the modern world, even, and more specifically, of our day.

----■■■----

To reveal it, we must introduce another set of players into the mystery, the most peculiar and contradictory of peoples.

Chapter 5

THE MYSTERY PEOPLE

THERE IS SOMETHING about the Jews. There is now and has always been. They have never quite fit into the world. Even from the beginning, when they journeyed in the wilderness to the Promised Land, it was said of them:

> A people dwelling alone, not reckoning itself among the nations.[1]

The Anomaly

The Jewish people have always been a mystery to the world. No people have ever known so much rejection, antipathy, and hatred. Joined to one land as no other people have ever been so joined to a land—and yet separated from their land and landless as no other people have been so separated from a land or landless. Dwelling apart and separate from the nations as no people have ever been so separate—and yet so intertwined with the nations and critical to world history as no other people have been so intertwined and critical. No people have ever been so connected to their times and their space, and yet no people have so transcended the parameters of time and space to become near timeless and universal.

They have been the weakest of nations and yet the strongest—the most vulnerable of peoples and most often in danger of extermination—and yet the most enduring of peoples. No people, while on earth, have ever so known the presence of God and glories of heaven—and yet no other people have ever so known the depths of hell. They are an enigma, an anomaly, a paradox, a mystery people.

A Kingdom of Priests

Why? What makes Israel unique among the nations, and the Jews, separate among the peoples? The answer is God. Though the Jews are known as "the Chosen people," the label can be misleading. It was not as if they existed among other peoples and were then chosen by God. Rather, the Scriptures record that God called them into existence. They were not chosen for any special attribute they possessed. If God called another people, that people would end up being the Jews. So why did they come into existence? The reason was given at the dawn of their history at Mount Sinai:

15

> And you shall be to Me a kingdom of priests and
> a holy nation.[2]

Israel was called into being to be a holy people, a kingdom of priests. A priest is a minister of God's purposes. So Israel was to be a vessel of God, a central conduit and instrument for the fulfillment of His plans and purposes for the world. It came into the world for the sake of every other people and nation, that, in them, all nations would be blessed.[3]

And so it was to Israel that the revelation of God was first received and then, through them, given to the nations. It was through the prophets of Israel that the word of God was given to them, and then, through them, to the world. It was through the Jewish people that much of the world received its sense of history and time and the sanctity and worth of human life. It was through Israel that much of the world was given the spiritual foundation on which its values and laws would rest, its concept of faith, prayer, meaning, and purpose. It was through Israel that the knowledge of God was given to the world. And it was through Israel that people from every land, of every tribe and tongue, were transformed, given hope, freedom, and purpose.

Witnesses of the Existence

According to the Scriptures, Israel stands at the center of God's purposes— not only in past and ancient times but in all times. They occupy the center point of history and prophecy. And beyond all this is something even more foundational. In the Book of Isaiah, God says to the people of Israel,

> You are My witnesses.[4]

And thus beyond any work or accomplishment of the Jewish people is something still more critical and transcendent—*their existence*. The very existence of the Jewish people is a witness testifying to the existence of God. It is because of God that they came into the world and, by Him, that they continue to exist in a world long hostile to their presence within it.

-------------------■■■-------------------

So we now have the mystery of two opposing realities, a people in whom is the mystery of God and a being in whom is the mystery of evil. What happens when they come together? What will happen is an explosion and a war that have determined and altered the course of world history and long mystified those who have sought to understand it.

THE ANTI-SEMITIC ANGEL

OUR FAMILIARITY WITH the world can blind us from seeing in clarity one of its most dramatic phenomena. For that we must temporarily remove ourselves from our planet.

The Eyes of an Alien

Imagine we have arrived in the world from another planet. We know nothing of its culture, nothing of its faith, nothing of nations or human history. We are told of only two things: first, that there is a spiritual entity that wars against the purposes and works of God and does everything in its power to thwart, attack, and destroy them; and second, that there is a people especially brought into the world as a work of God and who exist to fulfill His purposes.

Having no knowledge but of these two things, what would we expect to happen on the earth? We would expect that the entity that wages war against the purposes of God would especially wage war against the people brought into the world for the purposes of God. He would seek to wipe them out of existence that he might destroy the witness of God's existence.

As the name *Satan* means the Opposer, it was inevitable that the Jews would become the most opposed people on earth. Those who had been called to occupy the focal point of God's purposes on earth would inevitably occupy the focal point as well of the Enemy's fury. He would seek to thwart them, oppress them, persecute them, nullify them, exterminate them. He would inflame others with his hatred and use them to serve as his vessels in accomplishing those ends. And so the people called into existence for God's purposes would become the most hated of all peoples, and their existence, the most warred-against existence of any people in human history. They would dwell in this world in continual danger of annihilation.

The Devil in Hebrew

What we have just described as the logical conclusion of a hypothetical exercise is the actual history of the Jews. That we could so describe it without having any knowledge of it, only the awareness of a spiritual war, reveals how powerfully the events of this world are impacted and determined by the realities that lie beyond it.

If God were to choose a people through which He was to accomplish His purposes—then He already has. And if the Enemy was to focus the full force of his wrath and hatred onto one people above all other peoples of this world—then he too already has. What might seem to be the plot of a science fiction story is actually the very real matrix behind one of the most critical and longest-running dramas of world history.

It was all there from the beginning. The very fact that the name *Satan* comes from Israel is no accident. Not only does it refer to the Enemy, Opponent, and Adversary—but it does so in Hebrew. Among the inhabitants of this world, Satan is first the Adversary of Israel, the Enemy of the Jewish people. The Devil is first the Devil to the Jewish people, their Opponent, their Archenemy.

An Ancient Virus

Taking into account the reality of the spiritual realm, it is no accident that the people who brought God and His Word to the world should become the most hated and opposed of peoples. Nor is it an accident that they have, from the ancient world to the modern, walked the earth in danger of extermination. So hated are they among peoples that the hatred has its own name—*anti-Semitism*. But the hatred long precedes the name. They were hated and warred against in the medieval world, so too in the ancient world, and no less so in the modern world, to the present day.

The reasons and rationale given to explain this hatred have never been consistent. In the Communist world the Jews were hated for being capitalists. In the capitalist world they were hated for being Communists. Among the extreme Right they were hated for being of the Left, and among the extreme Left, for embodying the traditional, or conservative, values of the Right. They have been hated for keeping to themselves, for exclusivity, and, at the same time, for their engagement and involvement with the larger culture, for their universality, for not keeping to themselves. The truth is, they are hated because they exist.

It is the most resilient and undying of spiritual viruses. And as does a virus, it mutates from generation to generation, taking on new forms, always reviving and yet always maintaining its toxic and deadly core. And even in those times when it appears to have subsided, it is always there, waiting for the next opening through which to rear its head and infect the next generation. It is a light sleeper.

The Primeval Anti-Semite

The war against Jewish existence is unlike any other. It knows no bounds of space or time. It is not rational or natural. It happens no matter what, no matter when, no matter who, and no matter where. It is supernatural and irrational, the dark and virulent offshoot of the mystery of evil. It is the work of a fallen, twisted, inverted spiritual and supernatural being.

The truth is, the first of all anti-Semites was an angel.

All who hate the Jewish people, all the anti-Semites of every place and time—he is their father, and they, his children. The words they speak against the children of Israel are his words. The acts they commit against them are his acts. And so if we look through the ages at the attacks launched and battles waged against the Jewish people, we would expect to find there his footprints. And his footprints are exactly what we find.

The Accused

> For the accuser of our brethren, who accused them
> before our God day and night, has been cast down.[1]

So he is described as the accuser of the brethren. His nature and role as the caster of accusations is, as we have seen, intrinsic to the name *Satan* and *Devil*. Therefore, we would expect the Jewish people to become the most slandered people in human history, the eternal focal point of accusation, allegation, vilification, and demonization. And so they are. It is the distinctive marker of the Accuser.

Beyond that, as he is a liar, we would expect the Jewish people to become the focal point not only of accusation but of *false* accusation, lies, and fabrications. And so they have. In the ancient pagan world they were accused of atheism and sacrilege. In the Middle Ages they were accused of poisoning wells and extracting the blood of their victims. In the modern world they are accused of masterminding virtually every major evil and conspiracy for the purpose of world domination. It matters not how groundless or far-fetched the accusations are. Their origins, as we have seen, are not rational. But they are consistent with the one in whom *there is no truth*.

The Methodeia

The rage against Israel and the Jewish people has been called the oldest of hatreds. An ancient phenomenon must have an ancient cause. In the Book of Revelation the word *archaios* is used to describe the Enemy. It can be translated as *from the beginning* or *primal* and, in this case, is commonly rendered as *ancient* or *old*. And as the hatred of Israel and the Jewish people is the most enduring of hatreds, spanning the millennia, so there is only one suspect whose existence, likewise, spans the millennia—the Enemy. And as the Enemy never rests, so anti-Israel and anti-Jewish hatred, likewise, never rests and is undying.

As the Enemy is not bound by time or space, by physical or geographic parameters, so too the ancient hatred transcends all physical and geographic parameters. It can be found everywhere in the world, in virtually every land and culture, and can erupt at any given time or place.

In the Book of Ephesians it is written:

> Put on the armor of God, that you may be able to
> stand against the wiles of the devil.[2]

The word translated as *wiles* is the Greek word *methodeia*, from which we get the English word *method*. It speaks of a carefully devised plan, a well-crafted strategy, as in a scheme created for the purpose of deception and evil-doing. The Enemy is a schemer. Thus we would expect the Jewish people to become the target and victims of schemes designed to harm or destroy them. And so the Jewish people have been exactly that, the target and victims of such schemes from century to century, age to age.

The Destroyer's Target

From the tents of Assyrian generals to the palaces of Roman emperors to the planning rooms of the Spanish Inquisition to the administrative offices of Imperial Russia to the bunkers of Nazi Germany and the underground tunnels of Hamas in Gaza, the Enemy has woven together schemes against the children of Israel—schemes of murder.

He is, as we have seen, a *murderer from the beginning*, the Destroyer. So then, we would expect him to launch not only wars of words, defamation and calumny, against the Jewish people—but wars of destruction. And so the Jews have been not only vilified and persecuted but slaughtered, anni-hilated—from the casting of Hebrew children into the Nile to the leading of Jewish men, women, and children into the gas chambers of Auschwitz. It is not natural. It is satanic.

His Dark Children

And thus we have the smoking gun. The pages of Jewish history are cov-ered with the Enemy's fingerprints. And above and beyond all of the Ene-my's attributes is the attribute of evil. Therefore, we would expect that the war against the Jewish people would be especially and uniquely connected to evil. We would expect that those powers and people especially used to wage that war would especially manifest and uniquely embody the Enemy's nature—evil.

This too is exactly what we find—from the Pharaohs of ancient Egypt to Josef Mengele, from Heinrich Himmler to Saddam Hussein, from Joseph Stalin to Osama Bin Laden to Al Qaeda, to the White Aryan Supremacists, to ISIS, to Hezbollah, to the violent revolutionaries and dictatorships of

Marxism, to the gunmen of Hamas. Even though they represent often dia-metrically opposed ideologies, they, strangely, share the same specific ani-mosity and hatred of the same specific people, the Jews—just as does the Enemy. And as with the Enemy, each of these have been perceived as person-ifications and embodiments of evil.

And then, of course, is the one who belongs at the head of the list—whose name, more than any other, has become synonymous with evil: Adolf Hitler. It is no accident that the person most universally recognized as the most evil figure in world history was, at the same time, the most driven, inflamed, and possessed by the fury and mission to destroy one specific people—the Jews. As with the others on the darkened list, he bore the traits of his spiritual father, the inverted angel.

That evil should be so strongly connected to the specific hatred of this one particular people reveals its origin and wellspring—the ancient entity in which the two, evil and the hatred of Israel, are likewise joined. It goes back to the mystery of evil. It is an unwarranted and irrational hatred, a rage that, as with the entity from which it springs, should not exist—but does.

-----■■■-----

We will now open up a two-thousand-year-old prophecy to reveal the war as it was, as it is, and as it will be, and with it the mystery of an ancient and deadly creature.

Chapter 7

THE RED DRAGON PROPHECY

THE BIBLE CLOSES with the Book of Revelation. The word *revelation* comes from the Greek word *apokalupto*, meaning *the removal of the veil*. In the twelfth chapter of Revelation the veil is removed in the form of a vision concerning the Enemy and God's ancient people.

The Celestial Woman

> Now a great sign appeared in heaven: a woman
> clothed with the sun, with the moon under her
> feet, and on her head a garland of twelve stars.[1]

Who is the woman? Though some have interpreted her as a representation of the church, and though the vision certainly has relevance for the church, the woman is something else, and more ancient. She is identified by her garments. She is clothed with the sun, with the moon under her feet, and crowned with twelve stars. The imagery first appears in the Book of Genesis:

> Then he dreamed still another dream and told it
> to his brothers, and said, "Look, I have dreamed
> another dream. And this time, the sun, the moon,
> and the eleven stars bowed down to me."[2]

The dreamer was the Hebrew patriarch Joseph. The sun represented his father, Jacob; the moon, his mother, Rachel; and the eleven stars, his eleven brothers, who, along with him, made up the twelve sons of Israel and from whom came Israel's twelve tribes. It is among the first of symbolic representations of Israel given in the Bible. Later on, in the writings of the prophets, Israel is often symbolized as a woman. So here we have a woman clothed with the sun, with the moon at her feet, and crowned with twelve stars. The woman is, first and foremost, Israel.

The Red Dragon

> And another sign appeared in heaven: behold, a
> great, fiery red dragon having seven heads and ten
> horns, and seven diadems on his heads.[3]

22

The second of the vision's symbols is a monstrosity. The word used to describe it is the Greek *drakohn*, from which we get the English word *dragon*. The Greek can also be translated as *the seeing one*. The Greek also indicates a serpent-like being, as in a large constricting or venomous snake. As to the identity of the Dragon in Revelation, the Scriptures leave no doubt:

> The great Dragon was cast out, the Serpent of old, called the Devil and Satan.[4]

As a dragon or serpent, the Devil is a terrifying being, a devourer, poisonous, venomous, and deadly. The dragons of Greek mythology appeared in varied forms and typically possessed supernatural powers. They were often described as having toxic or fiery breath. And yet the Dragon of Revelation is unique. Its body is red—the color of fire, destruction, bloodshed, sin, fury, and war. Its appearance is monstrous with seven heads, ten horns, and seven crowns. The Dragon is both supernatural and unnatural, a turned and altered creature. As dragons are typically depicted as creatures of deadly ferocity and fury—so too is the Devil. Finally, as a dragon is a monstrous being—so too is the inverted being that wars against creation and existence.

The Child

The woman is pregnant:

> Then being with child, she cried out in labor and in pain to give birth.[5]

The image of a woman with child again points to Israel, the calling of which was to bring forth the Word, the revelation, the presence, and the knowledge of God to the world. That calling reaches its pinnacle in the nation's bearing into the world the child who would bear the name *Yeshua* and would be known to much of the world as *Jesus*.

> She bore a male Child who was to rule all nations with a rod of iron. And her Child was caught up to God and His throne.[6]

That the child will rule all nations makes it clear that He can only be the Messiah. This is another marker as to the woman's identity. The church did not give birth to the Messiah but rather was born of Him. But Israel did give birth to the Messiah. Nor, as some have interpreted it, could the woman be summed up in Mary. For according to the vision, she is alive not only at the time of His birth but also at the end of the age. The woman can only be Israel, and her child, only the Messiah.

The Persecutor

> And the Dragon stood before the woman who was
> about to give birth, to devour her Child as soon as
> it was born.[7]

The Dragon waits by the woman to devour her child upon its birth. So the Enemy wars against the purposes of God and seeks to destroy them at their inception. The scene corresponds, among other things, to the attempt of King Herod to kill the baby born in Bethlehem.

> And when the Dragon saw that he had been cast
> to the earth, he persecuted the woman who gave
> birth to the male Child.[8]

The vision centers on two periods of time, one at the time of Messiah's birth and the other, yet to come, at the end of the age. They comprise two battles in an age-old war. The vision and the war thus span the millennia. The war is that which has been waged against the Jewish people for ages. The vision reveals its hidden and spiritual underpinnings.

The Dragon's rage against the woman is manifested in *persecution*. And so it is no accident that Jewish history, more than any other, is joined to the word *persecution*. One must keep in mind that the vision was written down ages before the innumerable persecutions, atrocities, and slaughters that would mark Jewish history, particularly in the modern era.

The Hunter and the Hunted

The Greek word used in Revelation to describe the Dragon's attack on the woman is *dioko*, which can be translated as *to persecute*, but also as *to pursue, to aggressively chase, to hunt down* as a hunter in pursuit of his prey. As the Dragon persecutes, pursues, and hunts down the woman, so the Enemy would persecute, pursue, and hunt down the Jewish people.

The persecution of the Dragon against "the woman who gave birth to the male Child" implies a special rage against her derived from that fact. It was Israel's bearing the child Yeshua into the world that spread the knowledge of God throughout the earth and that would alter world history. Thus behind the persecution of the Jewish people down through the ages is an ancient rage and vendetta for their having brought into the world not only the revelation of God but the Messiah.

The Flood

And the Serpent spewed water out of his mouth
like a flood after the woman, that he might cause
her to be carried away by the flood.[9]

As the attack originates in the creature's mouth, so the persecution of the
Jewish people throughout history has often been initiated through the mouth,
through words, slander, falsehoods, edicts, decrees, orders, and deadly propaganda. The Dragon unleashes a flood against the woman. So the Jewish
people have found themselves, time and time again, on the receiving end of
a toxic flood of hatred, overwhelmed by persecution, and crushed in a deluge
of evils and calamities.

At the same time, the vision reveals a principle of redemption. Though the
woman is attacked, she is provided a refuge. Though a flood comes against
her, the earth opens up and swallows it. The principle can be seen as well
throughout Jewish history. When one nation has turned against the Jewish
people, expelled or warred against them, another has opened up to give
them refuge. When one power has warred against them, another has fought
against their adversaries.

The Dragon's Orgidzo

And the Dragon was enraged with the woman.[10]

The word *enraged* is a translation of the Greek word *orgidzo*. It can also
be translated as *fury, wrath, hostility,* and *violent passion*. It has been used to
describe a long-held, long-simmering, undying anger as well as a desire for
vengeance. And so it is no accident that in every generation the Jewish people
have been subject to an ancient, undying anger, a long-simmering fury. And
though it may hide itself for a season, it always manages, in time, to rear its
head. Its aim is bloodshed, death, and destruction. What has defined the
ages of Jewish history on earth, from the slaughters of ancient enemies to
the horror of the gas chambers, is the orgidzo, the madness of a monster, a
raging dragon.

———— ■■■ ————

As the vision of Revelation refers to the Enemy as the *Dragon*, so too will he
often be referred to here by that description and name. The prophecy of the
Dragon will provide the key to unlocking a mystery of what is yet to come
and what is now beginning.

Part III

THE
DARK
RESURRECTION

Chapter 8

DAYS OF THE VISION

THE VISION OF Revelation 12 has a requirement essential to its fulfillment. What is it?

Specificity

In the vision the Dragon stands in a specific place at a specific time. The woman flees into a specific wilderness, where she stays for a specific number of days. Both the woman and the Dragon exist in specific places and times. Normally that fact would be a given and of little significance. But this case is different.

For most of the past two thousand years the Jewish people have not existed in one time and place. Instead, they were scattered throughout the nations. Nor for most of those two thousand years has there been a nation of Israel in the world, existing as a unified body or polity. The vision's fulfillment is based on that unified or cohesive state. There would have to be a nation or state of Israel in the world in one place and time.

The Jewish Odyssey

The vision's beginning, with the woman giving birth to the child, corresponds with the beginning of the age. So Messiah was born in an Israel that existed as a unified polity in the land of Israel. But after His coming everything changed. He Himself foretold what would happen:

> But when you see Jerusalem surrounded by armies, then know that its desolation is near....They will fall by the edge of the sword, and be *led away captive into all nations*. And *Jerusalem will be trampled* by Gentiles until the times of the Gentiles are fulfilled.[1]

In AD 70 the armies of Rome destroyed the Temple of Jerusalem and razed the city to the ground. The Jewish people were taken captive into the nations. It was the beginning of their nearly two-thousand-year exile from their homeland. They would undergo an unprecedented odyssey. Without a land, a government, an army, they were scattered throughout the world from ancient times to the modern world. Messiah's prophecy was fulfilled.

"From One End of the Earth to the Other"

And yet it was all foretold long before it happened, not only in the words of Yeshua, Jesus, but as far back as Moses in the days of the Exodus:

> The LORD will *scatter you among all peoples, from*
> *one end of the earth to the other.*[2]

It was not only the magnitude of the scattering that was unique, nor the fact that it was all foretold in the Scriptures. Just as unprecedented was what happened to them in the lands of their dispersion. That was foretold as well:

> Your life shall hang in doubt before you; you shall
> fear day and night, and have no assurance of life.[3]

So in their wandering the earth, the Jewish people would undergo a persecution that would span the world and the age.

"Your God Will Gather You"

But as unprecedented as all these things were, what happened next would be still more unprecedented. And though this would only come to be fulfilled in the twentieth century, it too was foretold in the ancient Scriptures:

> The LORD your God will *bring you back* from
> captivity, and have compassion on you, and *gather*
> *you again from all the nations* where the LORD your
> God has scattered you....The LORD your God will
> *bring you to the land* which your fathers possessed,
> and you shall possess it.[4]

According to the prophecy, after being scattered to the ends of the earth and after "many days,"[5] the Jewish people would be brought home. God Himself would gather them back to the land as a shepherd gathers his flock. So it is written:

> Behold, I will bring them from the north country,
> and gather them from the ends of the earth....They
> shall come with weeping, and with supplications I
> will lead them.[6]

And so they came just as was prophesied, from the north country and the ends of the earth, women with children, the lame, and with weeping.

In Defiance of History

It had never before happened. An ancient people of refugees strewn throughout the globe with no natural bond to hold them together, nor any natural defense to sustain them, and with all hell arrayed against them, were brought back to their homeland according to the ancient prophecy:

> Hear the word of the LORD, O nations, and declare
> it in the isles afar off, and say, "He who scattered
> Israel will gather him, and keep him as a shepherd
> does his flock."[7]

In the Latter Days

The return of the Jewish people to the land of Israel is connected to what the Bible calls the "last days." In the Book of Hosea it is prophesied that the children of Israel will be for "many days" without a kingdom or temple. But after that,

> ...the sons of Israel will *return* and seek the LORD
> their God and David their king; and they will
> come trembling to the LORD and to His goodness
> in the *last days*.[8]

In some of the prophecies the connection is explicit; in others, implicit; but the gathering of the Jewish people after many days back to the land of Israel is implicitly joined to what are called the end times. Therefore, the generation that sees that return is witnessing a biblical sign, the sign of the end times.

This brings us back to the vision of the Dragon. Though the vision begins with the birth of Messiah at the beginning of the age, its focus is, rather, on the end of the age. So the vision's fulfillment requires that the Jewish people return to their ancient homeland, Israel. That this has now actually happened as prophesied in the Bible, the door has been opened for the final act in the war of the Dragon and the woman.

It will begin in a valley of dry bones.

Chapter 9

DRY BONES RISING

THE PROPHET WAS taken in a vision into the midst of a valley filled with dry bones. The Lord told him to prophesy. So he did. And as he did,

> …there was a noise, and suddenly a rattling; and
> the bones came together, bone to bone. Indeed, as
> I looked, the sinews and the flesh came upon them,
> and the skin covered them.[1]

The Valley of Dry Bones

So opens the vision given to Ezekiel of the valley of dry bones. At the word of the prophet, the bones become skeletons and the skeletons, bodies of flesh and blood, but with no breath. The prophet is then told to prophesy to the Spirit. The Spirit, or breath, then enters into the lifeless bodies, and they come to life and rise to their feet as an "exceedingly great army."[2] The Lord then reveals the meaning of the vision:

> Then He said to me, "Son of man, these bones are
> the whole house of Israel. They indeed say, 'Our
> bones are dry, our hope is lost, and we ourselves are
> cut off!' Therefore prophesy and say to them, 'Thus
> says the Lord GOD: "Behold, O My people, I will
> open your graves and cause you to come up from
> your graves, and bring you into the land of Israel."'"[3]

Though the vision spoke of the regathering of the Jewish people to the land of Israel, the imagery was not of a regathering—but of a resurrection. The regathering of the Jewish people would be part of a resurrection.

"I Will Open Your Graves"

The children of Israel never died as a people. But the *polity, state,* or *kingdom* that embodied it in ancient times was destroyed and, in that sense, died. But Ezekiel's vision foretold its rising—another impossibility. Gone from the world for nearly two thousand years and of a land that had become a barren, forbidding wasteland, Israel appeared to be as dead as any nation has ever been dead.

During His crucifixion the words *King of the Jews* were nailed on the cross over Messiah's head.[4] The crucifixion led to resurrection. A nation is to follow its king. If the King of the Jews was resurrected—so too would be His nation.

In a world still staggering from the Second World War, with the United States and Soviet Union beginning the first tense chapter of the Cold War, with the empires of Europe in a state of collapse, and with the Jewish people emerging from the horrors of the Nazi Holocaust, the ancient prophecies and visions of Scripture were about to come to fulfillment.

The nation that had closed its eyes to a world of flaming arrows and Roman emperors now opened its eyes to a world of nuclear weapons and superpowers. In the midst of Ezekiel's vision the Lord had asked the prophet, "Can these bones live?"[5] On May 14, 1948, the question was answered. The dry bones had risen from the valley of death. The nation of Israel was resurrected from the dead.

The Rising Skeleton

Beyond foretelling Israel's resurrection, Ezekiel's vision revealed *how* that resurrection would come about. At the command of the prophet, the disconnected bones begin attaching one to the other. So Israel's resurrection would commence as the nation's scattered remnants began returning to the land and joining themselves one to another. The dry bones then formed skeletons. So Israel's resurrection was, at first, skeletal. First came the framework, a skeletal culture, a skeletal army, a skeletal structure of dwellings, a skeletal nation. And then came the flesh and blood as Israel transformed into a living and fully functioning nation.

Natural organisms are born; they grow and develop until they reach their fully formed state. They become what they have never been. But with a resurrection, everything happens in reverse. It begins with the end, with the structure of a fully formed state. Ezekiel's dry bones do not grow and develop. They start out fully formed. The resurrected army is restored to its former state of being. What came into the world in 1948 was an ancient nation coming back to life, resurrecting into that which it had already been.

Resurrection Land

It was a national resurrection made up of many smaller ones. In the course of history, a nation's language comes first and then is codified in a dictionary. But in the case of Israel, the dictionary came first and then the language. The language came together, piece by piece, as in the assembling of dry bones. In the case of nations it is the parents who teach the children the native language. But in the case of Israel's resurrection it was the children who taught their parents the native language.

It was not only the nation that was resurrected but the land. Forests sprang up on the same ground on which ancient forests had stood. Fields of grain and vineyards blossomed on the same soil on which the ancient fields and vineyards had once blossomed. And cities rose up on the ruins of ancient cities and bore their names. Even the nation's currency was resurrected from its ancient currency—the shekel. And the ancient image of the menorah, the seven-branched lampstand that the Romans had engraved in stone to celebrate their destruction of Israel, now became the seal of its resurrection.[6]

The Return of the Israelite

And beyond the land and the polity was the resurrection of a people. The new Israelites bore the resurrected names of the ancient Israelites who had inhabited the land thousands of years before. Even the man who led Israel in its return and who became its first prime minister, Ben-Gurion, bore the name of the ancient leader who had led the nation in its ancient destruction.[7] And even the nation's name, *Israel*, was part of the resurrection, having been borne thousands of years before by its ancient counterpart.

Resurrection was everywhere—resurrected Israeli farmers again reaping their harvests, resurrected Israeli fishermen again casting their nets into the Sea of Galilee, resurrected Israeli vine tenders again tending their vineyards, and resurrected Israeli brides and grooms again rejoicing in the city streets. The ancient prophecies had foretold that in the day of their restoration the people of Israel would again "go forth in the dance of the merrymakers."[8] And so on May 14, 1948, the people of Israel again went forth and danced in their dances of joy. Even their dances were resurrected, as was their joy.

In order for all these things to come to fulfillment, there had to be a convergence of world events, mass movements, colossal forces, the coalescing of countless lives, two world wars, and the rise and fall of world empires. It was beyond the control of any one person, any one nation, organization, kingdom, or power. *All things* had to be set in motion and perfectly in place by the moving of an unseen and ancient hand.

———■■■———

But there would be another work, birthed in opposition to the first and of entirely other origins.

Chapter 10

THE MIMIC

WITH ISRAEL'S RESURRECTION the stage was set for the fulfillment of end-time prophecy. Its regathering into one specific place and time was the requirement needed for the vision of Revelation 12 to be fulfilled. It would mean that the Dragon's war against the woman, the Enemy's war against the Jewish people, could now enter its final stage.

The Latter Wars

Even beyond the vision in Revelation, what is revealed throughout the Scriptures would be enough for us to conclude that the nation's return in 1948 would carry massive ramifications. If the Enemy wars against the works, vessels, and purposes of God, then he would, all the more, war against a resurrected Israel. It would pose a special threat to his existence. It was when Israel existed in a single polity that the Scripture was given, the prophetic word imparted, the Spirit of God poured out, and the Messiah given to the world. And the mere fact that the Jewish people were now concentrated into one place and time would mean that the Enemy's war against them would become increasingly focused and concentrated.

The Orgidzo's Metamorphosis

It would mean that anti-Semitism would increasingly be merged with and morph into anti-Zionism. The age-old animosity toward the Jewish people would increasingly transform into a hatred toward the newly resurrected nation of Israel. And the newly manifesting hatred for Israel would become as universal, as deadly, and as satanic as anti-Semitism had been for ages—and more so. The Dragon's war against the woman would cause the resurrected Israel to become the most warred-against nation on earth.

The Great Imitator

We are now about to open a long-hidden mystery that lies behind some of the most critical events of modern times. It set in motion events that threatened to rupture the global order and bring the world to war. It still does. And it all goes back to the Dragon.

If the Dragon was to war against Israel's existence, how would he do so? He would use vessels, pawns, and players—human agents. He would stir up animosity, hatred, and fury against the resurrected nation. More specifically, if the Dragon was to wage war, literal war, against Israel, how would it come? The answer lies in the Dragon's essence and nature—and goes back to the dawn of ages.

It is the nature of the false to imitate the true, to take on its form and appearance that it might ultimately take its place. A deceiver can only deceive by making what is false appear to be true. A lie must seek to appear as the truth, and a liar as a truth teller—they are all mimics. So too the Enemy seeks to appear as his opposite. The apostle Paul writes of his strategy:

> For Satan himself transforms himself into *an angel of light*.[1]

So the angel of darkness appears as an angel of light—and more than that.

"I Will Be Like the Most High"

The prophet Isaiah describes the fall of the one called *Lucifer* and his vow and mission against God. Of him it is said:

> You have said in your heart: "I will ascend into heaven, I will exalt my throne above the stars of God....I will ascend above the heights of the clouds, I will be like the Most High."[2]

The Enemy's ultimate aim is to become *like the Most High, as God*—that he might dethrone Him. He is the dark mimic of God.

———— ■■■ ————

We will now begin assembling the pieces of the puzzle. The Devil seeks to be like God, to take His place, to mimic His appearance and works. As the inverter, he seeks to turn the things of God in upon themselves, the works and ways of God against the purposes of God. And as the Enemy is the Dragon, he persecutes the woman; he wars against Israel. The return of Israel is to him a threat that he will seek to eliminate. How will he mimic the works of God, invert them, and war against the nation of Israel to destroy it? To accomplish these things, he will need a vessel.

———— ■■■ ————

As Israel not only returned to the world but was resurrected into it, so the Enemy would seek to nullify that miracle by using the same means—*a resurrection*.

Chapter 11

THE DRAGON'S RESURRECTION

WHEN GOD BRINGS forth a work into the world, the Enemy seeks to bring forth an alternate work, a false work, an anti-work, for the purpose of destroying the work of God. In the Book of Revelation the Dragon gives authority and power to the one called "the Beast," also known as "the Antichrist," or the Anti-Messiah. In the original Greek the word *Antichrist* signifies not only one who is against, opposed to, and the antithesis of the Messiah, but one who is His *substitute*, His *alternative*, one who would *take His place*. So the Antichrist will mimic the Messiah in order to nullify Him.[1]

The Dragon's Summoning

Thus if God brought forth the resurrection of Israel, the Enemy would seek to do likewise, to imitate Him—to bring forth another resurrection, his own resurrection, an alternate and substitute resurrection.

The Dragon's resurrection would be, on the one hand, an anti-resurrection, the inversion and antithesis of Israel's resurrection, and, on the other, its imitation. It would seek to nullify the resurrection of Israel and take its place.

As God took an ancient nation and placed it on the center stage of modern history, so the Dragon would likewise take another ancient nation and place it on the center stage of the modern world. As God took a nation that was long dead and raised it from its grave, the Dragon would do the same. He would cause it to come out of its grave—an anti-nation, an anti-Israel. And as the resurrected Israel would bear the resurrected name of its ancient predecessor, so the Dragon would resurrect a people who would, likewise, bear the resurrected name of their ancient predecessors.

A Word Before

Before we reveal the mystery and resurrection of this ancient people, a few things must be noted. The mystery is not about *the people themselves* but rather the force and agenda that are using them. It would be the same if we were dealing with Germany under the Third Reich or Russia under Communism. It would not concern anything intrinsic to either peoples. Rather, it would be about the forces that overtook them and the agenda by which they were manipulated and used. So the mystery we are now about to open concerns that which overtook and used a people for its own ends. The people themselves had no idea that they were being used. Nor did they realize the

37

agenda that impelled them and how it would lead toward their own destruction. In this they were pawns in the hands of a force beyond their knowing.

We are dealing primarily in the realm of peoples and nations, not individuals. A people may embark on a course that wars against the purposes of God. A nation may choose evil, and evil may choose a nation. At the same time, we cannot judge individuals by the nations of which they are part or by the course that such nations may choose to follow. And we must remember that the love of God reaches out to each and all without partiality. Those who follow God must, on one hand, recognize and oppose that which is evil and yet, on the other, extend mercy to those under its influence and spell. They must love those who hate them and pray for their redemption. For nations, peoples, and individuals have free will. They can change their course, and the mercy of God has no end or limitation.

The Tanim

So then, what people or nation would the Enemy resurrect? The Enemy's resurrection would be *the resurrection of an enemy*—the return of Israel's ancient enemy. The joining of *the Enemy* of God to the enemies of Israel goes back to ancient times. The Book of Jeremiah contains a prophecy concerning one of ancient Israel's most powerful enemies, King Nebuchadnezzar of Babylon. It says this:

> Nebuchadnezzar the king of Babylon....He has
> swallowed me up like a *dragon*.[2]

The same Hebrew word used of Nebuchadnezzar appears in another prophecy directed against another of Israel's ancient enemies, Pharaoh:

> I am against you, Pharaoh king of Egypt, the great
> *dragon* that lies in the midst of his rivers.[3]

The word in both passages is *tanim*, or *tannin*. It can be translated as *monster*. But it can also be translated as *serpent* or *dragon*. This is especially striking in view of how Revelation 12 speaks of the Enemy:

> So the great *dragon* was cast out, that *serpent* of
> old, called the Devil and Satan.[4]

As the word *tanim* can mean both dragon and serpent, so in Revelation the Devil is called both the *Dragon* and the *Serpent*. When the Hebrew Scriptures were translated into Greek, the Hebrew *tanim* became the Greek *drakohn*, or *dragon*. In the New Testament the word appears only in the Book of Revelation and mostly in one section—the vision of the Dragon and the woman of Revelation 12.

The Little Dragons

So then, the word used to identify the Enemy, Satan, in the Book of Revelation is a translation of the word used in Hebrew to speak of Israel's ancient flesh-and-blood enemies. What is the connection? The ancient enemies of Israel were used by the eternal Enemy of God. They were the flesh-and-blood agents employed by the Enemy to attack, invade, and bring death and destruction to the people of Israel.

In ancient times the Dragon warred against Israel by using peoples and nations to serve as his vessels, little "dragons" of flesh and blood. His war became their war, and in their war was his war. When they attacked Israel, it was the Dragon attacking Israel. When they invaded the land, it was the Dragon invading. And when they raged against God's people, it was the raging of the Dragon. So as he used ancient people to war against an ancient Israel, he would use a resurrected people to war against a resurrected Israel. And he would time and calibrate the resurrection of the enemy to coincide with the timing of Israel's resurrection. So as Israel rose from its ancient tomb, others would likewise rise from their ancient tombs.

It would all begin in the waters of the Aegean.

Part IV

THE RETURN OF THE SEA PEOPLES

Chapter 12

THE SEA PEOPLES

OF ALL THE enemies faced by Israel in ancient times, the one most deserving of the title *archenemy* was the people known as the *Philistines.*

The Archenemy

No other people so continually warred against the Israelites, raiding them, oppressing them, taunting and provoking them, and terrifying them, as did the Philistines. None were so ever present in their history or so continually warred against their presence in the land.

The Philistines overcame and mutilated the Israelite hero Samson. They stood in battle against the Israelite shepherd boy David. They warred against Israel's first king, Saul, and pursued him to his death. They battled Israel's subsequent kings and remained the nation's sworn and archetypal enemies century after century.

Who were they?

The Pileshtim

In their first known appearance in ancient inscriptions, they are listed as one of those known as the *Sea Peoples.* It is generally accepted that they originated in southern Europe, the Mediterranean, and, more specifically, in the lands surrounding the Aegean Sea. They appear to have been connected to the ancient Mycenaean or proto-Greek civilization.[1]

In the late Bronze Age they invaded Egypt and battled against the Pharaoh's armies. Egyptian inscriptions call one of the invading Sea Peoples the *Pulasti,* or the people of *Peleset,* or *Palusata.*[2]

In Hebrew they are called the *Pileshtim,* the plural of the word *Pilishti,* a dweller of the region called *Pilashet.* It is believed that from the Hebrew *Pileshtim* came the Greek word *Philistinoi.* And from the Greek name came the Latin *Philistinus,* and from the Latin, the English word *Philistine.*

The Parallel Appearings

The first known appearance of the word *Israel* outside of Scripture occurs in the inscriptions of the Egyptian Pharaohs. It occurs in the victory stele of Pharaoh Merneptah. In it the Pharaoh boasts of conquering his enemies in the land of Canaan:

Canaan has been plundered into every sort of
woe....*Israel* is laid waste.[3]

The first known appearance of the word *Philistine* also occurs in the
records of an Egyptian Pharaoh, Ramesses III. On the walls of Ramesses'
mortuary temple, *Madinat Habu*, the *Peleset*, the Philistines, appear as enemies of the Egyptian empire. They are portrayed as warriors bearing double-
edged swords, long spears, and round shields, and wearing feathered head-
dresses.[4] They appear at the same time in the writings of *The Great Harris
Papyrus*, in which Ramesses claims,

> I extended all the boundaries of Egypt; I overthrew
> those who invaded them from their lands....The
> *Peleset* [the *Philistines*] were made ashes.[5]

Both *Israel* and *Philistine* make their first-known appearances in the annals
of the Egyptian Pharaohs. Most striking is the timing. The first appearance
of *Israel* is dated to the end of the thirteenth century BC. The first appearances of *Philistine* are dated soon after, to the middle of the twelfth century
BC. For all intents and purposes, they come into the world together—first
the Israelites, then the Philistines.

Three thousand years later, when Israel returned to the world in modern
times, it would all replay. They would reappear together—first the resurrected Israel and then the resurrected Philistines.

A Deadly Relationship

The Pileshtim, or Philistines, occupied the portion of the land of Canaan bordering Egypt, or the Sinai Peninsula. They dwelt on the shores of the Mediterranean Sea on the lowland of Israel's southwestern coast. It would become
known as *Philistia*.[6] Though it was part of the land God had promised to
Israel, the Israelites were never fully able to gain lasting possession of the
region. And so the region was, for ages, a thorn in the nation's side.

The fact that the Philistines also claimed the land given to Israel made
their conflict with the Israelites especially intense, relentless, and dangerous.
The Scriptures allude to the Philistines' deep bitterness and hatred for Israel.
They carried on and transmitted that hatred from generation to generation.
And at the right or wrong times it would erupt with deadly consequences.

Resurrecting the Philistines

When King Nebuchadnezzar of Babylon invaded the land of Israel in the late
seventh and early sixth centuries BC and, in the process, destroyed the cities
of Philistia, it spelled the beginning of the end of the Philistines.[7] They would

soon vanish from the records of history, thereafter existing as a memory of a vanished people.

But if God was going to resurrect the nation of Israel that had likewise vanished in ancient times, and made it known in biblical prophecy that He would do so, it would follow that the Enemy and imitator of God would likewise seek to resurrect an ancient nation, that of Israel's ancient enemies. It would follow that he would seek to raise from the dead the most embittered, persistent, and relentless of Israel's ancient enemies. He would bring back the people who likewise laid claim to the land and unceasingly warred against Israel's claim.

If God were to open Israel's ancient grave as was foretold in Ezekiel's vision, it would follow that the Dragon would seek to counter that opening by opening the graves of those who, more than any other people, comprised the nation's archenemies. And having raised them up, he would use them to hinder, to thwart, to strike, to war against, and to seek the destruction of that resurrected Israel. And that is exactly what would happen.

———■■■———

The name has become the center of a deadly controversy raging in the modern world. But few know its ancient and still more ancient origins and the reason behind its existence.

Chapter 13

THE ANTI-LAND

IF THE ENEMY were to raise up the Philistines, how would he do it?

It was in ancient times, at the time of Israel's destruction, that God sowed the seeds of its resurrection. So too it was at that same time that the Dragon sowed the seeds of the Philistine resurrection.

The Unholy City

The destruction of the Temple of Jerusalem in AD 70 was a defining and cataclysmic moment in Jewish history. The holy city was left in ruins, the land was ravaged, the nation of Judea was wiped off the earth, and multitudes of Jewish people were either killed or taken captive into the nations. And yet there was still a sizable remnant of Jewish people living in the land. In AD 132 the Jews in the land again revolted against Rome led by a man named Simon Bar Kochba. In AD 135 Bar Kochba was killed and the revolt brutally crushed.[1]

In terms of strategy, if the Enemy's mission is to destroy the works of God and to nullify His purposes, and if the purposes of God are most specifically connected to the Jewish people and the city of Jerusalem and, more specifically, to the *dwelling* of the Jewish people in the city of Jerusalem, then we would expect that he would do everything in his power to separate the Jewish people from Jerusalem. And that is exactly what happened.

In the aftermath of the Bar Kochba Revolt, the Roman Empire banned the Jewish people from setting foot in Jerusalem. To further obstruct the purposes of God, the city was renamed *Aelia Capitolina*, the word *Capitolina* referring to the god Jupiter.[2] Jerusalem was now dedicated to the chief of the Roman pantheon. The holy city of Israel was rebuilt and renamed as a pagan city of Rome.

"Land of the Philistines"

But there was more. It wasn't only the city that was joined to God's purposes but the land. So we would expect the Enemy to do everything in his power to separate the one from the other. The exile of the Jewish people from the land would not be enough—the land had to be renamed. It had to be given a new identity. Its connection to the people of Israel had to be expunged from history.

The land of Israel would now bear the name of the enemy of Israel—the

Philistines. It would be the Roman version of the name that had once denoted Israel's southeastern coast, the region once occupied by the Sea Peoples. But now the entire land of Israel, the Holy Land, was to be renamed *the land of the Philistines.*

The Anti-Name

The change was artificial and anti-historical. The land was to be retroactively named after a people who had not existed for half a millennium. The change was not about the Philistines. They were only being used. Nor was it about the Romans. They had little knowledge of the ancient people who had once warred against Israel. They were also being used. It was the Enemy's attempt to erase the connection of the people of Israel to the land of Israel and to obstruct God's future purposes for both.

It was an anti-name of what was to be an anti-land, the anti-Promised Land of the anti-god, the Enemy. God had named the land after the people of Israel. The Enemy had named the land after their enemies. The great nullifier had nullified the Promised Land. The Destroyer had now renamed the land of God's people after the people who were bent on destroying them. The mystery had ordained it.

Palaestina

In the Hebrew Scriptures the coastal strip was called the land of the *Pilishtim,* or *Pilashet.* Translated into other languages, the basic root *p-l-s-t* remained. In Greek it became the word *Palaistine,* and in Latin, *Palaestina.*

In English it was rendered *Palestine.*[3]

For nearly two thousand years the Promised Land would be called *the Land of the Philistines, Palestine.* But the name was about more than erasure and nullification. It was the first seed of the Dragon's sowing toward a future counter-resurrection.

———————■■■———————

The counter-resurrection would imitate the resurrection of Israel, paralleling it, unfolding at the same time, side by side.

Chapter 14

THE FILASTIN

A S THE WORDS *Satan* and *Devil* denote the one who opposes, so the Devil was to bring into existence a people to oppose and war against Israel's existence. But when Israel returned as a nation into the world, the Philistines had not existed for nearly two and a half thousand years. So out of what would he orchestrate his resurrection?

Becoming the Philistines

Though the modern state of Israel is overwhelmingly made up of the flesh-and-blood descendants of ancient Israel,[1] the resurrection went beyond genetics. It was a resurrection of a *nation*, its form and structure, its culture, its nature, its characteristics, its land, its name, its icons, its institutions, its functions, its calling, its identity, and its role among the nations. Not every citizen of the resurrected nation was of its ancient bloodline. These became Israelis.

The Philistine resurrection would be based on the identity of the ancient Philistines, their characteristics, their role, their nature, their functions, their culture, and their name. It would be a resurrection in which a people would be raised up and conformed into an ancient image.

The pattern of "becoming the Philistines" was actually begun in ancient times. The Philistines were originally an Aegean people who settled on Canaan's southwestern coast. But modern research has revealed that over time the genetic makeup of Israel's enemies changed to reflect that of the more native Canaanites.[2] Yet, even with a different and Canaanite genetic composition, they were still the Philistines—of the same culture, the same national characteristics, the same customs, ways, nature, role, and identity. So it would be with their resurrection into the modern world.

At the same time it must be noted that though their resurrection transcends genetics, genetics do play a part. Genomic studies have revealed that the modern inhabitants of the lands that made up ancient Lebanon, Syria, Israel, or Canaan bear genetic connections to the ancient inhabitants of those lands and to one another.[3]

The Reappearings

We would expect the Dragon, as the mimic of God, to join the Philistine resurrection to the resurrection of Israel. Israel's return to the world as a national entity officially began with the birth of Zionism. Zionism, in turn, began in 1897 when Theodor Herzl convened the First Zionist Congress in Basel, Switzerland.[4] It was no accident that it was right after that seminal event that the word *Palestinian* began appearing in the Arabic language, ushering in its modern usage. The subsequent years would see its appearance in Muslim, Jewish, and Christian periodicals.

And so just as the *Philistine*, or *Peleset*, made his appearance in the ancient world right after the Israelite, each manifesting in the writings of the Pharaohs, so it was again that as the one made his reappearance in the modern world, so would the other.

As Israel's resurrection progressed in the early twentieth century, and specifically with the issuing of the British *Balfour Declaration* in support of a Jewish homeland, the words *Palestine* and *Palestinian* increasingly surfaced in books, pamphlets, and articles. Though the word carried more than one connotation, depending on who was using it, including Jewish people, it was increasingly employed to oppose the birth of a Jewish nation in the land.

The Other Return of 1948

The defining moment in Israel's resurrection came in 1948, when its first leader, David Ben-Gurion, read the nation's declaration of its independence and proclaimed its return to the world. Up to that moment, the word *Palestinian* could and did refer to any inhabitant of the land, Arab, Jewish, or other. But from then on, the word would become joined to the non-Jewish inhabitant of the land, namely the Arab.

The Jewish inhabitant of the land was now an Israeli. The Arab inhabitant of the land outside of the Jewish state would, in time, become a Palestinian. The full implications of what was happening were not evident in 1948. But they would, in due course, become unmistakable. The resurrection of the Israeli would give birth to the resurrection of the Philistine.

And yet the signs were there from the beginning for those with eyes to see. In the year of Israel's rebirth, another state was also born. It was called the *All-Palestine Protectorate*.[5] It was the earliest manifestation of a Palestinian state. It was formed in direct response to Israel's resurrection and was created with the specific aim of nullifying it. From the All-Palestine Protectorate came the All-Palestine Government and the All-Palestine National Council.

It was, again, a case of mimicry. As 1948 was the year of Israel's declaration of independence, so it was the year of the All-Palestine National Council's declaration of independence. And as 1948 was the year that Israel declared its return to the land, so it was the year that the All-Palestine Government declared full sovereignty over the same land and empowered a Holy War Army for the express purpose of destroying the newborn Jewish nation.[6]

The Filastin

The word *Palestinian* would, in time, become the official name used to label the non-Jewish, or Arab, inhabitants of the land. It would become the name that they themselves would use to identify themselves. In English the word is *Palestinian*. But those who used the word spoke Arabic. So what was the actual word they used?

In Arabic the word was pronounced *Filastinian* or *Filastini*.[7] The root word of both is the word *Filastin*. It cannot be overlooked that the pronunciation of *Filastin* is virtually identical to that of the English word *Philistine*. In fact, in English dictionaries the pronunciation of the word *Philistine* will often be represented as exactly that—*Filastin*. And for that matter, the Arabic word for Palestine is *Filastin,* as in *Philistine.*

Since *Filastin* is the actual word used by the people known as the *Palestinians*, it will be used throughout this book.

———————■■■———————

So for the first time since ancient times, there would be a people in the world and in the land of Israel bearing the name *Philistine* or *Filastin*. And as with Israel's resurrection, the defining moment in the Philistine resurrection came in the year 1948. That year would begin a dark metamorphosis by which Israel's ancient enemy would begin manifesting in the land.

Chapter 15

METAMORPHOSIS

THE RESURRECTION OF the Philistines would imitate Israel's resurrection to the point of mimicking the pattern of Ezekiel's vision in the valley of the dry bones. It would begin with bones, the pieces of an identity connected to the ancient Philistines. The bones would then begin coming together to form a skeletal structure. And then flesh would cover them.

The Stage

At the time of Israel's rebirth most non-Jewish inhabitants of the land saw themselves as Arabs rather than Palestinians. The first attempt to form a Palestinian state, the All-Palestine Protectorate, would ultimately fail but would set the stage for a coming transformation.

In 1947 the United Nations approved a partition plan by which the land of Israel would be divided between a Jewish and an Arab state. The portion offered to the Jewish people was a fraction of their biblical homeland, but they accepted it. But the Arab world rejected it. They would not accept the existence of any Jewish state but demanded sovereignty over the land in its entirety.[1]

On the day of Israel's return to the world, the newborn nation was attacked from every side by the armies of multiple Arab nations committed to its destruction. Miraculously, it survived the onslaught and won the war. What then happened to the land's Arab inhabitants?

Those living within the borders of Israel were granted citizenship. During the war Egypt seized the coastal strip bordering the Sinai. Those living in that region would come under Egyptian sovereignty. Those in the Golan Heights in the north were under Syrian sovereignty. As for those living in what would be known as the *West Bank*, they would come under the sovereignty of Jordan, which had seized the region. They were now Jordanians.[2] For the resurrection of the Philistines to come to its fruition, there would have to be a major transformation.

The Deadly Child of Jerusalem

Israel's center is and has always been its eternal capital of Jerusalem. It was there that stood the Holy Temple, there that its kings sat on their thrones, and there that the people gathered to worship the Lord. Even in their agelong exile from the land, not a year went by when they failed to pray, "Next year in Jerusalem."

If the land of Israel was the focal point of God's purposes on earth, Jerusalem was the center point of that center. It was from Jerusalem that God's purposes went forth to the world—the Word, the Spirit, the gospel. Thus we would expect that Jerusalem would likewise become the focal point of the Enemy's purposes. So it was in Jerusalem that the Enemy birthed a new entity devoted to those purposes.

It was in 1964 that the Arab League initiated the bringing forth of a new organization to be called the *Palestine Liberation Organization*, or the PLO. It would be born in Jerusalem. The name summed up its purpose. The land it called *Palestine* was to be "liberated" from Israel. The only way that could happen was for Israel to be destroyed. Therefore, another organization was founded to accomplish that end—the PLA, the Palestine Liberation Army.[3] What happened in Jerusalem in 1964 would play a central and pivotal role in the Philistine resurrection, and yet it would be another event that would prove even more critical.

1967

According to the ancient prophets, the Jewish people must return not only to the land of Israel but to Jerusalem. The biblical prophecies concerning the end times could not be fulfilled until that happened. But with Jordan in control of biblical Jerusalem and the Islamic world claiming the ancient city for itself, it was virtually impossible for such a thing to happen. But the prophecies said otherwise.

In the spring of 1967 the nations that surrounded Israel began threatening its destruction. The threats were followed by military action as the combined armies of Israel's enemies began amassing at its borders. In order to avert destruction, Israel decided to act first. And thus began the Six-Day War.[4]

On the third day of that war, for the first time in nearly two thousand years, the soldiers of Israel entered the gates of Jerusalem. They made their way through its streets and corridors until they reached the Western Wall of the Temple Mount, where they prayed and wept.[5] The ancient prophecies were fulfilled. It was another critical moment in the raising up of the dry bones. Israel's restoration could never be complete without Jerusalem. So the return of the holy city was another defining moment in that rising.

The Inadvertent Resurrection

But as the Enemy imitates the works of God, we would expect the same defining moment in Israel's resurrection to produce a defining moment in the Philistine resurrection. And so it did. In Israel's victory over Egypt, Syria, and Jordan, the lands occupied by those nations were released. The Arabs of the coastal strip were no longer under Egyptian rule; those in the north, no longer under Syrian rule; and those in the West Bank, no longer under Jordanian rule. And so the return of the Jewish people to Jerusalem inadvertently opened the door for a new identity to take possession of the Arab inhabitants of the land—that of the *Palestinian*.

The Return of the Philistine Warrior

Key to the next stage of the Philistine resurrection was the man named *Yasser Arafat*. Born in Cairo, Egypt, Arafat would, as a student, come under the influence of anti-Zionist ideology. At the time of Israel's rebirth, Arafat was a militant Arab nationalist and fought to destroy the Jewish state at its inception. In the late 1950s he founded the militant faction known as *Fatah*, an acronym for *Harakat al-Tahrir al-Watani al-Filastini*, "the Palestinian National Liberation Movement."[6] In the early 1960s Arafat based his operations in Syria and, from there, launched raids into Israel.[7]

Days after the end of the Six-Day War, he crossed the Jordan River and entered the West Bank to recruit fighters in his war against Israel. He would wage that war increasingly through acts of terror against Israeli civilians. It was at that time that his forces pioneered the tactic of suicide bombing. And it was then that Egyptian president Gamal Abdel Nasser proclaimed Arafat the leader of the Palestinians. In February 1969 Arafat became the head of the PLO and later the commander of the Palestinian Revolutionary Forces.[8] Thousands of young Arabs were now recruited into his army and indoctrinated into his cause.

The Raiders

As the dry bones in Ezekiel's vision assumed the form of the fallen soldiers, and as the Israelis assumed the form of their ancient ancestors, so now the Arab inhabitants of the land began assuming the form of Israel's ancient enemies. They would be conformed, step-by-step, into the image of the ancient Philistines and the ancient Philistine soldiers. Taking on the name of the Philistines was just the beginning. Now they began taking on their identities, their ways, their roles, their strategies and tactics.

The Bible records that the Philistines warred against Israel by launching attacks, raids on its towns and civilians. Now, through Arafat, Fatah, and other guerrilla groups, the Filastin militants began resurrecting the ancient Philistine raids into the land of Israel, seeking to terrify its inhabitants.

An Ancient Possession

The Philistines were known as a people of war and violence. So it was no accident that the resurrected Philistines would increasingly become associated with the use of violence to accomplish their ends. Nor was it an accident that terrorism in the modern world would be especially linked to the Palestinian, or Filastin, agenda and rage against Israel. It was a deadly transformation. Those who would become known as Palestinians had not planned that which was now overtaking them. Nor did they choose the time of their metamorphosis. The Enemy had chosen it for them and was now taking them over. In that sense they were victims—victims of an ancient spirit. The possession of their ancient predecessors was now possessing them.

From the River to the Sea

God had given a promise to Israel concerning the land. He said:

> I will set your boundaries from the Red *Sea to the sea* of the *Philistines*, and from the desert to the *River.*[9]

The promise appears over and over again throughout the Scriptures, as do the words *river* and *sea*. Note also the appearance in that promise of the word *Philistines*. So the dark resurrection would produce a chant uttered by the Filastin peoples, a chant that multitudes around the world would shout along with them:

> *From the river to the sea*, Palestine will be free![10]

It is no accident that the same two key words given in God's promise to Israel concerning the land were used in the Filastin chant. It was the promise inverted. The fulfillment of that inverted promise required the elimination or annihilation of every Jew living in the land, from the river to the sea. It was, again, the Dragon's inversion—a promise to destroy the promise of God—an anti-promise.

The Shoah and the Nakba

Israel was resurrected in the wake of genocide, out of the ashes of the Holocaust, life from death. And so it is a typically satanic and brazen inversion that the greatest target of genocide in world history, the Jewish people, Israel, should, at every turn, be accused by their enemies and by the world of committing genocide—and by those who actually long for the genocide of the Jewish people.

Every year, the Filastin people commemorated Israel's rebirth as a day of evil and calamity they called the *Nakba*.[11] The nations of the world actually joined in this commemoration, as did the United Nations. The word for Holocaust in Hebrew is *Shoah*. It means *the catastrophe*. The word *Nakba* in Arabic means the same—*the catastrophe*. It is a revelation of the one behind it, he who inverts all things. For that which causes the Jewish people to rejoice is, to him, a catastrophe, and that which is to the Jewish people a holocaust is to him a cause for rejoicing.

The Israeli-Philistine Conflict

It should have been obvious. It was there from the beginning. But the world had little idea that *Palestinian* actually means *Philistine* or that *Palestine* actually means *the land of the Philistines*. The *Palestinian Authority* means the *Philistine Authority*, and the *Palestinian flag*, the *Philistine flag*; the *Palestinian cause*, the *Philistine cause*; and the *Israeli-Palestinian conflict*, the *Israeli-Philistine conflict*.

------■■■------

As the Jewish people were gathered back to the soil of their ancient homeland, is it possible that there was a second gathering happening at the same time—that of the resurrected Philistines back to the soil of their ancient dwelling place?

Part V

PILASHET

Chapter 16

PILASHET

WE WILL NOW see how an array of diverse forces and factors converged to cause a modern people to be conformed into the image of an ancient one.

The Coastal Plain

Sometime around the reign of the Egyptian Pharaoh Ramesses III, the Philistines settled the southeastern coast of the Mediterranean Sea just north of the Sinai Peninsula. The area had earlier been colonized by Egypt with the establishment there of a military garrison.[1]

Being a seafaring people, the Philistines tended to gravitate to coastal regions. So the Philistine settlement centered on a strip of land running north to south along the eastern Mediterranean coast. Though there were Philistines who would settle beyond this region, to the north and west of it, it was this coastal strip that would remain their headquarters and the center of their settlement in the land.

For the people of Israel, the region of the Philistines was hostile territory, an enemy land within the Promised Land. It would serve as the source of an agelong enmity and countless conflicts. It was this coastal plain that would become known as *Pilashet*, or *Philistia*, and that would become the source of the word *Palestine*.

Pilashet Rising

When Israel was reborn in 1948, Egypt invaded the newborn state through the coastal strip joining the two lands. Though Israel won the war, Egypt retained control of the strip. From the time of that war onward, tens of thousands of Arabs would relocate there under Egyptian rule. So massive was the influx that by the war's end, the region's population had tripled. Approximately one-quarter of Israel's Arab population was now living there.[2] And as the Jewish population then multiplied in the land of Israel, the Palestinian population would likewise multiply on that coastal strip. The increase was so great that by the early twenty-first century it was over *ten times* larger than it was before Israel was born.

It was that land that would become known as the *Gaza Strip*.

And though it came into the world's consciousness as if overnight and through the exigencies of war, the region was haunted by an ancient past.

The Gaza Strip was the land of the Philistines. By a quirk of history, the birth of Israel had led to a convergence of Arab inhabitants onto the same soil on which the ancient Philistines had once dwelt.

The Return of Gaza

Gaza was an ancient word. It appears in the Bible.[3] It was the name of a city that, in ancient times, stood in the land of the Philistines. The Philistines had built five major cities in Philistia: Ashdod, Gath, Ekron, Ashkelon, and *Gaza*.[4] More than once the Scriptures speak of Gaza as representative of Philistia and the Philistines. Gaza's modern incarnation would be known as *Gaza City*. So the city and region of Gaza would now again be teeming with inhabitants. And the Gaza Strip, once the concern of ancient Israel, would soon become the concern of the entire world.

The land of Philistia was located along Israel's western border. The Gaza Strip is located along Israel's western border. The land of Philistia ran down, southward, along the eastern shore of the Mediterranean Sea. The Gaza Strip runs down, from north to south, along the eastern shore of the Mediterranean Sea. The land of Philistia ended at the Sinai Peninsula, bordering on Egyptian territory. The Gaza Strip ends at the Sinai Peninsula, bordering on Egyptian territory.[5] The modern re-creation and incarnation of ancient Pilashet, Philistia, the land of the Philistines, *is the Gaza Strip*.

The Philistine Ingathering

And so another piece of the ancient mystery was falling into place. The people who were to take on the name of the ancient Philistines, the Palestinians, were now brought back to dwell on the same soil on which the ancient Philistines had dwelt. In other words, Pilashet, Philistia, the land of the Philistines, was now again inhabited by a people bearing the name of the *Philistines*. It was, again, no one's plan or intention. The influx of the people to the Gaza Strip only happened because of war and because Egyptian forces happened to have seized that particular strip of land, which happened to be the same strip of land occupied by the ancient Philistines.

There were, of course, other Arabs living in the West Bank. But even this had an ancient parallel. The Philistines had, in ancient times, made inroads to the north and east, but their central dwelling and headquarters was the land that bore their name, the coastal Mediterranean strip extending down to Sinai, Philistia.

Each to Their Ancient Ground

There was another connection that manifested at the time of the Philistine resurrection. The All-Palestine Protectorate, coming into the world at the time of Israel's rebirth, was, as we have seen, the first state to bear the name *Palestine*. But what exactly was it? It was the *Gaza Strip*. In fact, the All-Palestine Protectorate was the Gaza Strip's first name. So now the land of the Philistines was, for the first time since ancient times, again inhabited by a people bearing the name *Philistine*—and it became so, after two and a half thousand years, at the moment of Israel's return to its ancient land.

Each return would take place in 1948. Each would be birthed in war. Each would be sealed with a declaration of statehood. And each would involve a massive convergence—the ingathering of the Jewish people to Israel and the ingathering of the Filastin people to Philistia. The mystery had ordained that everything would return to its ancient soil.

---■■■---

The modern Israelites now inhabited the land of the ancient Israelites, and the modern Philistines, the land of the ancient Philistines. All was now set for the possessing of ancient spirits and hatreds.

Chapter 17

THE ANCIENT HATRED

WHAT EXACTLY WERE the ancient Philistines like?

"When They See War"

One of the earliest references or clues to the nature or reputation of the Philistines comes from the Book of Exodus. It appears just as the Israelites departed from Egypt:

> Then it came to pass, when Pharaoh had let the people go, that God did not lead them by way of the land of the Philistines, although that was near; for God said, "Lest perhaps the people change their minds *when they see war*, and return to Egypt."[1]

The existence of the Philistines at the time of the Exodus altered Israel's journey through the wilderness. The shortest and most natural route from Egypt to the Promised Land was by way of the Gaza Strip, or Philistia. But an alternate route was chosen in order to avoid the land of the Philistines.

The reason is given in the phrase "when they see war." The Israelites, having just emerged from slavery, were not ready for war. There were other peoples in the region, but only the Philistines presented so great a danger that the entire journey had to be altered. And it was not "*if* they see war" but "*when* they see war." It was a certainty. The Philistines would wage war against them.

The Warlike

In defining the Philistines, one Bible commentator writes,

> Because the Philistines were a *warlike* and *aggressive people*, it was feared that Israel might be alarmed at meeting them.[2]

Another writes:

> By the time of the Exodus, the Philistines were known for their *savage, warlike nature*.[3]

In the descriptions of the ancient Philistines, the word *warlike* appears over and over again. The accuracy of the word is attested to in biblical accounts, in extra-biblical ancient records, and in archaeological finds.

Philistine culture revolved around war. Vast amounts of time, energy, and resources were poured into the acquisition and production of weapons. War was glorified, violence was celebrated, and brutality was rewarded. Those who excelled in the arts of war and violence, the most fierce and brutal among them, were revered as heroes. They were, as one commentator put it, among

> the most feared enemies of God's people. They were brutal warriors.[4]

The Veneration of Blood

If a modern people were to be conformed into the image of the Philistines, we would expect the metamorphosis to involve the reappearance of the characteristics that most defined their ancient prototypes. We would expect that they would become increasingly warlike and predisposed to violence. That is exactly what would happen. We are not here speaking of a people's intrinsic nature or inborn trait. Every society and people are made up of individuals of diverse natures, tendencies, and traits. But cultures can assume specific and distinct characteristics. What we are referring to is the transformation of a culture and, through it, of a people.

For the Dragon to wage war against Israel's existence, he would need vessels of flesh and blood willing and able to execute it. It was not enough to resurrect the identity of an ancient people or their land. He would need to resurrect their ways and culture. He would seek to make his resurrected vessels into a warlike people. He would weave together a culture in which the shedding of blood was glorified and venerated.

The Darkening

The most prominent Palestinian leader of modern history was Yasser Arafat. Arafat was a violent man. But when he first set out to create his Palestinian army, few of his associates were adept at fighting. But in a matter of years the Palestinians would boast of thousands of young men trained for war and predisposed to violence.[5]

The people who now bore the name of the Philistines and dwelt on their land began morphing into their image and nature. A darkening came over them. They grew increasingly embittered, consumed with the desire not to build a prosperous culture but to execute vengeance. And as it was with the culture of the ancient Philistines, their culture now glorified violence and warfare.

As did their ancient predecessors, the resurrected Philistines poured massive amounts of time, energy, and resources into obtaining and producing weapons. As the society of ancient Philistia venerated its warriors, so modern Filastin, or Palestinian, society glorified those who had shed the blood of Israelis. And as ancient Philistine culture rewarded brutality, so modern Filastin culture did the same. Those who had killed Israeli citizens were rewarded with large sums of money by their government in a policy condemned by observers as "pay for slay."[6] As the metamorphosis progressed, the Palestinian, Filastin, people became increasingly focused on death. Countless polls revealed that the overwhelming majority of them were in favor of terrorist attacks and the slaughter of Israeli civilians.[7]

The Ancient Hatred

In order to use a people as vessels of rage, the Enemy had to transmit his hatred of the Jewish people to the resurrected Philistines. As the nature of the Accuser is to accuse and that of the demonic to demonize, so Palestinian culture became saturated with the demonization of the Israeli and the Jew, a culture of hatred, vilification, and rage.

With that mindset any action taken against the Israelis was justified as an act of vengeance. Even killing them was justified since the Israelis had been dehumanized. The rage of the ancient Philistines became that of the modern Filastin. And even in this, the ancient dynamics were resurrected. In the Book of Ezekiel it is written of the Philistines:

> This is what the Lord GOD says: "Because the *Philistines* acted in *vengeance* and *took revenge* with *deep contempt*, destroying because of their *ancient hatred*..."[8]

The ancient Philistines were known for harboring an "ancient hatred" against the people of Israel. So it was inevitable that in the resurrection of the Philistines the ancient hatred would be revived as well. Of the Philistines' ancient hatred one Bible commentary says this:

> It was *a hatred to the name and being of Israel*, they would *cut them off*...with *a perpetuated, endless enmity pursuing them*.[9]

The exact same words could be spoken of the Palestinian hatred for the name of Israel.

"Vengeance When They Could"

The commentary notes that the ancient Philistines

> took the opportunity to revenge themselves when
> the Jews were weak and low.[10]

So the modern Filastin people would likewise seek to exact vengeance on Israel when the Jews were "weak and low" or in a position of disadvantage or unpreparedness. Another commentary on the ancient Philistine hatred says this:

> It was an *old grudge they bore*, they had *spite and malice in their hearts*, and wanted an opportunity to vent it; *having determined to take vengeance when they could*, and *utterly destroy them*.[11]

Again, the same exact words could be spoken of the Filastin people of the Gaza Strip and of Hamas—they sought to exact "vengeance when they could." They were possessed by that which possessed their ancient predecessors and what another commentary referred to as "their thirst for revenge."[12]

Warriors of Black and Green

In Ezekiel's vision of Israel's resurrection the dry bones became not only a nation but an army, a nation of soldiers. So too did the resurrected Philistines. As the Israelis put on their army fatigues to defend their nation, the resurrected Philistines covered their faces in black and green cloth to hide their identities as they set out to bring death to the Israelis.

Behind the "endless enmity" and "ancient hatred" of the Palestinians for the Israelis was that of the ancient Philistines for the Israelites. And behind that was the still more ancient hatred, the orgidzo, of the Dragon for God and His people.

So we should not be surprised that the Filastin resurrection had produced an anti-culture, a culture of death that existed in negation and to bring about the nullification of Israel. They had become darkened, the unwitting vessels of the darkened angel.

One of the mysteries of the Philistine resurrection has to do with children. The first clue of that mystery will be an ancient giant.

Chapter 18

CHILDREN OF WRATH

THE SCRIPTURES GIVE us another clue into the warlike culture of the ancient Philistines. It appears in the account of David and Goliath.

"A Man of War From His Youth"

Goliath was a Philistine warrior. Day after day he stood before the armies of Israel, taunting them, challenging them to fight to determine which people would rule over the other. The soldiers of Israel were terrified. But a youth, the shepherd boy David, accepted the challenge. Israel's king, Saul, sought to dissuade him:

> And Saul said to David, "You are not able to go against this Philistine to fight with him; for you *are* a youth, *and he a man of war from his youth.*"[1]

The Hebrew word used for David's youth is *na'ar*. It speaks of a child, a boy, from infancy to adolescence. The word used for Goliath's youth is *na'ur*, derived from the same word, *na'ar*, and meaning the same. Goliath was thus described as a "man of war" from his childhood. We would assume it was not from infancy but from anytime thereafter until adolescence. Goliath's childhood centered on war. He was from boyhood a *man of war*.

Beyond revealing the nature of Goliath, the words reveal the nature of the culture in which he grew up. His induction into the ways of war would not have taken place in a vacuum. Nor would it have happened had it not been an accepted part of Philistine society. There is no indication that it was exceptional. It is a sign not only of a civilization that is predisposed to violence and war but one that is exceptionally so.

The Child Soldiers

Thus the Philistines undoubtedly trained their young children in the way of war. They inculcated their boys, from their earliest ages, into the practices and tactics of violence, battle, and bloodshed. They imparted into their children a mindset—a mentality of warfare and a brazen nature that could, without hesitation, initiate slaughter and destruction. It was this that made the Philistine warriors especially dangerous and deadly. And all the training had as its specific aim one target among all others—the Israelite.

If the ancient Philistines inducted their little ones into violence and war, we would expect the resurrected Philistines to do likewise. And that is exactly what they did. While in most cultures parents seek to shield their children from the ways of war, in Palestinian culture, as it was in the culture of the ancient Philistines, the children were dedicated by their parents and mentors into the purposes of war and destruction.

As Goliath was a "man of war" from his childhood, a child soldier, so of the modern Filastin children it is written:

> Palestinian children know they are expected to be
> child soldiers.[2]

Swimming, Arts and Crafts, and Killing Jews

For most children summer camp evokes images of play, sports, arts and crafts, boating, campfires, and new friendships. For the children of the Filastin, summer camp evoked different images—rifles, automatic firearms, military training, the loading of ammunition, and instruction given for the committing of murder.[3]

As for the staff and organizations running their summer camps, they were represented by such names as Hamas, Fatah, Palestinian Islamic Jihad, and Mujahideen Brigades. The Filastin children were indoctrinated and radicalized.[4] War was holy, and bloodshed was glorious.

As the ancient Philistine children were trained toward committing violence against a specific people, Israel, so it was with the training of their modern counterparts. They were trained to commit bloodshed against the Jewish people of Israel. So too they were taught to venerate terrorists as their role models in the hope that they would grow up to likewise commit acts of terrorism.[5] So the ancient thirst for vengeance spoken of in Ezekiel was transmitted to the children of the modern Philistines. And it was no accident that several of the camps had in their name the Arabic word for *revenge*.

The Darkened Kindergartens

The indoctrination came to the Filastin children not only through their summer camps but through their society and culture. It came through their television sets, through children's entertainment, cartoons, and storybooks. It even came through the curriculum taught in their public schools. Palestinian kindergartens were used to indoctrinate four- and five-year-olds into bloodshed. With toy guns in hand, they were trained to perform military operations and carry out mock executions of Israeli soldiers. One Palestinian schoolbook taught physics by showing the dynamics and forces involved in striking Israelis.[6] Others taught the Filastin children that Jews were evil, a danger, and a threat. Some of these lessons were given in classes funded by the United Nations.

Thus the dehumanization and demonization of the Jews began at the youngest of ages. And so it was no accident that Israeli survivors of Palestinian massacres would describe their killers as being totally devoid of any trace of humanity or mercy as they performed their atrocities. It was as basic to the invaders as was the alphabet that had been taught to them as little children, along with jihad and the waging of war against the Israelis.

Children on the Altars

The modern Filastin culture of death went beyond the celebration of their enemies' destruction. It celebrated, as well, the death of its own. The Filastin children were taught to long for their own deaths. They were taught that to be killed while seeking to shed Jewish blood was an act of glory. And so the Filastin children now dreamed of being killed. So too the Filastin mothers were taught to rejoice in the deaths of their children, while their little ones were led to perform mock funerals in which one of them would have the honor of playing the part of a corpse, having been killed while shedding Jewish blood.[7]

Among the gods worshipped by the ancient Philistines were Baal and Ashtoreth. Both were linked to child sacrifice.[8] And so as the Palestinians were progressively conformed to the image of the ancient Philistines, they would end up, as well, sacrificing their children to death. For the Dragon willed, above all things, for destruction. And so the Palestinians were, as well, the Dragon's victims. They were deceived by him, misled, used, abused, and consigned to destruction. For the Enemy is the enemy of all and wills for the destruction even of those he uses and who unwittingly serve as his instruments.

---■■■---

So after over two and a half thousand years the children of the Filastin people were again being baptized into the ancient hatred of Israel, and again, indoctrinated and trained into the ways of bloodshed on the soil of the Gaza Strip, on which they had received their training in ancient times. It was as if the spirit of the ancient Philistines had returned to their ancient shores to exact vengeance on their ancient enemies.

---■■■---

Vengeance would come through the sky.

Chapter 19

THE MISSILES

PROMINENT AMONG THE Philistine warriors were the archers. From
excavations of Philistine ruins we know that they used metal arrows as
opposed to those of wood and stone[1] and thus were especially lethal. The
archers allowed the Philistines to inflict deadly blows on the Israelites from
a distance.

Archers on Gilboa

The most celebrated moment of the Philistine archers took place at Mount
Gilboa in battle against the Israelite army of King Saul and his sons. Saul
had abandoned the ways of God and gone into battle without the favor of
God that had once rested on his life. The Book of 1 Samuel records the tragic
events that followed:

> Now the Philistines fought against Israel; and the
> men of Israel fled from before the Philistines, and
> fell slain on Mount Gilboa. Then the Philistines
> followed hard after Saul and his sons. And
> the Philistines killed Jonathan, Abinadab, and
> Malchishua, Saul's sons. The battle became fierce
> against Saul. *The archers hit him*, and he was
> severely wounded.[2]

Thus the Philistine archers brought an end not only to King Saul's life
but to his house and dynasty. By doing so, they ushered in the reign of King
David. For the Philistines the killing of King Saul and his house would stand
as the crowning moment in their wars against Israel, and for Israel, the most
infamous and traumatic.

The Long-Range Weapons of Philistia

Is it possible that the resurrected Philistines would employ a modern arma-
ment corresponding with the bows and arrows of their ancient predecessors, a modernized version of that by which they inflicted their most lethal
blow on ancient Israel? Since bows and arrows are no longer used in warfare,
what would be the modern equivalent? The bow and arrow belonged to a
small class of ancient armaments characterized as *long-range weapons*.[3] They

struck their targets over long distances. The Philistine archer would launch a projectile into the air; it would fly over the battlefield in the trajectory of an arc and, if successful, would bring death or destruction upon landing.

Is there a modern equivalent to the flying projectiles of ancient warfare? There is. We call them *missiles*. Missiles are the high-tech modern version of the arrows of the ancient archer. As did the arrow in ancient warfare, the missile stands at the forefront of the long-distance weaponry of modern warfare, and as did the arrows of the ancient warriors, the missile strikes its target over long distances.

The ancient launching device used to propel the arrows into the sky was the bow. In modern warfare, missiles are launched from launching pads and platforms. As the arrows of ancient warfare flew over city walls and battlefields in arch-like trajectories to bring destruction upon their landing, modern missiles likewise fly over battlefields, cityscapes, and regions in arch-like trajectories to bring destruction to their long-distance targets.

The Missiles of Gaza

The ancient Philistines fired deadly projectiles into the armies and dwellings of the Israelites. So the resurrected Philistines would do likewise, firing deadly projectiles into the cities and towns of modern Israel. Launching those projectiles were the Filastin militants and terrorists of Hamas, Fatah, and the Islamic Jihad. The victims of those missiles included, of course, those Israelis struck and killed by them, but also those suffering collateral damage. Studies would reveal that over half of the Israeli children in the regions under missile bombardment would suffer from stress disorders. The missiles began firing from Gaza into Israel in 2001. From then to the present time they have numbered into the tens of thousands.[4]

The majority of the ancient arrows fired by the Philistines at the people of Israel originated from Philistia. So in the Philistine resurrection the majority of the missiles fired into the cities and towns of Israel originated from modern Philistia, the Gaza Strip. They were forged or set in motion on the same soil on which, in ancient times, the arrows of the Philistines were forged and set in motion. And so the armaments of Philistia once again flew through the skies of Israel.

"Under Heavy Bombardment by the Missiles"

The connection between the weapons and tactics of the ancient and modern Philistines goes further. It is not only that the ancient Philistines fired arrows into Israel and the modern Philistines fired missiles that were *like* arrows. What is a missile? It is defined as this:

> An object which is forcibly propelled at a target,
> either by hand or from a mechanical weapon.[5]

The definition of an arrow is this:

> A *missile* shot from a bow and usually having a
> slender shaft, a pointed head...[6]

In short, an *arrow* is a *missile*. Thus the ancient Philistines fired missiles into the nation of Israel. So the resurrected Philistines did the same. In fact, one Bible commentary recounts the death of King Saul this way:

> After the fall of his sons, the archers discovered
> Saul, and *began to aim their missiles at him.*[7]

Another renders it this way:

> Saul...and his men now found themselves *under
> heavy bombardment by the missiles.*[8]

And so the ancient mystery replayed itself. As the Philistine warriors of ages past fired their missiles to bring death to the people of Israel, so now the resurrected Philistines again fired their missiles to bring death to the people of Israel. As the missiles of Gaza brought horror to the skies of ancient Israel, so now the missiles of Gaza again brought horror to the Israeli skies. And the resurrected people of Israel again "*found themselves under heavy bombardment by the missiles*" of the resurrected Philistines.

Missiles were not the only weapons used by Israel's resurrected enemies. They would use another, even more closely associated with the Jewish nation—the *kelah.*

Chapter 20

THE KELAH

I F FOR THE Philistines the crowning moment in their wars against Israel was the death of King Saul, the crowning moment for the Israelites was the victory of a shepherd boy.

The Shepherd Boy's Sling

The battle between the Israelite shepherd boy David and the Philistine warrior Goliath is celebrated not only by the people of Israel but by countless others throughout the world. So it is written:

> So David prevailed over the Philistine with a sling
> and a stone, and struck the Philistine and killed him.[1]

What was so shocking for the Philistines was that their most fierce and formidable of warriors was struck down by a shepherd boy using nothing more than a *kelah*, the Hebrew word for a *hanging* and in this case referring to a sling.[2]

Is it possible that the Philistine resurrection would preserve an ancient vendetta? Not that the modern Philistines would be conscious of the vendetta, but rather the spirit that possessed them would cause it to manifest.

The Inverted Kelah

In December 1987, in the land of the ancient Philistines, Palestinian rage erupted into what would be called the *First Intifada*, or uprising, against Israel. Because of its unique nature, it would also be known as the *Stone Intifada*. The same people who would later employ missiles and guns to war against the Israelis would, in this uprising, use more rudimentary weaponry—the stone and the kelah, the ancient sling.[3]

What did the two weapons have in common? They both went back to biblical times, and both were used in the wars of the Philistines and the Israelites. Now they were revived to be used in the war of the revived Philistines and the revived Israelites.

The stone and the kelah would again be used by the Palestinians in the Second Intifada. So the resurrected Philistines were now employing the same weapon employed by ancient Israelites against the ancient Philistines—to war against the resurrected Israelites.

Revenge of the Giant

It was as if, after three thousand years, a resurrected Goliath was taking revenge on a resurrected David by using David's weapon to do it. As David had used Goliath's sword against him,[4] so now the modern Philistines, the people of Goliath, were using the celebrated weapon of the Israelites, the sling of David, against the Israelites of the modern world. A pro-Palestinian Arabic observer wrote that the "Children of the Stones" had altered the world's perception

> by *inverting the symbol* of the Israeli David and the *Philistine* Goliath, *transferring the sling for the first time in history, to the hands of a Palestinian.*[5]

It is striking that the commentator was led to speak of the Israeli-Palestinian conflict in terms of the ancient conflict of the Israelites and Philistines. It was, in fact, a replaying of that conflict—an inverted replaying. It was Goliath's revenge. It was as if the spirit of the ancient Philistine had possessed the Palestinians to seek revenge. And so they chanted,

> *We want revenge* in the West Bank and Gaza, *with the sling and the slingshot.*[6]

The Dragon had resurrected an ancient nation from the dead to function as an anti-nation, to nullify Israel, and to take its place. It had always been the Enemy's will to turn the works of God against the works of God. So now he would invert the sling of David in war against David's people.

The Kelah as a Symbol

The Dragon was inverting the biblical account of David and Goliath to create an inverted narrative and, by that narrative, to stir up the world's hatred against Israel. The master of inversion had inverted the ancient story. He switched David for Goliath and Goliath for David. And the sling became, again, a most powerful weapon as swung by the hand of the Dragon.

The next mystery spans the age, from the melting pots of the ancient world to the computer defense systems of a modern nation.

Chapter 21

WARS OF IRON

ONE OF THE most important and least known factors in the wars of the Philistines against the Israelites was that of technology.

The Power of Metal

In the waging of ancient warfare, metal was critical. Archaeological excavations of the ruins of ancient Philistia have uncovered furnaces used for the smelting of metal.[1] Some believe that the Philistines also imported iron weapons from abroad to use against their enemies in the land. The Philistines sought to maintain their monopoly on metal weaponry. The Bible records:

> Now there was no blacksmith to be found throughout all the land of Israel, for the Philistines said, "Lest the Hebrews make swords or spears."[2]

So the Philistines did everything in their power to keep the Israelites from the practice of metallurgy. And when it came to war, this gave them a decisive advantage.

The Ancient Furnaces

Is it possible that the modern Philistines would follow in the footsteps of their ancient predecessors in this as well? They would. Under the leading of Hamas, the Palestinians of the Gaza Strip would learn the secrets of metallurgy. And as the ancient Philistines learned those secrets for the purpose of producing weapons and waging war, so too would their modern counterparts. As the ancient Philistines of Philistia produced those weapons specifically for the purpose of striking the Israelites, so the resurrected Philistines did so for the purpose of striking the modern Israelites. And they did so on the same soil as did their ancient predecessors.

Those who uncovered the ruins of the ancient Philistines found in their dwellings furnaces and facilities for the melting and forging of metal for the production of weaponry. So in the dwellings and underground chambers of modern Philistia, the Gaza Strip, the modern Philistines built furnaces and facilities for the melting and forging of metals for the production of weapons for the purpose of war and terror.

The Iron Key

There was one metal above all others that gave the ancient Philistines their greatest advantage in their wars against the Israelites—iron. The world was, at that time, moving from the Bronze Age to the Iron Age. Weapons of iron were more durable and destructive than those made of bronze. The Philistines were ahead of the Israelites in employing the new technology. So they kept the people of Israel away from the production of metal weaponry and, most specifically, away from the production of iron weaponry. And as one writer put it:

> As long as the Philistines maintained this monopoly, Israel could not hope to dislodge them from the plain.[3]

So iron would play a central role in the wars of the Israelites and the Philistines. Could it again play a central role in the wars of the resurrected Philistines and the resurrected Israelites?

Beating Plowshares Into Swords

In order to prevent the Gazans from producing weapons to be used against Israeli citizens, a ban was put into effect on the import of *iron* and the *iron alloy steel*.[4] In ancient times the Philistines kept the Israelites from making weapons of iron. In modern times the saga continued, as Israel sought to keep the Filastin people of Gaza from, likewise, producing weapons of iron.

But as did their ancient predecessors, they made them anyway. And as in ancient times it happened in Philistia, in the region of the Gaza Strip. They took scrap iron, one of their main exports, and repurposed it for weaponry. They took old iron cannon shells and turned them into rockets. They took the massive inflow of money sent them from around the world to be used for humanitarian purposes and used it, instead, to forge weapons to be used against the people of Israel.[5]

The Iron War Resurrection

It was the reign of King David, slayer of Goliath, that brought the age of Philistine domination of war to an end. David's victories would bring much-needed supplies of iron ore to his nation. Iron would now be used to Israel's advantage, to withstand the attacks of the Philistines and to overcome them.

So too in the modern wars of the resurrected Philistines and Israelites, *iron* would again play a central role—not only in the iron and steel weapons of Hamas but in Israel's response to them.

Israel's protective shield against incoming rockets and used extensively against those launched from the land of the Philistines, the Gaza Strip, would be called the *Iron Dome*.[6]

Israel's defense system aimed at keeping the Filastin Hamas from expanding its tunnels into Israeli population centers, its underground *Iron Dome*, would be called the *Iron Spade*.[7]

Israel's protective barrier against the Filastin militants and terrorists in the Gaza Strip would be called the *Iron Wall*.[8]

And Israel's added defense against not only rockets but drones and rounds of mortar sent in from the land of the Philistines would be called the *Iron Beam*.[9]

High-Tech Sling of David

In view of how critical a part was played by iron in the ancient wars of the Philistines and Israelites, it is striking to note how many of the defensive systems and weaponries used by the resurrected Israelites in their war against the resurrected Philistines bore the same name: *iron*.

And in view of the fact that it was King David who proved to be the most critical leader in the ancient wars of Israel and the Philistines, the king who turned the tide of those wars in favor of Israel, it is also striking that the Israeli military system designed to intercept the medium- to long-range rockets fired into the land was called *David's Sling*.[10]

-------------- ■■■ --------------

To the ancient Israelites, Philistia was the wellspring in which deadly evils were conceived and from which they were sent forth. And so from the resurrected Philistia new evils would be conceived and again be sent forth.

Chapter 22

THE CAULDRON

WE ARE ABOUT to see the mystery erupt in an explosion that would shake the world. Before we do, we must take note of one more puzzle piece of the ancient resurrection.

The Dangerous Separation

Though the clashes of Philistines and Israelites were many, the two peoples largely dwelt apart. And though Philistia was part of the Promised Land, to the Israelites it was a foreign land—enemy territory. The two peoples lived and functioned in two different worlds.

The separation between the two peoples might have seemed a means for peace. But in the case of the Philistines it was a dangerous thing. For it was in the Philistines' separation, in their separate world, that they were able to nurture their "ancient hatred" of Israel and their desire for revenge and then to manifest in violence and bloodshed.

So Philistia became for Israel the launching pad of calamities.

The Gazan Cauldron

So too in the Philistine resurrection, Gaza, or Philistia, became an entirely separate world from that of the Israelis. And in that separation the modern Philistines would nurture the ancient hatred and would devise plans of vengeance that would explode into acts of violence, of death, of destruction.

Philistia would again become the land of deadly schemes, the launching pad of calamity. It was no accident that it was from ancient Philistia that the first Intifada was birthed and that thousands of missiles would be sent from there into the land of Israel. In the third decade of the twenty-first century, it would again serve as the matrix of another evil, birthed and conceived on its soil, to be sent into the land of Israel. Philistia would again become a cauldron of evil.

The pieces of the ancient mystery would converge to produce a calamity that would shock the world.

Part VI

PREDATORS AND PREY

Chapter 23

THE PREDATOR

IT IS IN the very first pages of the Bible that the Enemy is personified as a serpent. In the very last pages of the Bible he is actually *called the "Serpent."*[1] In the letter of 1 Peter he is spoken of as a *"roaring lion."*[2] In Revelation 12 he is called *the "Dragon."*[3] And one can find, in the scriptures referring to wolves, another allusion to his nature.[4]

Serpents, Dragons, and Wolves

What do all these—serpents, dragons, and wolves—have in common? They are all predators. Each seeks a victim. Each is fierce. Each is, by nature, a killer. Each waits for the right moment to strike. Each launches its attacks against its victim to immobilize, kill, and devour it.

All these are, as well, attributes of the Enemy. The Enemy is a predator. He seeks for prey. He is, by nature, a killer. He waits for the right moment to strike. And he launches his attacks to wound, kill, and devour.

And so it would never be enough for him to resurrect a people to serve as an obstacle, a substitute, an imitation, or an enemy to the nation of Israel. He would resurrect them to become predators, to attack and destroy. They would wait for the right moment to strike. Then, at that moment, they would launch their attack to wound, kill, and bring terror to the inhabitants of the land.

The Invaders of Habitats

Another attribute shared by the creatures representing the Enemy is that they all infiltrate, they all break in, they all invade the dwellings of their prey to bring destruction. Serpents invade nests, lions invade watering holes, and wolves invade sheepfolds. So the Enemy would impel his resurrected vessel to invade the dwellings of Israel, to draw blood and bring death. Therefore, we would expect that at a time of vulnerability, a strike would come, an invasion, led by the spirit of the predator.

------- ■■■ -------

As to the prey, they would have no idea until it was too late.

Chapter 24

THE PREY

THE BORDERS SEPARATING ancient Philistia from the rest of Israel were never fully defined. That made it all the more dangerous for those Israelites living in such regions.

The Dangerous Lands

Not far from the dwellings of the Philistines were Israelite cities, villages, settlements, and homes. While most of the Philistines lived on Israel's western coast, on or near the Mediterranean Sea, the neighboring Israelite dwellings would have been located just east or inland of them. And while Philistia represented the center of Philistine life, the neighboring Israelites were living on their nation's outposts.

They were thus especially vulnerable to a Philistine attack or invasion. Though they would live their day-to-day lives with the appearance of normalcy, the truth was, their existence was in continual danger. And the lives they knew could, in an instant, be wiped away.

In the resurrection of Israel and the Philistines, the ancient dynamics would replay. Israelite civilians would again live in towns and villages that bordered the modern-day land of Philistia, the Gaza Strip. Several of those were kibbutzes or moshavs, communal settlements, with names such as *Be'eri, Nir Oz, Netiv HaAsara, Kfar Aza, Alumim,* and *Ein HaShlosha.* And as in ancient times the Israeli dwellings were located just east and inland of the Filastin dwellings.

Though the people of these villages and kibbutzes would live their day-to-day lives with the appearance of normalcy, the truth was that, just as it was for the Israelites who lived in the borderlands, they lived their lives in danger. Everything they knew could, in an instant, be wiped away—*and at a time when they least expected it, it would be.*[1]

The Fortified Cities

In order to protect the cities of Israel on the borders of Philistine or enemy territory, the kings of Israel fortified them. So it is written of King Rehoboam:

> He fortified the strongholds, and put captains in them.[2]

They would become known as the *fortified* or *fenced cities*.[3] So too the Israeli government sought to fortify the nation and the Israeli villages and cities that bordered the Gaza Strip by building a protective barrier between Israel and ancient Philistia, the Gaza Strip. The barrier would be referred to as the *security wall* or *security fence*.[4]

As King Rehoboam had stationed soldiers to watch over, guard, and protect the cities and towns of Israel in the vicinity of Philistia, so the Israeli government stationed soldiers to watch over and guard the cities, towns, and kibbutzes near the Gaza Strip. They were there on a Saturday morning in October when what they had long feared began to unfold.[5]

The Predator Invasion

The dynamics that had played out in ancient times between Philistia and the Israelite villages by its borders were about to replay—and with a vengeance. As the ancient Philistines were, at opportune times, able to neutralize and overcome the fortifications set up for the security of the Israelite villages, so the resurrected Philistines would, at the opportune time, be able to neutralize and overcome the security barrier that Israel had put up to protect its people—to the deadliest of consequences.

———————■■■———————

The result would be *October 7.*

Chapter 25

THE INVADERS

THE PHILISTINES, ALONG with the other Sea Peoples, wreaked havoc on the eastern Mediterranean world at the end of the Bronze Age. They raided the port cities of Syria, Anatolia, Cyprus, and Egypt.[1] They were raiders.

The Return of the Raiders

Even after settling down on the coast of Canaan, they still raided the land. They still invaded the villages and cities of those who lived inland of Philistia. And in their wars with Israel, raiding would play a prominent part. So it is written:

> So, the Philistines were subdued and they stopped
> *invading Israel's territory.*[2]

The implication of the passage is that Philistine invasion of Israelite dwellings was the normal state of affairs. It was the forcible ending of their raiding that was noteworthy—and temporary. They would, in time, resume.

King Jehoram of Judah was an evil monarch. He led the nation away from the ways of God. Judgment would come in the form of invading Philistines:

> Moreover the LORD stirred up against Jehoram
> the spirit of the Philistines....They came up into
> Judah and invaded it, and carried away all the
> possessions that were found in the king's house.[3]

The brazenness of their raid is evidenced by the fact that it was directed against the nation's capital, Jerusalem, and the king's palace itself.

From the Shores of Philistia

The raids continued from generation to generation. The chronicles of Israel record that later on, in the reign of King Ahaz, the Philistines conducted massive raids against the Israelite cities and villages of the nation's southern territories.[4]

So would the revived Philistines raid the land of the revived Israelites? The mystery would ordain that they would. And so they did on October 7, 2023.

It would catch Israel by surprise and leave the world in shock. But it should not have been unexpected. It is exactly what would have been expected to happen if the ancient mystery was to be replayed.

The Breach

In the verse quoted at the beginning of this chapter, the Hebrew word translated as *territory* is *gebul*. Beyond territory it means *boundary*, *border*, and *coast*. On October 7 the people bearing the name of the Philistines invaded Israeli territory, attacked from the coast, overwhelmed the border, and broke through the boundary. The Hebrew word translated as *invaded* is *baqa*. *Baqa* means *to break out*, *breach*, *burst*, and *break through*. All these things would likewise manifest on October 7.[5]

Philistine Warriors in Israeli Villages

As the ancient Philistines invaded the land to frighten, shock, and terrorize their Israelite victims, so their modern counterparts on October 7 did likewise.[6] The ancient Philistine invaders raided the land of Israel from the coast, moving eastward, inland, to wreak havoc and destruction on the Israelite towns and villages in their path. On October 7 the resurrected Filastin invaders, likewise, raided the land from the coast, moving eastward, inland, to wreak havoc and destruction on the Israeli towns and villages in their path.

In the ancient raids the contrast between the invading Philistine warriors and the unprepared Israelite villages could not have been any greater. The conflict was asymmetrical. So too on October 7 the ancient dynamics replayed themselves as the unprepared Israeli villages were overtaken by the warlike invaders from the coast.

As it had been for the ancient Israelites, the Philistine coastal plain, the Gaza Strip, had become for the modern Israelites the source of horror.

Could there be an ancient mystery that determined the location, the land, and the soil on which the calamity of October 7 would take place?

Chapter 26

GHOSTS OF THE SHEPHELAH

WHICH OF ISRAEL'S ancient towns, cities, and villages stood most vulnerable to the Philistine invasions?

The Negev

In the account of what appears to be the most massive of Philistine raids, we are given a clue. It is recorded in 2 Chronicles 28:

> The Philistines also had invaded the cities of *the lowland and of the South of Judah*, and had taken Beth Shemesh, Aijalon, Gederoth, Sochoh with its villages, Timnah with its villages, and Gimzo with its villages; and they dwelt there.[1]

The passage identifies a number of the cities and villages attacked by the Philistines but also describes the vicinity. They were located in "the South of Judah." The Hebrew rendered as *south* is even more specific. The word is *Negev*—as in *the Negev desert*, the vast stretch of arid land in Israel's southernmost region.[2] So the Philistines invaded Israel's southernmost villages and cities, those in the land of the Negev.

The Shephelah

The passage gives us another clue, another word to identify the region. The invaders targeted the dwellings of *the lowland*. What exactly were the lowlands? The Hebrew behind the translation is the word *shephelah*. *Shephelah* is the specific name given to one of Israel's regions. There are some who expand or restrict its application, but the simplest and most general understanding of the word appears in one of the most authoritative Bible commentaries. Accordingly, the Shephelah is:

> The name given to the land between the mountains of Judah and the Mediterranean Sea.[3]

Another commentary further defines its borders with regard to the land of Judah:

> "The valley" or the Shephelah, is bounded on
> the south by the Negev, on the west by the
> Mediterranean, on the north by the plain of Sharon,
> on the east by "the mountains."[4]

All this matches what we know of the Philistines and their dwellings that centered on the land's southwestern and coastal region. In the Book of Joshua the Bible identifies a number of the cities located in the Shephelah. Two of them appear as well in the previously quoted account of the Philistine raids on the land in 2 Chronicles 28—*Sochoh* and *Gederoth*.

"Gaza With Its Towns and Villages"

The cities and villages mentioned in Joshua at the end of the list and referring to the southernmost part of the Shephelah are of special note:

> And in *the Shephelah*....From *Ekron* to the sea...
> *Ashdod* with its towns and villages, *Gaza with its
> towns and villages.*[5]

These last three cities are especially significant as they were located in Philistia. So the Philistines, at the very least, lived in the lowlands on the border of the Shephelah and, by the most literal and simplest understanding of the text, within its parameters.

So which of Israel's towns, cities, and villages were most vulnerable to be targeted by the Philistine invaders? Those *nearest to*, *bordering*, and *just east and inland of Philistia*—and those towns, cities, and villages of the *Shephelah* and the *Negev*. Note the last region to be mentioned is *Gaza with its towns and villages*. What would this correspond with? The *Gaza Strip*.

On October 7, 2023, the war that had begun ages before the birth of the Roman Empire broke out before the eyes of the world. The people being transformed into the image of the ancient Philistines committed the ancient acts. Who would be their victims?

To the East of Philistia

The ancient Philistine invaders attacked the Israelite villages and dwellings bordering their region, just inland and to the east of Philistia.

On October 7 the resurrected Philistines, likewise, attacked and raided the Israeli villages, kibbutzes, and homes bordering their region, just inland and east of the Gaza Strip, Philistia. The ancient Philistine invaders attacked and raided the Israelite villages and dwellings in Israel's southernmost region. On October 7 the modern Filastin invaders attacked and raided the Israeli villages, kibbutzes, and homes of Israel's southernmost region.

The Convergence Ground

The ancient Philistine attackers invaded the Israelite villages and dwellings located in the lowlands and desert, in the region of *the Shephelah and the Negev*. The Shephelah, as identified in the Book of Joshua, extends *southward* to *Gaza*. The Negev extends *northward* to *Gaza*. Where do these two regions, the Negev and the Shephelah, intersect? *They intersect at Gaza.* More specifically, they intersect on the ground bordering and just east of, just inland of, the *Gaza Strip*.

It was at this very intersection, the convergence of the Negev and the Shephelah, just east and inland of the Gaza Strip, the ground targeted by the ancient Philistines, *that the Filastin attackers of October 7 invaded and brought destruction—the same ground.*

The Ancient Mystery on the Ancient Ground

It was on that same ground, most vulnerable to the ancient Philistine invaders, that the Israeli youths gathered to take part in their music festival when the invaders from Gaza turned their celebration into calamity.[6] *And it was that same ground* on which stood the villages, kibbutzes, and homes of Israeli families that would be devastated on October 7.

The resurrected Philistines had done to the resurrected towns and villages of the resurrected Israelis who dwelt in that ill-fated region just as had the ancient Philistines to the ancient Israelites. Those who watched it on their television and computer screens had no idea they were witnessing in real time the playing out of *an ancient mystery on the same ground as it played out thousands of years before.*

---------------◼◼◼---------------

Could the replaying of the mystery involve not only exact locations but exact strategies and acts?

Chapter 27

THE CAPTIVES

THE RAID ON King Jehoram's house provides an important detail involved in Philistine invasions.

Carried Away

The account of 2 Chronicles 21 reveals what else the invaders were after beyond the riches of the king's house:

> And they came up into Judah and invaded it, *and carried away...his sons and his wives*, so that there was not a son left to him except Jehoahaz, the youngest of his sons.[1]

What happened at King Jehoram's house was not an exception. It was the common practice of the Philistines to take Israeli captives from the lands and dwellings they invaded.

The Case of Ziklag

One of the most famous biblical accounts of an ancient raid resulting in the taking captive of Israelite civilians concerns the town of *Ziklag*. Though the raid was carried out by another of Israel's ancient enemies, the Amalekites, the account gives us more detail into what such raids involved.

As David and his men returned from battle to Ziklag, where they had left their wives and children, they discovered their loved ones were gone:

> So David and his men came to the city, and there it was, burned with fire; and their wives, their sons, and their daughters had been taken captive. Then David and the people who were with him lifted up their voices and wept, until they had no more power to weep.[2]

The enemy had invaded the town and taken its inhabitants, the women and children, captive. Then they set it on fire.

What was the purpose of taking civilians captive? The invaders could turn the captives into slaves or sell them into slavery to others. The captives could be used as bargaining chips, as security or leverage to force or stay the hand of an opposing power. And they could be taken captive simply as an act of dominance, vengeance, brutality, and rage.

"That You May Remove Them"

In a prophecy given in the Book of Joel, identifying the sins of varied ancient peoples, the evil of the Philistines is exposed:

> What have you to do with Me...all the coasts of Philistia?...*The people of Judah and the people of Jerusalem you have sold...that you may remove them far from their borders.*[3]

The Philistines took the people of Israel, or Judah, captive, then sold them as slaves to other nations, taking them far from their homeland. A commentary written on Amos' condemnation of the Philistines notes that the Philistines

> made frequent *incursions upon the Jews and Israelites.* And it is probable from this passage that they were guilty of some *injustice and cruelty, beyond the usual practice of war, in making captives.*[4]

From these and other scriptures, it is clear that for the Philistines to take civilians as captives was not exceptional but typical. It was their common practice. And the central targets of these abductions were Jewish or Israelite civilians. They were taken bound from their homes or villages and brought back to Philistia to be enslaved, sold, or put to death. Most would never return to see their loved ones, nor would ever again be seen by them.

The Autumn Captives

In the Enemy's resurrection of the ancient Philistines, we might expect the taking captive of innocent civilians to again manifest. And so it did. Who would we expect the captives to be? The resurrected Israelites. And so they were. How would they be taken captive? From an invasion originating in Philistia. This is exactly what would happen on October 7. The modern Filastin invaders would come from Philistia, Gaza, raid the Israeli villages, and those of the Israelis and their neighbors that they didn't immediately kill, they took away as captives.[5]

The captives of October 7 were to be used as human shields, security, bargaining chips, and leverage to force the hand of the Israeli government.[6] And beyond the strategic goals, the invaders took the Israelis captive to show their dominance, to humiliate and traumatize them, and as an act of hatred, vengeance, and rage.

It took place not in the midst of war but of peace. So a commentator on the ancient Philistine raids against Israel writes that they went beyond

> the usual practice of war, in *making captives*, perhaps taking the *peaceable inhabitants…*or, *making these incursions when Judah and Israel were at peace with them.*[7]

The Filastin invaders of October 7, likewise, focused their attack on *the peaceable inhabitants* and made them captives. The sleepy villages of the southern Israeli desert were awakened to an ancient nightmare.

"Their Wives, Their Sons, and Their Daughters"

The invaders of King Jehoram's Jerusalem took as captives the women and children, or youths, of the royal palace. The invaders of Ziklag took from David's men "their wives, their sons, and their daughters." Women and children were always most vulnerable to be taken as captives.

So in October of 2023 the world looked on in horror at the photographs and video clips of the Filastin invaders taking Israeli women, children, youths, and infants as their captives. Though there were no video clips of the ancient Philistines, their raids would have, no doubt, looked similar in the brutality and horror they produced.

"The Old and Infirm"

But the ancient Philistine invaders carried away more than women and children. The commentary continues:

> …taking the peaceable inhabitants *and all without distinction, the old and infirm* as well as the *young and healthy…*[8]

This too replayed on October 7. The modern Filastin invaders showed no distinction in their violence or their abductions. Video images showed them taking away the old, the frail, and the sick, white-haired Jewish grandmothers as their captives.[9] Among the elderly in the land that morning were those who could remember the Nazis rounding up their families in Germany and eastern Europe to send them to concentration camps. They had come to Israel to find refuge from those horrors but awoke that Saturday morning to find that the evil of their childhoods had never died and had now found them again.

"Burned With Fire"

When David and his men returned to Ziklag, they found that the invaders not only had taken away their women and children but had destroyed their village, as the account relates, "and there it was, burned with fire."[10] So when the rescue teams entered the villages and kibbutzes attacked on October 7, they found that the invaders not only had killed and abducted their inhabitants but, in many instances, had set their victims' houses on fire.[11]

Though we can't confirm its exact location, Ziklag was undoubtedly located in or by the Negev, in the southwest of Judah, and was originally occupied by the Philistines. In other words, the burned houses and desolated villages and kibbutzes of October 7 stood in the same region of the homes of Ziklag burned and destroyed thousands of years before. And it was, again, as if the spirits that had possessed Israel's ancient enemies had possessed another and, through them, had returned to the haunting ground.

Vayishbu

In the account of the Philistine raid on Jerusalem, the word used for the abduction of the royal family is *vayishbu*, from the Hebrew root word *shabah*. *Shabah* can be translated as *led, carried away,* or *transported into captivity.* The images of October 7 show the Filastin invaders leading away their victims into captivity on foot or transporting them in their vehicles.[12]

To where did the ancient Philistines take their Israelite captives? They took them back to Philistia. So on October 7, after wreaking destruction on the Israeli villages of the region, the Filastin invaders brought their hostages back across the border into the Gaza Strip—to Philistia.[13] There they would do with them as they pleased.

In the case of Ziklag, David would lead an attack against those who had taken the women and children captive, and would set them free. But in the case of Jehoram, he would never again see the members of his family whom the Philistines had taken away. They had decided to murder them. As for the captives of October, their fate and their lives would hang in the balance between those two outcomes.

———————————■■■———————————

We will now find, on Israel's southwestern shores, the footprints of the deadly creature described in ancient prophecy as a *monster.*

Part VII

DAY OF THE DRAGON

Chapter 28

THE REPTILIAN

THAT WHICH THE Dragon of Revelation 12 holds for the children of Israel, the Jewish people, the *orgidzo*, encompasses everything from antipathy, hostility, long-simmering anger, wrath, fury, rage, and madness to violent passion. On October 7, they would all manifest.

The Day of the Dragon's Wrath

As the Dragon is spirit but must war against a physical nation with physical instruments, flesh-and-blood enemies of Israel, his orgidzo, his fury, would have to take hold of them. It would have to possess them, take them over, inflame them, cause them to rage against the people of Israel as does the Dragon. And so it did. On October 7 the Dragon's orgidzo exploded upon the people of Israel. It would lead to a frenzy of violence. It would overrule any natural constraint of conscience. Those impelled by it would commit acts devoid of humanity and mercy, crimes against humanity.

The Cold-Blooded

In Revelation 12 the Dragon attempts to strike and devour the child of the woman, the child of Israel.[1] On October 7 the spirit of the Dragon moved on the Filastin invaders to strike the children of Israel. Though dragons are mythological creatures, they are reptilian and thus cold-blooded. And so on October 7 the Dragon's vessels would act in cold blood, committing cold-blooded acts of sadism on the children of Israel. In their raging was the Dragon's rage; in their cruelty, the Dragon's cruelty; and in their hatred of Israel and the Jews, the Dragon's hatred of the woman and her children. It was a day of horrors, as it was the day of the Dragon's orgidzo.

———————■■■———————

And yet what happened that October was the next step of the dark resurrection. Even the most evil of acts committed on that day were bound to a mystery of ancient origins.

Chapter 29

THE TERRORS

IN EZEKIEL 32 the prophet gives a unique glimpse into the fate of those nations that warred against the ways of God.

"Who Caused Terror in the Land of the Living"

They are spoken of as descending into the realm of the dead. Most of these nations are cited elsewhere in Scripture as enemies of Israel. And most share a common theme. Of the Assyrians it is written that they

> caused terror in the land of the living.[1]

Of the Elamites, they

> caused their terror in the land of the living.[2]

Of Meshech and Tubal, they

> caused their terror in the land of the living.[3]

And of the Sidonians, they will go down in shame

> at the terror which they caused by their might.[4]

What they all hold in common is *terror*.

The Khitit

The word translated as *terror* is the Hebrew *khitit*. It comes from the root word *khatat*, which means *to break down* as by *violence* or *confusion*, or by *instilling fear*, by *terrifying*. Israel's ancient enemies brought terror to the land. They did so as a by-product of their savagery and bloodshed and as a means of breaking the nation's will and causing it to submit to conquest and subjugation. The state of terror could be brought about by the sword or by psychological warfare. The Philistines employed both tactics.

They Were Terrorized

One of their most famous attempts to instill terror among the Israelites took place in the Valley of Elah and involved the giant Goliath. As the most dreaded of Philistine warriors, of colossal stature, and bearing colossal armor and weaponry, his presence was enough to provoke panic throughout the Israelite army. But it was also his words. Every day, he would stand before the Israelite soldiers, challenging, intimidating, and taunting them to fight him. The Scripture records:

> When Saul and all Israel heard these words of the
> Philistine, they were *dismayed* and greatly afraid.[5]

The word translated here as *dismayed* is *khatat*, the same Hebrew root word signifying the inflicting of *terror*. The Israelites were terrorized.

The Return of the Terrorist

If the Enemy was to resurrect the ancient enemies of Israel, we would expect him to also resurrect their ancient tactic—terror. It is worthy of note that one of the enemy powers mentioned in Ezekiel's prophecy to have *caused terror in the land of the living*, ancient Assyria, is considered the father of what, in the modern world, is known as *terrorism*.[6]

And so if Israel was to return to the modern world, we would expect it to be confronted with the modern counterpart of the ancient terror—*terrorism*. Further, we would expect the return of terror, or terrorism, to the modern world to be especially connected to the Middle East. We would expect it to be especially directed against Israel. And so it is.

As the ancient Philistines employed terror against Israel, we would expect the resurrected Philistines to become likewise joined to it. And so they were. It is no accident that the most famous Filastin leader, Yasser Arafat, was, for much of his life, the most famous terrorist in the world. Nor is it an accident that the Palestinian governments of both Gaza and the West Bank were rooted in terrorism and terrorist organizations. These, in turn, have inducted multitudes of their people into the doctrines and tactics of terror.[7] And that terror was intended to be directed against one nation, one people, Israel.

The Day of Khitit

As in ancient times, the terror of October 7 came from the coastal plain. As in ancient times, it came through armed warriors. And as then, it came from the land of the Philistines, from the Gaza Strip, from Philistia.

October 7 would constitute the worst single day in Jewish history since the Holocaust.[8] It was thus inevitable that the atrocities committed that day would be compared to those committed by the Nazis. Terror was everywhere, on the streets, in the home, in the children's rooms. October 7 would become Israel's day of khitit, the day it was *broken down* by *violence, confusion, fear—terror.*

The Monster's Day

Ezekiel's prophecy against those who caused *terror in the land of the living* centers on Pharaoh king of Egypt and begins with these words:

> Son of man, take up a lamentation for Pharaoh king of Egypt, and say to him...you are like a *monster* in the seas.[9]

The word here rendered as *monster* is *tanim*, the Hebrew word for *serpent* and *dragon*. So the prophecy of those who *cause terror in the land of the living* is connected to the words *drakohn* and *serpent*, the same words used of the Enemy, the Devil. The master of terror and father of terrorists is the Dragon. Combine this with the fact that the Greek translation of that word, *drakohn*, appears in the Bible's last book to speak of the one who wars against the nation of Israel, and one is led to the conclusion that the Dragon would wage war against Israel through the use of terror. And so October 7 was the day of the Tanim, the day of the Dragon's terror and the Serpent's atrocities. It was the day of the Monster.

———————■■■———————

One of the mysteries behind October 7 goes back to an event recorded in the Book of 1 Samuel when the Israelites found themselves overwhelmed in the face of a Philistine invasion.

Chapter 30

THE PITS

O N THE MORNING of October 7 young Israelis and their friends were gathered in the Negev desert near Kibbutz Re'im for the Supernova music festival. It took place just three miles from the Gaza Strip.[1] It was the same region where the ancient Philistines had invaded and terrorized the ancient Israelites.

Palestinian Invaders and Fleeing Israelis

At about sunrise rockets began firing over their heads in the desert skies. Then came the sirens, and then, the men from Gaza. They came in trucks, motorcycles, and paragliders. They blockaded the roads that could have served as escape routes.[2]

The Israelis went into hiding. Some hid in trees, some in bushes, some in undergrowth, some in orchards, and some in a nearby forest. Some covered themselves with sand. Some hid in vehicles. Some made their way to nearby bomb shelters. Some were slaughtered in their hiding places; others survived. Some survived by pretending to be dead.[3]

It was unprecedented. Never had masses of Israelis fled for their lives before masses of Palestinian gunmen. Never had they taken off in desperate flight in every direction to escape their Palestinian pursuers.

Philistine Warriors and Fleeing Israelites

But there *was* a precedent for what took place. It was an ancient one and recorded in Scripture:

> When the men of Israel saw that they were in danger (for the people were distressed), then the people hid in caves, in thickets, in rocks, in holes, and in pits.[4]

In the face of a multitude of armed militants, the ancient Israelites fled in terror, seeking places to hide. From whom were they hiding? *The Philistines.* It was the massive armed Philistine militants that had sent them fleeing for their lives and in search of places to hide.

On that October morning, the ancient drama replayed. The resurrected

Philistines had again invaded the land, and the resurrected Israelites had again gone into hiding, keeping silent and still in fear of their pursuers.

"They Fled in All Directions"

The following words describe what happened on October 7 with regard to the Israelis in the face of the invading Palestinians:

> They fled in all directions....Most took refuge in the hiding-places.[5]

But those words were not written of October 7 but of an event that took place three thousand years earlier. They are from a Bible commentary on the ancient flight of the Israelites from the Philistine warriors, when *they fled in all directions.*[6] The following words, though, *were* written of the events of October 7:

> *They fled in all directions*—some into the open desert or surrounding orchards.[7]

They fled in all directions—the same exact words used to describe the ancient event and its modern replaying by its resurrected players.

Into the Woods and Thorn Bushes

Of the ancient event one commentator writes that the Israelites fled the pursuing Philistines by hiding in *woods and forests.*[8] Of the Israelis who fled the Filastin militants three thousand years later one would recount,

> *I started to run into the forest and hide.*[9]

One of the words used in the Scripture to describe where the Israelites hid from the Philistines can be translated as *thicket, briar,* or *thorn bush.* As one commentary says regarding the site of the conflict:

> There was a very great number of *brambles and thorn bushes.*[10]

Of the Israelis who fled the October 7 gunmen it was recorded:

> She would...seek shelter in some *bushes* to hide from roaming Hamas gunmen.[11]

And,

> others dispersed into the wilderness, scrambling *under cactus scrub and bushes.*[12]

"Anywhere They Could"

On the ancient conflict with the Philistines, one Bible commentator writes:

> At this time of crisis the Israelites *hid anywhere they could.*[13]

Of the Israeli victims of October 7, it was recorded

> hundreds of attendees were fired upon from all directions, scattering and *hiding wherever they could.*[14]

"The Holes Where They Have Hidden"

In 1 Samuel 14 the Scriptures record a confrontation between Jonathan, the son of the Israelite king Saul, and a Philistine garrison. Jonathan and his armor bearer appear before the soldiers of the Philistine fortress:

> And the Philistines said, "Look, the Hebrews are coming out of *the holes where they have hidden*".[15]

Of the Philistines' remark, one Bible commentary says this:

> The Philistines offer this mocking, denigrating statement for they were aware of the *terror their presence had produced in the Hebrews.*[16]

The presence of the Philistines had produced terror in the Israelites. The result of that terror was that the Hebrews hid themselves in holes to save themselves. It matches up with the earlier-mentioned account, when the Israelites hide themselves in *holes* and *pits*.

"The People Hid...in Holes and Pits"

Could this ancient and specific element in the war of the Philistines and the Israelites manifest again in the resurrection of both peoples? Could the phenomenon of Israelites hiding themselves in holes and pits in the face of Philistine terror appear now, in the modern world?

The following are accounts describing what the Israelis did in the wake of the invading Filastin gunmen of October 7:

> *He hid in a pit* to save himself.[17]

> Then I saw a *hole*, like it was dug by someone. *We went into it.*[18]

> *A man hiding in a pit* during the Oct. 7 Hamas assault...said he heard someone nearby screaming.[19]

> *She hid in a hole* and pretended to be dead to survive.[20]

> *Yuval hid in a hole* in the ground for hours and survived the horrible Nova massacre.[21]

> *People were hiding in ditches.*[22]

And from 1 Samuel 13, describing the attempt of the Israelites to survive in the wake of the Philistines:

> Then *the people hid...in holes, and in pits.*[23]

And so the ancient mystery again played itself out on the stage of the modern world. The resurrected Philistines terrorized the resurrected Israelites, and the resurrected Israelites hid for their lives *in caves, in thickets, in rocks, in holes, and in pits*, just as had the ancient Israelites. Each had done exactly as they had in ancient times.

——————■■■——————

The next mystery will begin with the acts of ancient Middle Eastern invaders and end on computer screens across the world.

Chapter 31

THE ACT OF GALAH

THE LORD GAVE the prophet Isaiah a strange command:

> "Go, and remove the sackcloth from your body,
> and take your sandals off your feet." And he did so,
> walking naked and barefoot.[1]

The Naked Prophet

It would seem a most inappropriate directive—for a man of God to walk naked in public. But it was a prophetic act:

> Then the LORD said, "Just as My servant Isaiah
> has walked naked and barefoot three years for a
> sign and a wonder against Egypt and Ethiopia, so
> shall the king of Assyria lead away the Egyptians
> as prisoners and the Ethiopians as captives, young
> and old, naked and barefoot."[2]

Isaiah's nakedness was a sign foreshadowing the fall of the Egyptians and Ethiopians at the hands of the Assyrians. They would be taken captive, stripped naked, and humiliated.

The Captive's Humiliation

When God's Word pronounces judgment on the Philistines, it cites their carrying away the people of ancient Israel as captives. We have already seen how the modern-day Filastin invaders carried away the Israelis captive. But there was more to the mystery.

Behind the words *carried away captive* is the Hebrew word *galah*. The word can rightly be translated as *to take captive*, but its meaning goes deeper. It literally means *to uncover, to unclothe, to denude, to strip naked*. So the same Hebrew word meaning *to take captive* also means *to strip naked*. The connection between the two translations is that it was a common practice among the enemies of ancient Israel to strip naked their captives. It was an act of humiliation, disgrace, domination, and debasement. The implication is that the Philistines not only took the people of Israel captive but humiliated them, uncovered them, stripped them naked.

The Act of Galah

The Filastin militants who entered the land of Israel on October 7 did more than take Israelis captive. Many of their female victims were found stripped naked. The invaders had humiliated them, sexually assaulted them, brutalized them. Some were raped; some were beaten; some were tortured; most were killed. Their bodies were found in their homes or on the sands of the Negev unclothed.[3] Those with years of experience in rescue work would be shocked on October 7 and in the days that followed with the number of victims they found stripped naked. But it was an evil that stretched back thousands of years into the past, an act of degradation performed by Israel's ancient enemies. What confronted them was *the act of galah*—a word especially associated with the ancient Philistines.

Among the most famous and earliest images of the October 7 atrocities was that of a young Israeli woman who had attended the Supernova music festival. Soon after the invasion a video surfaced showing Hamas militants riding in the back of a pickup truck with the body of a young woman. It was her. She had been stripped near naked.[4]

Galah.Com

Beyond stripping their captives naked, the enemies of Israel would typically take them back to the land from which they had come and parade them naked through the city streets.[5] So on October 7 the Filastin invaders took their captives and victims back to the Gaza Strip. They proudly displayed the body of the young Israeli woman in the pickup truck beyond the streets of Gaza as they posted images of her body on the internet, paraded on computer screens and paraded throughout the world.

It was not that the modern Filastin invaders had any idea of the prophecy foretelling the judgment of the Philistines or the ancient act that invoked it. Nevertheless, they performed the act of *galah* and did so before the world.

The next mystery of October 7 begins on the mountain of a slain king.

Chapter 32

SPECTERS OF GILBOA

THE DAY AFTER King Saul was struck down by the Philistines on Mount Gilboa, his enemies discovered his body. The Bible records,

> They found Saul and his three sons fallen on Mount Gilboa. And they cut off his head and stripped off his armor, and sent word throughout the land of the Philistines, to proclaim it in the temple of their idols and among the people. Then they put his armor in the temple of the Ashtoreths, and they fastened his body to the wall of Beth Shan.[1]

The Headless King

Though they found their enemy slain, it was not enough. They stripped his armor, placed it in the temple of their goddess, Ashtoreth, and fastened his body to the city walls. And as an act of total dominion, they cut off his head. They did similarly with the bodies of his three sons. Such acts were in keeping with the Philistines' reputation for brutality.

But there was more to the story. At the time of King Saul's death, another battle would have still been fresh in the Philistines' collective memory—and another beheading. When their most feared warrior, Goliath, was struck down, the Israelite shepherd boy David took up the fallen giant's sword and cut off his head. The champion of Philistia was beheaded by a boy representing King Saul's army.

But now, at Mount Gilboa, the tables were turned. As a soldier of King Saul had cut off the head of a Philistine warrior, now Philistine warriors cut off the head of King Saul. Whatever the motives, the most celebrated victories in the war of the Philistines and the Israelites each involved decapitation.

King Saul's Head in the Temple of Dagon

What then happened to the head of King Saul? The answer is found in the Book of 1 Chronicles:

> [The Philistines] took his head and his armor, and sent word throughout the land of the Philistines....
> They...fastened his head in the temple of Dagon.[2]

105

His head was taken back to Philistia and, it is believed, to the city of Ashdod, in which stood the great temple of Dagon. The king's head was fastened to the wall of the pagan sanctuary as the crowning trophy of their victory, the spoils of war, a gift to Dagon, and a sign proclaiming the supremacy of their gods over the God of Israel.

For the Israelites, the displaying of their king's head in the temple of their enemies had to be one of the most demoralizing consequences of the war. The Philistines used it to full effect to torment their enemies. So the act of decapitation played a central, strategic, and symbolic role in the wars of the Philistines and the Israelites. Could the crowning act of the ancient wars make its way into the modern world? Could the resurrected Philistines resurrect it?

The Ancient Barbarities

When the Filastin militants invaded Israel on October 7, they came with guns and explosives. But they also came with knives and other implements of cutting. What they were about to do did not happen on the spur of the moment but was planned out before they set foot into the land.

They came to do more than kill or take captive. They came to perform decapitations. And so they did. They cut off the heads of those who battled them. They cut off the heads of those who didn't and were defenseless. They cut off the heads of the Israeli villagers. They cut off the heads of Israeli fathers and mothers. They cut off the heads of the Israeli women they sexually brutalized. They cut off the heads of Israeli children. They even cut off the heads of Israeli babies.[3]

The resurrected Philistines had reenacted the dark acts of their ancient predecessors. The Dragon had possessed them to take on the role of the ancient Philistine invaders. And now he conformed them into their ancient barbarities.

———————■■■———————

When one finds fingerprints at a crime scene and one can match them to those found in other crime scenes, one will likely be able to identify the criminal. What happens if we do that with the fingerprints of October 7?

Chapter 33

THE DRAGON'S FINGERPRINTS

WE HAVE SEEN more than one writer describe the ancient Philistines as a people of "brutal warriors." One of their brutal acts of war was that of mutilation.

The Mutilations

The fact that two of the most famous leaders of ancient Israel suffered mutilation at the hands of the Philistines confirms not only the violent nature of that ancient people but their tendency to perform that particular act—mutilation. Not only did they commit the act; they publicly displayed it.

On October 7 the ancient act of the Philistines was performed on the people of Israel—the act of mutilation. Again, those recovering the bodies from the calamity were shocked and traumatized by what they discovered. A major element of the invasion was mutilation. It was so consistently performed on the victims of that day that it had to have been planned out by those who orchestrated the invasion.[1]

Elisha's Prophecy

The prophet Elisha reproved one of Israel's ancient adversaries for the barbarities he would commit against the people of Israel:

> I know the evil that you will do to the children of
> Israel: *Their strongholds you will set on fire*, and
> their *young men you will kill* with the sword; and
> *you will dash their children*...[2]

Every one of the acts spoken by the prophet would be committed by the invaders of October 7. Israel's resurrected enemies would "set on fire" Israeli strongholds. Young Israeli men they would "kill." Israeli children they would "dash." Hamas invaders were not reading the Scriptures of Israel when they planned their invasion or their atrocities. Yet on that day, they would repeat the acts of their ancient counterparts.

The Dragon's Other Crimes

It was the hour of the Dragon's savagery. It evoked his other savageries, crimes, and atrocities against the children of Israel. When the young Israelis hid themselves behind anything that would conceal them, it evoked the days in which their relatives had hidden themselves from the Einsatzgruppen, the Nazi death squads that had hunted them down in fields and house to house.[3] But it was also there in the prophecy of the Dragon in Revelation 12. It was implicit in the word *dioko—to aggressively chase, to pursue as a hunter seeking his prey.* And when the Filastin invaders stripped their Israeli victims naked, it evoked not only the *galah* of the ancient Philistines, Assyrians, and Babylonians, but the stripping naked of the Jews of Europe by Hitler's SS, the act of *galah* in the concentration camps of the Third Reich.

***

Though it shocked the world, what happened on October 7 was only the most recent manifestation of a war that had begun in the days of cuneiform inscriptions and stretched forward to the days of electronic media. What happened that day bore witness to the transcendence of evil and of the creature that embodied it.

***

Could a story that many of us heard as little children contain an ancient mystery behind October 7?

Part VIII

THE
MYSTERY
OF
GAZA

Chapter 34

THE DARK MATRIX

WE HAVE SPOKEN of the region known as the *Gaza Strip*. We now focus on the heart of that region, its de facto capital, the *city of Gaza, or Gaza City*. There we will find a mystery and a template stretching back to ancient times. Appearing numerous times in Scripture, Gaza was, for Israel, a continual source of evil, conflict, and anguish.

A Womb of Evils

With the resurrection of Israel came the return of Gaza as the matrix of conflict and evil for the Jewish people. When Israel was reborn on its ancient land, the Gaza Strip was born from the ancient city. It was there that the Palestinian National Council and the All-Palestine Government convened. It was from there that Arab troops went forth to destroy the newborn Jewish nation. It was from there that the first major Palestinian uprising against Israel was birthed. It was from there that missiles were fired to bring terror into the land of Israel. And it was from there that the invasion and atrocities of October 7 were planned, prepared, and sent forth.

───────■■■───────

What happened on October 7 and its connection to the Philistines and the city of Gaza go back to an ancient event predating the Hamas invasion by over three thousand years. It centers on an Israelite named *Sunshine*, or *Shimshon*. We call him *Samson*.

Chapter 35

THE SHIMSHON PROTOTYPE

THE STORY OF Samson is ingrained in the world's collective consciousness. But could it contain a mystery and key to an event of the modern world?

The Gazan Plot

The setting of the story is Philistia, the borderlands of Israel, and *Gaza*. That too was the setting of October 7.

The story is driven by the conflict between the Philistines and the Israelites—so too the events of October 7.

In the story of Samson, the Philistines seek to find a way to bring down the power of Israel as embodied by its strongman and hero, Samson. On October 7 the resurrected Philistines, likewise, sought to bring down the power of Israel. So it is written:

> When the Gazites were told, "Samson has come here!" they surrounded the place and lay in wait for him all night at the gate of the city.[1]

The plot to kill Samson was devised and set in motion in the city of Gaza. The subsequent plot that would actually bring about Samson's downfall would again center on Gaza. So the plot of October 7 that was intended to shake Israel to its foundation was devised and set in motion from Gaza.

In the Bible the people of Gaza are called the *Gazites*. Their resurrected counterparts are known in English as the *Gazans*—two versions of the same word. Each was involved in a plot against Israel's power.

"The Philistines Are Upon You!"

The Philistines knew they could never beat Samson in a face-to-face confrontation. Their plan was to catch him off guard in a moment of weakness, unguarded, and bring him down. So the Filastin terrorists of Hamas knew they could never beat Israel in a face-to-face confrontation. Their plan was to catch it in a moment of weakness, unguarded, and bring it down.

The Philistines exploited that moment of weakness to attack Samson. Samson heard the words "The Philistines are upon you!"[2] In seeking to fight off the attack, he found his strength was gone. On the morning of October 7 the Israelis awoke to the horrifying realization that *the Filastin invaders were upon them.* At other times they could have expected a prompt response from the nation's defense forces. But Israel was caught off guard. The victims found themselves without help. They found their strength was gone.

Blinding the Israelite

Then the Philistines took him and put out his eyes.[3]

The Philistines executed another act of mutilation. To put out the eyes of Samson was an act of humiliation and degradation. It was also an act of disabling—it was to nullify Israel's strongman. On October 7 the Filastin invaders did likewise. One of the atrocities committed on October 7 was the same as that which the Philistines performed on Samson—the Filastin invaders gouged out the eyes of their Israeli victims.[4] And as the putting out of Samson's eyes was connected to the city of Gaza, so on October 7 the putting out of eyes was likewise connected to the city of Gaza.

Blinding a Nation

There was another blinding performed that day. It took place in the realm of high technology. The putting out of Samson's eyes by the Philistines rendered him unable to resist and fight against them. The nation of Israel had installed an intricate high-tech defense system along its border with Gaza. But on October 7 it failed. One of the reasons it did so was that the first act of the invaders was to render it *blind*. Using drones, grenades, and other explosives, they neutralized the security sensors and cameras meant to alert the Israel Defense Forces (IDF) of a coming attack. The following are from news accounts of that day. Notice the word that keeps reappearing:

> The control centers were *blinded* and could not tell where the breaks through the physical obstacle were taking place.[5]

> Hamas most likely targeted these towers to "*blind* Israeli commanders and prevent communication among their units."[6]

> The soldiers that were supposed to protect them were *blind* to the unfolding disaster, or had been killed or kidnapped.[7]

As the ancient Philistine attackers blinded their Israelite nemesis, Samson, so the resurrected Filastin invaders now blinded the Israel Defense Forces. They had each disabled Israel's power and blinded the strongman.

The Nechushtayim

They...bound him with bronze shackles.[8]

The ancient Philistines would bind their captives to restrict their movements and prevent escape. The word used to describe the shackles by which they bound Samson is the Hebrew *nechushtayim*. The word is not singular but plural and, more specifically, denotes duality. It may refer to the binding of hands and feet. It is most literally translated as *two shackles*.

The most well-known shackle of the modern world is the handcuff. As in the account of Samson, the handcuff is a metal shackle and, as in the ancient account, is almost always referred to in the plural and, specifically, as shackles, as in a *pair of handcuffs*.

As the Philistine assailants bound their captive, Samson, in shackles, so the Filastin attackers of October 7 did likewise. They bound their captive Israelis in handcuffs. Some were shackled and blindfolded at the same time.[9] As the ancient Philistine attackers blinded and immobilized their Israelite captive, Samson, so did the Filastin attackers three thousand years later on October 7.

<hr>

This was not, of course, the end of Samson's story. Nor was it the end of what happened on October 7.

Chapter 36

THE PRISONER

The Philistines took him and put out his eyes, and brought him down to Gaza.[1]

THE ANCIENT STORY could only conclude in one place: the city of Gaza. Gaza would become Samson's prison, and Samson its prized trophy, the Gazan captive. As Gaza embodied the power of the Philistines, Samson embodied the power of Israel and the power of God. In Gaza, Samson appeared weak and helpless, a pathetic shadow of his former self. In Gaza it would all be put on display. It was in Gaza that the power of Israel was to be brought down.

On October 7 Gaza's famous ancient role as the city of the Israeli captive was resurrected. The Filastin terrorists took their captive Israeli men, women, and children back to Gaza just as the ancient Philistines had brought their captive Samson there. And now again, it was in Gaza that the Israeli captives appeared weak and helpless, debased, as was the captive Samson.

Beit Ha-Asorim—the House of Prisoners

The Hebrew words in the account of Samson's captivity translated as *prison* are *beit ha-asorim*.[2] It literally means *the place of captivity, the house of the captives*, or *the place of the bound*. It can include any chamber of captivity, anyplace where captives are kept, restrained, or bound. On October 7 Gaza was filled with chambers of captivity, aboveground and below, where hundreds of miles of the tunnels built by Hamas would serve as an elaborate prison house.[3] For the Israeli hostages, Gaza became their beit ha-asorim, their prison house, as it had been for Samson.

The Transgressions of Gaza

And yet Gaza's connection to the captive Israelis transcends the story of Samson. In the first chapter of Amos the evil of *Gaza* is exposed:

> For three transgressions of *Gaza*, and for four, I will not turn away its punishment, *because they took captive the whole captivity.*[4]

Gaza was representative of the Philistines. Its evil was undoubtedly that of all Philistia. At the same time, the prophecy specifically cites Gaza, and so it must first be applied to that ancient city.

What was Gaza's evil? It was the taking of captives from Israel. The ancient Philistine invaders would bind the Israelite civilians and transport them to Gaza.

On October 7 the resurrected Filastin invaders transported their Israeli captives to the same city. It was the ancient "transgression of Gaza" playing itself out in the modern world and, again, carried out by those who did so unknowingly.

"Because They Took Captive Whole Communities"

The invaders of October 7 had, as their goal, to kill or take captive entire Israeli communities. In view of this, it is especially striking to read the various translations of the scripture exposing the sins of Gaza:

> Because she [Gaza] took *captive whole communities.*[5]

Another translation reads,

> The people of Gaza have sinned....They sent *whole villages* into *exile.*[6]

So on October 7 the captives came from the Israeli villages. *Whole communities* and *whole villages* were invaded and their survivors taken captive to Gaza.

"Defenseless Judaean Villages Were Overpowered"

Another commentary on the prophecy explains the sin of Gaza in terms of the *extreme barbarity* committed on the bordering Jewish villages. It involved

> *border warfare, in which defenceless Judaean villages were overpowered.*[7]

This too matches what happened on October 7. It was then that Gaza waged *border warfare in which defenseless Judaean villages were overpowered and acts of extreme barbarity performed.*

The Prophetic Image

Reading the following Bible translation of Amos' prophecy against Gaza, the parallel to October 7 is striking:

> For three transgressions of *Gaza* [*Philistia*] and for
> four...I will not reverse its punishment or revoke
> My word concerning it, because...*they took captive
> the entire* [*Jewish*] *population* [*of defenseless
> Judean border villages, of which none was spared*].[8]

What would happen if we simply took the key words given in the Bible translations and commentaries concerning Amos' prophecy against Gaza? What would we get? We would get this:

> Philistia [the Gaza Strip]...border warfare...
> incursions upon the Jews...border villages...raids
> made upon the villages of Judah...defenseless
> villages...villages were overpowered...cruelty
> beyond the usual practice of war...the old and
> infirm as well as the young...they took captives...
> taking the peaceable inhabitants...Gaza...extreme
> barbarity...none was spared.

The ancient evils of Gaza end up producing a composite picture of exactly what happened on October 7.

———————■■■———————

Could the story of Samson have even foreshadowed what would break out in Gaza, the West Bank, and other parts of the Middle Eastern world in the wake of the calamity?

Chapter 37

THE SPECTACLE

THE CAPTIVITY OF Samson caused the people of Gaza and the rest of Philistia to rejoice.

The Gazan Celebration

> Now the lords of the Philistines gathered together to offer a great sacrifice to Dagon their god, and to rejoice. And they said: "Our god has delivered into our hands Samson our enemy!"[1]

They held a great celebration to give thanks to their god Dagon, whom they credited for their victory. But the celebration wasn't complete without its cause being present:

> So it happened, when their hearts were merry, that they said, "Call for Samson, that he may perform for us." So they called for Samson from the prison, and he performed for them.[2]

"That He May Entertain Us"

So they sent for Samson to be taken out of the prison house to *perform* for them. The Hebrew word translated as *perform* is *sakhak*. It means *to laugh* or *laugh at* especially in the context of scorn, contempt, and derision. Some translations render the directive as, "Call for Samson, that he may entertain us, amuse us, make us laugh." They wanted to put Samson on display as an object of mockery, to make of him a spectacle.

When one compares this with what the Philistines did to King Saul, a pattern emerges. In Saul's case they put his armor, his body, and his head on display. In each case the spectacle involved mutilation, a severed head and a captive with his eyes gouged out.

The ancient pattern would reemerge on October 7. More than one observer would note the difference between the Nazis and the Filastin invaders—namely, the Nazis sought to hide their atrocities from the world. But the resurrected Philistines boasted in them and displayed them. They made spectacles of their atrocities before cheering crowds and on the internet across the world.[3]

"Rejoice Not Thou, Whole Palestina"

But it wasn't just the spectacle that stands out in the ancient account but the Philistines' joy and celebration over the humiliation and mutilation of their captive:

> The lords of the Philistines gathered together...*to rejoice.*
>
> When *their hearts were merry...*
>
> That he might *make us laugh.*

The joy and celebration were not a fluke. They were so much a part of Philistine practice or culture that they were noted in the Hebrew Scriptures on more than one occasion. Upon the death of a Judaean king a word is given to the Philistines through the prophet Isaiah:

> Do not *rejoice*, all you of *Philistia*, because the rod that struck you is broken.[4]

The King James Version renders Isaiah's prophecy this way:

> Rejoice not thou, whole *Palestina* [Palestine].[5]

"Lest the Daughters of the Philistines Rejoice"

So upon the death of King Saul and his sons at Mount Gilboa, David sings a song of sorrow and mourning. The song opens with a word concerning the Philistines:

> How the mighty have fallen! *Tell it not in Gath, proclaim it not in the streets of Ashkelon—lest the daughters of the Philistines rejoice, lest the daughters of the uncircumcised triumph.*[6]

Gath and Ashkelon were two of the chief cities of the Philistines. David uses them to speak of all the Philistines. David knew that when they heard of King Saul's death, there would be rejoicing in the streets of Philistia—the Gaza Strip.

The Dark Celebrations

From the captivity of Samson to the death of King Saul to the oracles of Isaiah, the calamities of Israel produced celebrations and joy among the Philistines. The dark celebrations of Philistia would continue until there was no more Philistia and no more Israel in the land. All three had vanished from the world.

But with Israel's resurrection and that of the Philistines, it was only a matter of time before the dark celebrations of Philistia would return. On October 7 the ancient phenomenon again manifested and at full strength. The streets of Philistia were again filled with rejoicing and celebrations over Israel's calamity. Throughout the Gaza Strip, ancient Philistia, Palestina, as well as the West Bank, the resurrected Philistines rejoiced.

"You Clapped Your Hands"

The rejoicing of Israel's ancient enemies over its calamities is described, as well, in the Book of Ezekiel:

> Because *you clapped your hands, stamped your*
> *feet, and rejoiced in heart with all your disdain for*
> *the land of Israel.*[7]

Upon hearing the news of Israel's calamity, her enemies clapped their hands and stamped their feet in joy over Israel's disasters. So on October 7 Filastin revelers sang and chanted in the streets. They clapped their hands and stamped their feet in unison in joy over the day of Israel's horrors.

"They Praised Their God"

In the story of Samson the people of Gaza rejoiced over Israel's tragedy. On October 7 the people of Gaza again rejoiced over Israel's tragedy. In the ancient account, when the people of Gaza saw what had been done to Samson, it is written,

> They praised their god; for they said: "Our god has
> delivered into our hands our enemy."[8]

So on October 7, when the people of Gaza heard of the attack on Israel, they praised their god. They declared, "Allah is great!" and thanked him for delivering the Israelis into their hands.[9]

The Children's Play

In the ancient account the people of Gaza rejoiced over Samson's mutilation. On October 7 the people of Gaza and Philistia rejoiced over the day when the Israelis were mutilated.

David had told the people of Philistia to not rejoice over the death and beheading of King Saul. But on October 7 the people of Philistia, the Gaza Strip, rejoiced over the day that the Israelis were beheaded. David's lamentation specifically mentions the rejoicing of the *daughters of the Philistines*. On October 7 the Filastin sons and daughters, youth and little children, were brought into the celebration and rejoiced with their parents over what had been done to the Israelis.[10]

They would continue to rejoice in the days and weeks that followed as their schoolteachers led them in lessons that celebrated the atrocities of that day with songs, plays, arts and crafts, fun, and games.[11]

The Dragon's Joy

The rejoicing that broke out in Palestinian cities over October 7 was seen on television and computer screens by millions. To most of those millions it was a shocking addendum to the day of horrors. But what they were seeing was a phenomenon as ancient as the Bible, the dark celebrations of Philistia. The only thing new was its reappearance. Another puzzle piece in the dark resurrection had fallen into its ancient place.

We must now ask a question: For whom is calamity a cause for rejoicing, and evil the cause of joy? For whom is atrocity a cause for celebration? Such things are inversions. More than evil, they are satanic. Those who participated in such things were only vessels. They had all become partakers in the Dragon's joy.

Could the ancient story have presaged a manifestation of vengeance so precise that it would involve exact numbers?

Chapter 38

THE RETURN OF THE GAZANS

THE BLINDING, THE captivity, the mocking, and the degradation of Samson was not, of course, the end of the story.

The Fall of Dagon's Temple

So they called for Samson from the prison, and he performed for them. And they stationed him between the pillars. Then Samson said to the lad who held him by the hand, "Let me feel the pillars which support the temple, so that I can lean on them."[1]

After asking the Lord for the restoration of his strength, Samson braced himself against the two pillars that supported the Temple of Dagon and pushed with all his strength. The temple collapsed. In its fall it struck down the "lords of the Philistines"[2] and the multitude of Philistines celebrating the degradation of their blinded enemy.

The fall of Dagon's Temple at the hands of Samson and the resulting fatalities caused by that fall would constitute the most dramatic defeat ever suffered by the Philistines at the hands of an Israelite and on their home soil of Philistia and, in particular, in Gaza. Is it possible that the event could have repercussions for a subsequent age?

The Revenge of Gaza

If it could be said of the Philistines that they have *dealt by revenge and have taken vengeance*, and if their revenge and vengeance could span the ages, then what about the massive calamity they suffered in Gaza, the bringing down of Dagon's Temple by Samson? Could there be a modern event corresponding to and answering it—an act of revenge?

The ancient event involved a massive death toll. The corresponding event would likewise involve a massive death toll. The ancient event was part of the conflict between Israel and the Philistines. The corresponding event would involve the same conflict. The ancient event centered on Gaza. The corresponding event would also be centered on Gaza.

As death came to Gaza from Israel through Samson, could it mean that death would now come to Israel from Gaza? And could it involve the people of Gaza bringing death to the people of Israel? There *would* be a corresponding event—it would be October 7—the revenge of Gaza.

The Festival

> Now the lords of the Philistines gathered together
> to offer a great sacrifice to Dagon their god, and
> to rejoice.[3]

The Philistines and their leaders had gathered together to celebrate and give thanks to their god Dagon. Samson would bring calamity to Gaza on the day of its celebration.

So on October 7, when the Gazans brought calamity to Israel, they would, likewise, do so on *Israel's day of celebration,* when the people were celebrating a festival and giving thanks to God.[4]

Simcha

> Now the lords of the Philistines gathered together...
> to rejoice.[5]

The Gazans gathered together "to rejoice." The word used in the account and translated as *rejoice* is the Hebrew *simcha.* The calamity would come upon the Philistines in Gaza on the day of a celebration marked by the word *simcha.*

On October 7 it would all be reversed. The resurrected Philistines of Gaza would bring calamity to Israel on a Jewish holiday in which Israel was to *rejoice.* In fact the very name of the holiday, *Simchat Torah,* comes from the exact same word used to describe the Philistines in the account of Samson—*simcha.* So the vengeance of the Philistines would come upon Israel, likewise, on *the day of simcha.*

The Day of One Sacrifice

> Now the lords of the Philistines gathered together
> *to offer a great sacrifice.*[6]

The account relates that the Philistine leaders planned to offer *a single sacrifice* to their god. Samson brought calamity to Gaza on the day of the sacrifice.

October 7 was both a holiday of rejoicing, *Simchat Torah,* and a holy day known as *Shemini Atzeret. Shemini Atzeret* is unique among Hebrew holidays in that it ordained that *a single sacrifice be offered* to God. So as did Samson to Gaza, now Gaza brought calamity to Israel, likewise, on a festival day on which *a single sacrifice was to be offered.*[7]

The Return of the Three Thousand

How many Filastin militants invaded Israel on October 7? It took some time for the Israel Defense Forces to make that determination. The assessment came almost one month after the attack. An article sums up the findings:

> A new assessment by the IDF holds that the number of Hamas terrorists who invaded Israel is much higher than the initial estimates. *About 3,000 Hamas terrorists* invaded the Western Negev from dozens of infiltration points on the morning of October 7.[8]

The number refers to the actual Hamas-led invaders of October 7, specifically the armed men who entered the land. (A mob of unarmed Palestinians would follow their lead, coming in later.) So the number of Filastin militants who entered the land on October 7 was, in the words of the IDF, *about three thousand.*

How many Gazans did Samson kill by bringing down the Temple of Dagon?

There is only one number given in the account of the destruction in the Book of Judges. It's the number of the Gazans on the roof watching Samson "perform":

> ...*about three thousand* men and women on the roof watching while Samson performed.[9]

The number of Gazans in the ancient account was *about three thousand.* On October 7 the number of Gazans who invaded the land to slay the people of Israel was *about three thousand.*

It is not only the same number—it is *the exact same phrase.* The ancient Hebrew reads *shiloshet alfanim*, the exact translation being *about three thousand.* The number of Gazan militants who invaded Israel on October 7 was given by the IDF as *about three thousand.*

The Dragon's Conjuring

So the Dragon's resurrection involved not only the return of the ancient Philistines but, on October 7, *the return of the exact same number—the return of the three thousand Gazans.* In other words, the Palestinians of Gaza were now conformed specifically into the image of the three thousand ancient Gazans that Samson slew. The invaders had long committed themselves to vengeance, but it was now as a vengeance that spanned three thousand years from the fall of the Temple of Dagon.

It was as if the Dragon had summoned the three thousand into the modern world that they might rise from the dead to exact their vengeance on the children of Israel.

———————■■■———————

If the invaders of October 7 were the most recent players in an ancient war, is it possible that there was a direct line of succession leading up to their coming? Is it possible to find predecessors, forerunners, who passed their torches and mantles on to them? And if that ancient war is ultimately a spiritual one, is it possible that we might even find the familiar spirits that possessed them, one after the other?

We will now find a line that stretches from the Gaza Strip on October 7 to the beer halls of Munich, Germany.

Part IX

THE TRANSMISSION OF SPIRITS

Chapter 39

THE MUFTI

IF BEHIND THE world's rage against the Jewish people is a spiritual entity as represented by the Dragon, we would expect that that war would transcend any one person, movement, organization, kingdom, or power.

The Dragon's Torch

Through the passage of time the war's central core and inner essence would remain the same, but the names would change and the forms would morph. The war would be waged from one generation to the next and one land to the other. We would thus expect to see the handing down of mantles, the overlapping of players, the converging of movements, and the passing on of ancient torches. In the case of the Philistine resurrection, we would expect that other currents and manifestations of the Dragon's war and fury would prepare its way, converge with it, anoint and empower it. What happens then if we go deeper into the origins of October 7 and the Philistine resurrection? Will we find forerunners and the handing down of the Dragon's torch?

The Grand Mufti

Mohammed Amin al-Husseini was born at the end of the nineteenth century in Ottoman-controlled Jerusalem. It was not long after his birth that the word *Palestinian* began appearing in the Arabic language. He would play a critical part in the Philistine resurrection.

In the First World War, he fought in the Ottoman army. After the war he returned to Jerusalem and focused on derailing all movement toward the birth of a Jewish nation in the land. His inflammatory speeches incited violent Arab riots, leaving several Jewish people dead.[1] From 1921 onward he would be known as the "Grand Mufti of Jerusalem."[2] In the ensuing years he would continue to play a central part in violent Arab uprisings with a trail of Jewish blood in their wake. The last of these, in the late 1930s, would result in a warrant for his arrest. He escaped prosecution by fleeing to Lebanon, then Iraq—and then to Nazi Germany.[3]

Natural Allies

The Mufti was an early admirer of Adolf Hitler. In 1933, shortly after Hitler's rise to power in Germany, the Mufti expressed his support for the new

government, stating that the Palestinian Muslims were enthusiastic sup-
porters of the Nazi regime and looked forward to the spread of fascism
throughout the Middle East. He was especially in favor of the Nazis' anti-
Jewish campaigns. He appealed to Hitler to rid Palestine of Jewish settlements.[4]

In 1940 the Mufti drafted a document he hoped the Nazi government
would approve in which the Arab countries would be given the right to *solve
the Jewish issue* in their lands *as the Nazis had solved it in Germany.* In
November 1941 the Mufti obtained a meeting with Hitler in the Reich Chancellery in Berlin. He told Hitler that the Arabs were his natural allies, as they
had the same enemies, most specifically the Jews. He asked Hitler to commit
to the elimination of a national Jewish homeland. Hitler affirmed his com-
mitment to destroying the Jewish element residing in the Arab sphere at the
right time.[5] The Holocaust was to be taken to the land of Israel.

The Mufti's Holocaust

Al-Husseini was increasingly drawn to Hitler's SS, the prime agents of the
Holocaust, and to Heinrich Himmler, its prime overseer. The German dip-
lomat Fritz Grobba recorded that in July 1942 the Mufti visited a Nazi concentration camp and was favorably impressed. Throughout the Holocaust the
Mufti would work tirelessly to block the routes of Jewish people trying to
escape its horrors. He was personally responsible for preventing the escape
of five hundred Jewish children, consigning them to their deaths in the Arbe
concentration camp.[6]

"Wherever You Find Them"

During the war al-Husseini worked for the Third Reich, broadcasting Nazi
propaganda throughout the Arab world. The Nazis, in turn, took up the task
of distributing his writings, including a pamphlet he wrote for the SS calling
for the total destruction of the Jewish people. He implored his Nazi employers
to bomb Tel Aviv and Jerusalem in order to kill the Jews residing in those
cities. He worked with Himmler to organize Muslim SS killing squads in the
Balkans.[7] He publicly exhorted the Muslim world to follow the example of
the Nazis in a "definitive solution to the Jewish problem."[8] He had hoped for
a Nazi victory in the Middle East by which the Holocaust could reach the
land of Israel. Near the end of the war the Mufti broadcast from Radio Berlin,
"Arabs...kill the Jews wherever you find them."[9]

Accused of having committed war crimes, the Mufti would again escape
prosecution by fleeing to Egypt, where, upon his arrival, he was given a
hero's welcome. During his time with the Nazis his popularity among the
Arabs had only increased. He resumed his leadership in the Arab world and

worked extensively with the Muslim Brotherhood. At the time of Israel's resurrection in 1948 he actively worked for its destruction.[10]

The Nazi-Arabian Convergence

The Mufti served as a conduit through which the virulent toxicity of Nazi anti-Semitism merged with Arab nationalism and Islamic fanaticism. The racial doctrines of the Third Reich, the belief in a Jewish global conspiracy, and the conviction that there could be no negotiation or peace made with the Jewish people, only annihilation, now infected the Arab and Islamic world—and would, in the years to come, bring the Middle East and the world to the brink of war.

In terms of the spiritual forces at work behind the transmission, the orgidzo, the Dragon's rage that had inflamed and empowered the evil and madness of Nazism, would now ignite the Arab and Islamic world. And as it had with the people of Germany, it set the Middle East on fire with a satanic fury centered over Israel and the Jewish people.

From Munich to Gaza

And yet there was more to the connection. Not only was the Mufti *a leader* in the Arab world; he was *the leader* of the *Palestinian* world. He has been called, with good reason, the "father of Palestinian nationalism."[11] When Israel was resurrected in 1948 and, at the same time, the first Palestinian, or Filastin, state was founded, the president of that state was the Mufti.[12] And so from Hitler's ascension in 1933 to the meeting in the Reich Chancellery to the killing squads of the SS to the resurrection of the Filastin soldier, from the beer halls of Munich in the early 1920s to the shores of Gaza on October 7, the line runs straight and deep, the connections are central and intrinsic, and the Dragon's fingerprints are all over them.

The Dragon's Employees

The end of the Second World War saw the demise of Hitler and the leaders of the Third Reich. But the Mufti survived and remained an active agent of Nazi anti-Semitism throughout the Arab world. One prominent Muslim leader at the time proclaimed, "Germany and Hitler are gone, but al-Husseini will continue the struggle."[13] How could radical Islam and Nazism, two conflicting ideologies, constitute the same struggle? They could if they were two branches of the same spiritual root. They could if they shared the same overriding goal—which they did—the destruction of the Jewish people. It was the same goal shared by the spiritual entity that empowered them. The struggle and war belonged to the Dragon. Nazism and radical Islam were vessels of that war.

It is no accident that the father of Palestinian nationalism was an agent of Nazism, nor that Adolf Hitler was the employer of the man who set in motion the Palestinian agenda. Each were, in turn, employees of the Dragon. The Mufti longed for a second Holocaust, one that would wipe out the Jews of the Middle East and destroy the nation of Israel before its rebirth. What the Enemy had failed to do through Adolf Hitler he would now seek to do through radical Islam, by inflaming the Arab world and then resurrecting an ancient enemy from the dead.

The Disciple

In 1946, the year after the Holocaust's end, after the Mufti fled from Germany and Europe to Egypt, he met an Arab teenager attending a secondary school in Cairo. He took the teenager under his wing and recruited him to his cause. The youth became his disciple. His name was *Yasser Arafat*.[14]

The Mufti indoctrinated Arafat and his associates into his hatred of the Jewish people and his ideology of extermination. So Yasser Arafat was taught and discipled by the man who worked with and for Adolf Hitler. Arafat would take al-Husseini's mantle. He would become *the* leader and face of Palestinian nationalism and Palestinian terrorism. He too would be critical in the Philistine resurrection, taking up where al-Husseini left off.

The Aryan Guides

To train Arafat in the ways of violence and war, the Mufti secretly brought in a former Nazi commando to Egypt.[15] The commando taught Arafat and his comrades how to launch attacks against the Jewish people of Israel, how to wage guerrilla warfare, and how to shed Jewish blood. Arafat would thus be trained in the tactics of both the Nazis and the ancient Philistines.

Arafat would continue in al-Husseini's footsteps, recruiting Nazi instructors into the Palestinian agenda. They would include Erich Altern, a leader in the Gestapo's Jewish affairs section, and Willy Berner, a member of the Matthausen concentration camp SS.[16] Only in later years would it be revealed that the Palestine Liberation Organization was working with and employing several other Nazi and neo-Nazi agents.

The Dragon's Chain

And so we have a chain that stretches back to a beer hall in Munich, Germany, and forward to the shores of Gaza. Within that chain we have a man cited as "the father of Palestinian nationalism," a paid employee of Adolf

Hitler, a Nazi agent also known as "the father of Arab terrorism." Hitler's employee would, in turn, disciple and raise up Yasser Arafat to wage a war of terrorism on the people of Israel. So we have on one end of the chain Yasser Arafat and October 7, and on its other, Adolf Hitler.

The joining together of such disparate and conflicting ideologies and movements as German Nazism and Palestinian nationalism should not surprise us. For we are dealing with an ancient war of spirits. Nor should we be surprised by the timing of these events. It is no accident that it was just as Israel's resurrection was set in motion that Hitler and Nazism began their rise. Even the Mufti's birth was part of the mystery. It was in the year 1897 that Theodor Herzl convened the First Zionist Congress and officially inaugurated the movement of Zionism for the return of Israel. The Dragon would respond. It is believed that it was that same year, 1897, the child who would become the Mufti of Jerusalem was born.

———————■■■———————

The dark chain of cause and effect did not begin with Adolf Hitler, nor would it end with Yasser Arafat. It would continue into the present day. And it would involve yet another evil, this one birthed in an ancient city of darkness.

Chapter 40

CHILD OF THE BROTHERHOOD

HASSAN AL-BANNA WAS born in 1906 in a rural Nile Delta town northwest of Cairo.[1] He too would play a key role in the mystery.

The Brotherhood

Al-Banna's father was a teacher of Islamic doctrine, an imam in the local mosque. Upon reaching adulthood, al-Banna became an elementary school teacher. Disturbed over the abandonment of Islamic beliefs and practices in Egyptian culture, he preached a return to the teachings of the Koran. In March 1928 he founded an organization dedicated to Islam and jihad, the struggle or fight against the enemies of the faith. It would be called the *Muslim Brotherhood*. Within ten years the Muslim Brotherhood had branches throughout Egypt, and another ten years later, half a million active members and many more sympathizers.[2]

"My Jihad"

The Muslim Brotherhood was born at the same time that another movement was coming to power, Nazism. In the year of the Brotherhood's birth, the Nazis won their first seats in the German parliament. Like the Mufti, al-Banna was enamored of Adolf Hitler. He repeatedly wrote to him expressing his admiration and his hope that Islam and Nazism would become collaborators.[3]

From 1935 onward the Brotherhood would send delegations to attend the Nazi party's annual rallies in Nuremberg. Along with other anti-Semitic writings from the West, the Brotherhood translated Hitler's autobiography and diatribe against the Jews into Arabic. As for its title, *Mein Kampf* ("My Struggle"), they rendered it as *My Jihad*. It would become widely published throughout the Arab and Islamic worlds. Beginning in the 1930s Hitler financed the Brotherhood. Brotherhood members, in turn, functioned as Middle Eastern Nazi spies. The Nazis would also help the Muslim Brotherhood in its organizing, its dissemination of propaganda, and its waging of war.[4]

Metastasis

Al-Banna was also a great admirer of the Mufti, and the two would become collaborators in their war against the Jews. When the Mufti arrived in Egypt after working for the Third Reich, it was al-Banna who played the key part in the hero's welcome given in his honor. The Mufti's Nazi-influenced anti-Semitism would, in turn, influence the Muslim Brotherhood's ideas and ideology. The Brotherhood would, in turn, disseminate them across the Islamic world. Long after the end of the Third Reich, its anti-Semitism could be found throughout the Arab world and had become a central pillar of radical Islamic thought.[5] Behind the raging of radical Muslim preachers and terrorists against the Jews was the rage of Adolf Hitler, and behind Hitler's raging was that of the Dragon.

Holy War

The new radical Muslim incarnation of the ancient rage against the Jews was unique in that it was now framed as a holy war. And as it was for Hitler and Nazism, so too it was for the radical Muslim—Jewish extermination was not peripheral but a foundational principle of their entire worldview and purpose.

We would expect that the rage of the Nazi-infected Middle East would find its focal point in the return of the Jews to their ancient land. And so it did. The Mufti was appointed as al-Banna's official representative in Palestine and the overseer of all the Brotherhood's activities there.[6] Thus the man who served as the bridge between Nazism and Islam would also serve as the conduit in bringing the Muslim Brotherhood into Israel. At the time of Israel's resurrection Muslim Brotherhood troops entered the land to destroy the Jewish nation at its birth.

The Brotherhood's Child

If the Mufti's protégé and successor in his war against Israel was Yasser Arafat, the Muslim Brotherhood's protégé in Israel would come later. It would appear in the city that was to serve as the Mufti's headquarters as president of the first Palestinian state—the city of Israel's ancient enemies. It would be born in Gaza.

The Brotherhood would give birth to the *Islamic Resistance Movement*. In Arabic it was called *Harakat al-Muqawama al-Islamiya*.[7] The name was shortened into an acronym.

The Brotherhood's child was given the name *Hamas*.[8]

———■■■———

Is it possible that in the very foundation on which Hamas was born we can find the voice and the spirit of Adolf Hitler?

Chapter 41

THE MADMAN'S CHARTER

HAMAS WAS BORN in Gaza on December 10, 1987.[1] The place and timing of its birth were significant.

The Charter

As it was in Gaza that ancient evils were devised against Israel, so it was in Gaza that the First Intifada was launched against the Jewish nation. It exploded in early December 1987.[2] It was on the day following the first day of uprising and violence that Hamas was founded. The Palestinian child of the Brotherhood was born in a storm of hatred and rage.

Why did Hamas come into existence? The reason, along with its mission statement, was given in its founding charter in 1988. Central in that charter is the annihilation of Israel. It was all there at the very beginning, in the preamble, where it stated:

> *Israel will exist and will continue to exist until*
> *Islam will obliterate it.*[3]

Voice of the Fuehrer

As the Dragon's war is spiritual and transcends time and space, so Hamas' mission was not limited to the Israeli but was against all Jews, as the charter made clear:

> *For our struggle against the Jews is extremely wide*
> *ranging and grave.*[4]

And it was not only the Jews living in Israel who were the enemy but any Jew living anywhere on earth—just as it was for Hitler. The phrase "our struggle against the Jews" is noteworthy, as Hitler used the same words, "my struggle," "mein kampf," as the name of his autobiography. The reference is not an accident, as much of the charter could have been taken directly from *Mein Kampf*. Article Twenty-Two of Hamas' charter reads like a compendium of anti-Semitic calumny and Hitler's madness:

> *[The Jews] took control of the world media, news*
> *agencies, the press, publishing houses, broadcasting*

> *stations, and others. With their money they stirred revolutions in various parts of the world....They were behind the French Revolution, the Communist revolution and most revolutions....With their money they formed secret societies, such as Freemasons, Rotary Clubs, the Lions...for the purpose of sabotaging societies and achieving Zionist interests....There is no war going on anywhere, without having their finger in it.*[5]

A Jewish Conspiracy

And the following could have been lifted word for word from any number of Hitler's written and spoken words against the Jews:

> *They aim at undermining societies, destroying values, corrupting consciences, deteriorating character...Israel, Judaism, and Jews.*[6]

As did Hitler—it was not enough to declare war on the Jewish people—Hamas declared war even on Judaism. As for the classical Nazi and anti-Semitic charge of a Jewish conspiracy to take over the world, the charter features that as well:

> *Today it is Palestine, tomorrow it will be one country or another. The Zionist plan is limitless.*[7]

"Together Into Hell"

Hamas' charter makes clear that no peace can be made with the Jewish people—only war—in this life and even beyond:

> *"Ye shall be overcome, and thrown together into hell...." This is the only way to liberate Palestine.*[8]

The charter includes a number of quotes from Islamic writings to argue for the destruction of the Jews. Perhaps the most raw and revealing is this one:

> *I will assault and kill, assault and kill, assault and kill.*[9]

The words come off as a mantra of one satanically possessed. And in view of what we are dealing with, that is exactly what it should come off as.

Ghostwriters

If one wanted to destroy a particular people and one needed vessels of flesh and blood with which to destroy them, one would depict that people as evil by nature, the source of all evil, and whose very existence constitutes an existential danger. And so it is no accident that so much of Hamas' charter reads like Nazi propaganda and could have been written by Adolf Hitler. Without Hitler the charter could not exist. Nor could it exist without the Dragon. It was penned in his script and infused with his murderous intent. The founders of Hamas were only his ghostwriters.

The Long-Watered Seeds

It was no accident that Hamas was born in a city noted in the Bible for its evil and from which, in ancient times, came death and destruction to the Israelites. Nor was it an accident that October 7 so evoked the acts of the Nazis. Soon after the soldiers of Israel entered Gaza in response to the massacre, they discovered there an Arabic book with an image of Adolf Hitler on its cover—it was *Mein Kampf*.[10] What had happened on Israel's southern coast that October and what had happened in Nazi Germany each sprung from the same source. What happened on October 7 had been ordained from the beginning, from the moment Hamas was conceived. The invaders of that day were carrying out the words of its founding charter: *"I will assault and kill, assault and kill, assault and kill."*

It was the coming to fruition of the long-watered seeds of the Dragon's sowing.

------■■■------

Is it possible that Hamas is actually found in the Bible? And if so, what would it reveal?

Chapter 42

THE DARK PLACES OF THE EARTH

Though the name *Hamas* is an acronym for the *Islamic Resistance Movement*, it is also an ancient Middle Eastern word.

Hamas in Hebrew

In Arabic, *Hamas* means *zeal, strength, passion,* and *bravery*.[1] And that is how the leaders of Hamas would want their organization to be viewed in the Arabic world. But *Hamas* is unique in that it exists not only as an Arabic word but as a Hebrew word—an ancient Hebrew word that appears in the Bible. In Hebrew, *Hamas* means something very different—*violence, evil,* and *destruction.* And in the context of its specific usage in Scripture it can refer to *brutality, immorality, falsehood, lawlessness, injustice,* and *acts of cruelty, plunder, murder, slaughter,* and *terror.*

In 2007 the Gaza Strip came under the rule of Hamas. From a biblical and linguistic view, in coming under the rule of *hamas*, the Gazans came under the rule of *violence*. In being governed by a *hamas* government, the people of Gaza were governed by *lawlessness*. In being taught in *hamas* schools, the Gazans were taught in the schools of *terror*. In following their new *hamas* leaders, they were following *evil*. And in being trained in *hamas* paramilitary camps, they were being trained in *destruction*.[2]

Hamas in Scripture

The scriptural appearances of the word *hamas*, of course, in context refer to violence and evil as manifested in ancient times and as would be understood by the ancient Israelites. On the other hand, God's Word is filled with multiple layers of meaning and is given by the One with knowledge of all events—past, present, and future—including the future birth of the terrorist organization to be known by the name *Hamas*. What happens, then, if we look for the word *Hamas* in the original Hebrew of the Bible?

Psalm 140 opens with this prayer for deliverance:

> Deliver me, O Lord, from evil men: Preserve me
> from men of violence.[3]

But in the original Hebrew the second line could be more literally rendered

> Preserve me from the men of *hamas*.

"The Dark Places of the Earth"

The word *hamas* specifically described what Israel's ancient Middle Eastern enemies inflicted upon its people. One of those enemies would be given a prophecy of judgment and the reason for that judgment:

> For *hamas* against your brother Jacob, shame shall
> cover you, and you will be cut off forever.[4]

Hamas functioned in the dark. It hid its terrorist activities behind the cover of schools, hospitals, and other centers of civilian life. It converted the city of Gaza into a command center of terrorism. It dug into the city's earth to build over three hundred miles of tunnels for the purpose of violence, warfare, and terrorism.[5] Hamas operated in metaphorical, or figurative, darkness but also in actual physical darkness. Its operatives literally dwelt in the dark places of the earth. Psalm 74 says this:

> For the *dark places of the earth* are *full of the*
> *dwellings of hamas*.[6]

"A Rod of Wickedness"

On October 7 Hamas converted its members and agents into a unified and coordinated weapon of violence and evil against the people of Israel. When the prophet Ezekiel speaks of Israel's day of calamity, he says this:

> Hamas has *risen up into a rod of wickedness.*[7]

On October 7 the land of Israel, its towns and dwellings, were filled with violence, crimes, atrocities, and blood. Ezekiel's prophecy continues:

> For *the land is filled with crimes of blood*, and *the*
> *city is full of hamas*.[8]

Jeremiah prophesied the judgment of Babylon for the evil and destruction it brought upon the land of Israel. That evil is embodied in one word:

> Let the *hamas* done to me and my flesh be upon
> Babylon.[9]

But in the preceding verse, another word appears, just as significant. The word is *tannin*, or *tanim*. It is, again, the Hebrew word for *dragon*. Thus the words *hamas* and *tannin* are connected. The Dragon is the source of Hamas, and so Hamas bears the nature of its father.

"Hamas Shall No Longer Be Heard"

It is a striking thing that an organization dedicated to bringing evil, violence, and destruction to Israel should choose for its name an Arabic word that was, at the same time, the Hebrew word for *evil, violence,* and *destruction*. It had no idea that *hamas* was the same word used in the Bible to speak of what the enemies of God brought upon Israel, and the judgment and destruction that would come on those who did. But God always has the last word.

The prophet Isaiah was given a glimpse into the days when the kingdom of God will manifest on earth and Messiah will reign on Israel's throne. In those days war will no longer be known, and the children of Israel will, at last, find their peace. In Isaiah 60 the prophet specifically mentions one of those blessings, a blessing not of what will be but of what will be no more. The promise is this:

> *Hamas* shall *no longer be heard in your land, neither wasting nor destruction within your borders.*[10]

---■■■---

In that day, violence will no longer threaten and oppress the Jewish people or the children of Israel. And all those who warred against them, all those who tried to wipe them off the face of the earth, from Pharaoh to Hitler to Hamas, will have perished.

Their terrors will be long gone, their threatenings long past, and their evil and destruction long forgotten.

---■■■---

It was not only the invasion of October 7 that followed the ancient mystery but that which came after it. We will now see how the war that was triggered on that day was also foreshadowed ages before it happened. Along the way we will uncover a connection joining it all to the Book of Revelation.

Part X

THE DRAGON'S FLOOD

Chapter 43

FIRE ON THE WALLS

Because she took captive whole communities…
I will send fire on the walls of Gaza that will consume
her fortresses.[1]

T HE PROPHET AMOS not only exposed Gaza's sin but foretold its judgment.

Judgment by Fire

The judgment would come because of Gaza's transgression of taking "whole communities" of Israel into captivity and, according to varied Bible commentaries, for the *extreme barbarity*. In view of the fact that the ancient sins of Gaza were replayed on October 7, we would expect the replaying of the same dynamics, the invoking of its judgment.

How would that judgment come? According to the prophecy, it would come by fire. *"I will send a fire upon the wall of Gaza."*[2] And that fire would come through war.

Did the prophecy come true? It did. In the eighth century BC, the fire of war came to the walls of Gaza and Philistia through the armies of Assyria and, in the following century, through the armies of Egypt and Babylon.[3]

Wars of the Kings

But judgment would also come through the armies of Israel. The continual and immediate danger that Gaza and Philistia posed to the people of Israel was not sustainable. So it is recorded that King Uzziah

> went to war against the Philistines and broke down the walls of Gath, Jabneh, and Ashdod. He then rebuilt towns near Ashdod and elsewhere among the Philistines.[4]

King Hezekiah did likewise:

> Hezekiah defeated the Philistines *all the way to Gaza and the area around it*. He defeated all the Philistine cities—from the smallest town to the largest city.[5]

The Walls of Gaza

As of October 7 Israel was in a state of war. It would seek to rescue the hundreds of hostages taken in Gaza and drive Hamas from the land. It would call the people of the Gaza Strip to move southward to avoid being caught in the middle of battle.[6] The battle would be focused on Hamas to ensure that there would never again be another October 7. So the soldiers of Israel would enter the Gaza Strip and Gaza City with two objectives—to rescue the hostages and put an end to the danger and terror of Hamas.

In the autumn of 2023 the ancient dynamics as recorded in the books of Kings and Chronicles were replayed on the same soil, in the same way, before the eyes of the world. The people of Gaza and Philistia had again attacked the land of Israel, again raided its villages, again committed acts of bloodshed and atrocity, and again taken Israeli civilians as captives into the land of Philistia. And so again, their acts would invoke destruction. War would again come to the land of Philistia. And fire would again burn *on the walls of Gaza*. Its walls would again be broken, and fire would again *devour its palaces*.

Resurrected Soldiers in a Resurrected Land

The ancient wars between Israel, Philistia, and Gaza had ceased ages before Israel's rebirth in the modern world. But now they had returned. In ancient times the soldiers of Israel fought in the city of Gaza and the surrounding areas. So in the autumn of 2023 the soldiers of Israel were now again fighting in the city of *Gaza and the surrounding areas.*

The world did not know, but it was witnessing the resurrected soldiers of a resurrected nation fighting in a resurrected war in the resurrected land of its resurrected enemy.

------------■■■------------

Could the name given to the war between Israel and Gaza have unknowingly been taken from the wars of the ancient Israelites and Philistines?

Chapter 44

SWORDS OF IRON

IN THE BOOK of Ezekiel, God commands the leaders of the Jewish people to remove violence and evil from the land. It was a rebuke of their sins, an exhortation to the nation's rulers. But in the original language in which the command was given, something else appears.

"Get Rid of Hamas"

In Hebrew the command joins together two words: *hasiru* and *hamas*. *Hasiru*, in this context, can be translated as *turn away, put away, remove, rid, put an end to*. The direct object of the word *hasiru* is the word *hamas*. Thus the first words of the command can be rendered as:

> Put an end to hamas.
>
> Put away hamas.
>
> Remove hamas.
>
> Get rid of hamas.

In the wake of October 7, Israel's leaders came to the realization that they could not continue to allow Hamas to operate within striking distance of its population and that what happened on October 7 could never happen again. For that to be accomplished, they saw that their only answer was summed up in the prophet's words *Hasiru Hamas*. In other words, Hamas had to be removed from the land.

The Wall, the Sling, and the Dome

Critical in the ancient wars of the Philistines and Israelites, as we have seen, was the issue of iron. What happened in the autumn of 2023 constituted the greatest war of Israel and Philistia since ancient times. Could the issue of iron again become central in that war? It did. The October war would be especially imbued with "iron."

The war began when the Filastin invaders breached the Israeli security system known as the *Iron Wall*.

As Hamas fired thousands of rockets from ancient Philistia into the towns and cities of Israel, the central defense system attempting to shoot them down to avert destruction was the *Iron Dome*.

Assisting the Iron Dome in protecting the land from the missiles of Gaza and onward was the Israel air defense system known as *David's Sling*. Though David's original sling was certainly not made of iron, it was David who overcame the weapons of the Philistines and did so by employing iron.

The Beam and the Sting

The October war caused the development and first-time use of new Israeli weapons. One that went into accelerated development was a laser-based air defense system called the *Iron Beam*. Another that had never before been used in battle was the laser-guided mortar shell designed to minimize collateral damage in war by taking out specific targets with unprecedented precision. With Hamas militants using urban centers as their base of warfare and civilian buildings as their cover, the new weapon became especially important. It was used for the first time in late 2023 in the war against Hamas. It would be known as the *Iron Sting*.[1]

And so in the *Iron Dome,* the *Iron Wall*, the *Iron Beam,* and the *Iron Sting*, iron, the element so critical in the ancient wars of Israel and Philistia, again took center stage in the wars of their modern counterparts.

Swords of Iron

And there was more. We saw how the Philistines prevented the Israelites from forging weaponry of iron:

> There were no blacksmiths in Israel. The Philistines would not allow them because they were afraid the Israelites would make *iron swords*.[2]

The translation elucidates the heart of the issue by using the words *iron swords*. Though the original Hebrew is not as specific, the meaning is clear and implicit. The Philistines used *swords of iron* to defeat the Israelites and did all in their power to keep the Israelites from using *swords of iron* against them.

So in the autumn of 2023, in the greatest war waged by the soldiers of Israel against the soldiers of Philistia since ancient times, a name had to be chosen for the operation. It would be given the name *Swords of Iron*.[3]

The Book of Revelation describes how the Dragon wars against the woman. What we are now about to see is how one of the elements of that ancient vision played a central part on the morning of October 7.

Chapter 45

THE DRAGON'S FLOOD

I N THE VISION of Revelation 12 the Dragon seeks to destroy the woman by overwhelming her. The Dragon, also spoken of as the *Serpent*,

> *spewed water out of his mouth like a flood after the woman, that he might cause her to be carried away by the flood.*[1]

The Potamon

He spews water out of his mouth like a *potamon*. *Potamon* can be translated as *river, torrent, deluge,* or *flood.* "That he might cause her to be" *potamophoreton.* The word *potamophoreton* means *to be overwhelmed by a river, carried away by a flood, swept away by a deluge.* So the creature sends forth an evil of such magnitude and force that it threatens to overwhelm the woman, drown her, and carry her away in its current.

And so the Enemy will seek to destroy the Jewish people by sending a flood against them, an evil, a calamity so great and powerful that it will threaten their very existence. The vision is appointed for the future but, again, reveals a central strategy in the Dragon's war against the Jewish people. Jewish history is filled with floods, overwhelming disasters, deluges that have threatened destruction. Behind them was the mouth of the Dragon.

The October Deluge

It is of note that the Scriptures use the imagery of a flood to symbolize a mass invasion of Israel by the armies of its enemies. The Assyrians and Babylonians swept over the land in a flood of destruction, wiping away everything in its path.

In Revelation the flood is connected to the Enemy. It is one of his central tactics—a sudden calamity, an overwhelming evil, an invasion of darkness, a deluge of destruction. The link between the Enemy and the flood appears in a well-known scripture from Isaiah:

> The enemy comes in like a flood.[2]

Throughout this book the connection between the events of October 7 and the Dragon has been noted. But now we have an added one—the connection of October 7 specifically to the Dragon's *flood*. It is no accident that October 7 bore the properties of a flood.

It came with sudden ferocity. It was a mass invasion of the nation's enemies, a deluge upon the land. With its thousands of rockets and multiple breaches of the nation's protective wall, it came as a flood and overwhelmed the land. It swept over the land as a deluge of death and destruction and carried away its victims from their homes, their lives, and their existence.

The Day of the Tufan

Those who masterminded October 7 gave the operation a name. Within that name were the words *Al-Aqsa*, referring to the Islamic Mosque on the Temple Mount. The significance of those words we will soon uncover. But they were qualifiers, added to the name to describe what the operation, and what October 7, actually was.

The name given to the invasion by its creators began with the Arabic word *Tufan*.[3] The invasion was a *Tufan*. What does *Tufan* mean?

Tufan means *deluge, inundation, overflow, cataclysm.*

Tufan means *flood*.

So the name given to that which would overwhelm Israel on October 7 was *Flood*. Those who named it *Tufan*, or *Flood*, undoubtedly had no idea of the vision given in Revelation and the flood sent by the Dragon to destroy the woman, Israel. Nor were they pondering the Greek word *potamon*. Nevertheless, they named it *Flood*.

And so as the Dragon produced the *potamon*, Hamas produced the *Tufan*. The Enemy sent forth his *Flood*, a deluge of death and destruction, to overwhelm the children of Israel.

It was a shadow of the day that the Dragon will spew forth *water out of his mouth like a flood after the woman "that he might cause her to be carried away."*

———■■■———

The next stream of mysteries will bring that which was given to Israel at Mount Sinai—the *moedeem*, the appointed times, the Hebrew holy days—together with the desecrating angel.

Part XI

THE UNHOLY DAYS

Chapter 46

THE DESECRATOR

T HE DRAGON IS a desecrator and the father of abominations.

Father of Abominations

Desecration is the logical consequence of the Enemy's will. God is holy. The things of God are holy. The Enemy wars against God and the things of God. So his war is, by definition, an unholy one. To destroy that which is holy, he seeks to invert it, to turn it in upon itself. God makes what is holy. God consecrates. The Enemy seeks to turn the holy into the unholy. What God consecrates, the Enemy desecrates.

Days of Desecration

Again, we see the Enemy in his role as imitator. He desecrates the holy by creating an inverted imitation—lies in imitation of truth, false gods in imitation of God, and the darkness of the occult in imitation of the powers of the Spirit. It is for this reason that the occult is filled with what appear to be religious, or "sacred," elements, ceremonies, chants, and liturgies—inversions of the sacred and desecrations of the holy. The very concept of "Satan *worship*" is based on the worship of God. And as the calendar of God consists of holy days, so the Devil has his own calendar of unholy days, feasts, and convocations, his sacred days of desecration.

We will now open another dimension that lay behind what took place that October morning on Israel's coastal plain—the unholy days of the Desecrator.

Chapter 47

THE BLACK SABBATH

Thus the heavens and the earth…were finished.…
Then God blessed the seventh day and sanctified
it, because in it He rested from all His work which
God had created and made.[1]

The Shabbat

It was the seventh day that sealed God's creation. It was then that God rested from His works. Behind the word translated as *rested* is the Hebrew *shabbat*. The seventh day would come to be identified by the act of God's resting. So it would be called the *Shabbat*, the *Sabbath*.

"God blessed the seventh day." The Sabbath was thus the day of God's blessings. It was also the day of holiness. It is in connection to the Sabbath that the Hebrew root word for *holy* first appears in the Bible. God *sanctified* or *made holy* the seventh day. It was the first of all holy days.

The Holy Guest

At Mount Sinai, Israel was commanded to remember the seventh day and keep it holy.[2] The Sabbath was a sign of the nation's covenant with God. Since God blessed the creation on the Sabbath, the Sabbath also became a commemoration of the creation, and God's blessing upon it, a celebration of life, of peace, renewal, and restoration.

For the Jewish people the Sabbath was not simply to be observed—it was to be received. The Sabbath was to be welcomed into each Jewish home as if one were receiving a royal guest. Special prayers were to be recited upon its advent, welcoming the Sabbath's entrance into one's house with blessings, honor, and joy.[3]

As the seventh day was the final sealing of God's creation, it spoke of completion and perfection. And as the last of days it was seen as a shadow of the last of all things, the kingdom of God, the age of Messiah, the *Olam Ha Bah*, and the reign of heaven, when war would be no more, when peace would cover the earth, and when God's presence would fill every space and moment—and all would be *Shabbat*.

The Inverted Sabbath

As the Dragon wars against the woman, the Enemy against the people of Israel, we would expect that he would wage war, as well, against the Sabbath, the sign of Israel's covenant. And so it was, again, no accident that the darkest event in Jewish history since the Holocaust was launched on the Sabbath. It was the Devil's Sabbath.

As the Sabbath was to be a commemoration of God's creation of life, rest, and peace, the Enemy would invert it. The inversion of peace is war; the inversion of life is death. So on the day of rest for the Jewish people, their rest would be taken from them. Their Sabbath peace would be broken and replaced by war, horror, and devastation. And their commemoration of creation and life would become to them, instead, a day of death and destruction.

Day of the Uninvited

The day when God's blessing was to make its entrance into Jewish homes and when each home was to welcome in His blessing and presence, everything was reversed. October 7 became the day when something very different and dark made its entrance into Jewish homes. On the day that the presence of God and His angels was to be ushered into each Jewish home, it was the Dragon who entered the Jewish home and, with him, his servants. And instead of welcoming in their Sabbath guests, the Jewish families of that Sabbath fought to keep their Sabbath visitors from entering into their houses and then into their saferooms. It was the day of the uninvited, the unholy and unwelcome guests of a darkened Sabbath.

Shadows of Hell

The day given to commemorate and sanctify God's creation was hijacked by the Enemy—and the creation would be desecrated. On the day that stands as a shadow of God's kingdom on earth, when Messiah will reign and peace will cover the land, it was destruction that was king, the Devil that ruled, and blood that covered the land. The dark Sabbath of October 7 was not a foretaste of the kingdom of heaven but of hell.

The Tzod Desecration

The Sabbath desecrations of October 7 included the breaking of the laws of *tzod*. The laws of *tzod* forbade any trapping or forced confinement on the Sabbath day. These would normally refer to the trapping and confinement of animal life. But on the Sabbath of October 7, the desecrators broke the laws of *tzod* as they trapped innocent civilians, forced their confinement, and took them captive as hostages. The entire Sabbath was converted into a trap for the capturing of human life.

The Koshair Desecration

Then there were the laws of *koshair*, which forbade the binding together of two objects. On the Sabbath of October 7 the laws of *koshair* were broken as well, as the desecrators bound together their hostages and their hands behind their backs as they took them away into captivity.

The Hotzaah Desecration

Then there were the laws of *hotzaah*. These forbade the transferring of any object on the Sabbath day from one domain to another. One was not to take an object from a private domain into a public space or from a public space into a private domain. But on the Sabbath of October 7 the laws of *hotzaah* were broken, as the desecrators transported Israeli men, women, and children from the private domain of their houses into the public domains of the streets and thoroughfares—and from the public domains of open-air gatherings into the private domains of the hidden chambers of their captivity.

The Mavir Desecration

Then there were the laws of *mavir*. These forbade any form of igniting and kindling, the setting, fueling, or spreading of fires. So the invaders of October 7 broke the laws of *mavir*. Their guns fired through the igniting of gunpowder. They set off explosives for the purpose of destruction. And they lit Israeli homes, kibbutzes, and villages on fire.

The Shokhait Desecration

And then there were the laws of *shokhait*. These forbade the taking of life through slaughter or any other means. It goes without saying October 7 broke the laws of *shokhait*. The Dragon turned the Sabbath of God into a *Shabbat Shakhet*—a day that Israel would remember as a Sabbath of slaughter.

The Most Elusive of Days

Those who performed the desecrations had little, if any, knowledge of the detailed laws they were breaking. Nevertheless, they broke them, directly and specifically, one Sabbath desecration after the next.

It is ironic that the one people of all peoples who were specifically given a sacred day of peace and rest are the same for whom peace and rest have been most elusive. In returning to their ancient homeland, the Jewish people believed they had finally found their peace. The nation of Israel was, in fact, reborn on a Sabbath day. At the same time, Israel's enemies chose that Sabbath day to launch an all-out invasion aimed at annihilation. So the Enemy who seeks to bring calamity on Israel and the desecration of the holy would, on October 7, accomplish both.

The Black Sabbath

It was not long after the calamity that the people of Israel gave October 7 a Hebrew name. There is a phrase in English and other languages used to speak of a ceremonial gathering convened for the purpose of performing occult rituals, witchcraft, and the worship of the Devil. It denotes an unholy convocation, a satanic Sabbath.

The name Israel gave to October 7 was *HaShabbat HashHorah*. It is the same name given to a convocation of Satan.

They called it the *Black Sabbath*.[4]

------■■■------

But October 7 was more than a Sabbath. It was the day on which fell two of Israel's annual holy days—one among the most ancient and sacred, and the other among its most joyous. Could these have also played a part in the mystery?

Chapter 48

THE DRAGON'S HOLIDAY

T HE SATURDAY ON which the invasion took place was not only the first of all holy days given by God to Israel but also the last.

Shemini Atzeret

All of the *moedeem*, the sacred appointed times, or holy days, given by God at Mount Sinai are recorded in Leviticus 23. The last of these is the *Feast of Tabernacles*, known in Hebrew as *Sukkot*. At the end of Sukkot comes a sacred gathering that seals the festival as well as the sacred year. So it is written:

> On the eighth day you shall have a holy convocation....It is a sacred assembly.[1]

From this comes the holy day of *Shemini Atzeret*, or the *Gathering of the Eighth Day*.

The Day of Rejoicing

In Israel the day would also be known as *Simchat Torah*, or the *Joy of the Torah*. Simchat Torah marks the completion of the yearly reading of the Torah, the first five books of the Bible, as contained in the scrolls of the synagogue. On Simchat Torah the last scriptures of the old cycle are finished and the first of the new cycle begun.[2]

True to its name, the holiday is marked by joy and rejoicing. Its rejoicing takes the form of singing and dancing, the participation of children, the waving of banners, the giving out of candy and delicacies, exuberance, celebration, and jubilation. The joy of the holiday is not confined to the synagogue. It is customary for the celebrants to take their rejoicing outside the synagogue walls, to sing, dance, and rejoice in the streets of their cities and towns.[3]

In 2023 Simchat Torah fell on *October 7, 2023*.

The Sukkot Music Festival

As every Hebrew holy day begins at sundown "the night before," so it was with Simchat Torah. It began Friday night, October 6, and culminated on the day of October 7. It was that night before that a celebration of music and dancing was begun in the Israeli desert. Its official name was the Super-nova *Sukkot* Gathering. It was named after the Hebrew holiday that was then reaching its climax in Simchat Torah, the celebration of joy. But the Dragon had other plans.

Joy Inverted

How does one desecrate a holy day appointed for joy? How does one invert a time of rejoicing? One turns it inside out. And so came the inversion of Simchat Torah. The Enemy transformed Israel's day of joy into a day of sorrow. The sounds of laughter, rejoicing, and singing were replaced by wails of weeping and lamentation. God had promised to turn Israel's mourning into joy. So the Enemy turned her joy into mourning. He caused those who should have been rejoicing to go into mourning instead, and those who should have been mourning to rejoice.

The Unholy Simchat Torah

As the desecration of the holy creates a new unholy reality, so after desecrating God's holy day, the Devil created his own. The joy and rejoicing that should have taken place in Israel on Simchat Torah took place instead in Gaza and the West Bank. Mass celebrations erupted not over the completion of God's Word but over the blood of the Israeli youth and villagers. The exuberance and jubilation meant for Simchat Torah and that the Enemy had caused to cease could now be seen in the towns and cities of Israel's enemies. It was the Dragon's holiday.

As on Simchat Torah the Jewish people sing and dance for joy, so now, on the Dragon's holiday, it was Israel's enemies who sang and danced for joy.

As on Simchat Torah the Jewish people go outside their houses and synagogues to celebrate and rejoice on the streets, so on that day, it was the people of Gaza and the West Bank who went outside their houses and dwellings to celebrate and rejoice over the shedding of Jewish blood.

And so it was reported:

> A video from Al-Jazeera Network...titled: "Palestinians *overjoyed* with the Al-Aqsa Flood Operation," showed celebrations in Gaza, Nablus, Jenin, and Bethlehem.

In the West Bank city of Nablus:

> They fired their guns to *express their jubilation.*

The themes of joy and jubilation, as in Simchat Torah, came up in more than one account. One news agency described it as:

> *Happiness and jubilation* for the Al-Aqsa Flood.[4]

Child's Play

In the Orthodox celebrations of Simchat Torah, it is the men and boys who take the lead in the dancing and rejoicing of the day.[5] So on the streets of Gaza and the West Bank, it was the men and boys who predominated in the dancing and jubilation over Israel's calamity.

On Simchat Torah both young boys and girls may dance with their fathers. So on Simchat Torah the enemies of Israel brought in their young children to celebrate with them, lifting them on their shoulders as they danced for joy. The little children, in their celebration, even mimicked those who had brought bloodshed, as noted in a description of a scene caught on video from that day:

> A little girl can be seen waving a rifle and a handgun in the air.[6]

The Colorful Flags

The bearing and waving of colorful flags is unique to Simchat Torah. So on that Simchat Torah of 2023 the enemies of Israel employed the bearing and waving of flags in their celebrations, the flags of Islamic zeal, of Palestinian nationalism, and terror. And while no Israelis were then joyously waving their flags on that day, the Palestinian and Islamic celebrations that replaced the Jewish ones included joyously setting on fire the Israeli flag.[7]

The Day of Sweets

Another unique element of Simchat Torah is the handing out of sweets and candies. The practice actually became a major issue just before the calamity. In the days leading up to October 7 the Israeli government announced that it had launched a new initiative in observance of Simchat Torah. They would distribute bags of candies to 250,000 Israeli children.[8] In the wake of what had happened on the holiday, the giving away of candy was overwhelmed by sorrow.

And yet the unique practice of Simchat Torah, the giving of candy and sweets, *was* observed that day.

The Dragon's Candy

The Devil, as the master of imitation, mimicked the customs of the Jewish holiday he had desecrated. So the giving away of candy *was* observed on Simchat Torah—only not by the Israelis. The accounts of the Palestinian celebrations of October 7 include this detail:

> The Iranian-affiliated Mayadeen TV (Lebanon) aired a report about Palestinian celebrations in the West Bank, according to which *sweets were handed out* in Nablus.[9]

> A member of the Al-Quds Brigades *distributes candies* in celebration of the deadly Hamas terror assault on Israel...October 7, 2023.[10]

It was not, of course, that those involved had any idea that they were performing the appointed act *of Simchat Torah on Simchat Torah*. It was the Imitator who was causing them to unwittingly mimic it. The mimicry of Simchat Torah went beyond Gaza and the West Bank. One account reported,

> Across the Middle East, people *distribute treats, dance in streets and celebrate*....From Ramallah to Beirut, Damascus, Baghdad and Cairo, *people have distributed candies, danced and chanted*.[11]

People distribute treats, dance in streets, and celebrate. The words describe exactly what happens on Simchat Torah. Only now those words described the desecration of Simchat Torah. The Dragon had created a darkened version of Israel's holiday, as his celebrants danced in the streets and ate candy as they rejoiced over the Jewish blood that had been shed.

———————■■■———————

Could the mystery of the appointed times have determined not only the time of year in which the calamity would fall but the exact year in which it would fall?

Chapter 49

A MYSTERY OF JUBILEES

THE MOST DRAMATIC of Israel's appointed times comes only once every fifty years. In Hebrew it is called the *Yovel*. We know it as the *Jubilee*.

The Year of Restoration

The Yovel, or Jubilee, first appears in Leviticus 25:

> And you shall consecrate the fiftieth year, and proclaim liberty throughout all the land to all its inhabitants. It shall be a Jubilee for you; and each of you shall return to his possession, and each of you shall return to his family.[1]

The Jubilee was the year of release, freedom, return, and restoration. If one had lost one's ancestral land, in the year of Jubilee it was restored. Each would *return to his possession*. So the Jubilee was the year of return, when the dispossessed would return to that from which they were separated.

The Prophetic Jubilee

No other people have been so greatly and so long separated from their ancestral possession as have the people of Israel from the land of Israel. No other people have ever so dramatically returned to their ancestral land as have the children of Israel to the Promised Land. And to no other nation was such a law given ordaining the return to one's ancestral land. Is it then possible that the two could be connected—the ancient ordinance to return to one's ancestral possession, and the return of the Jewish people to their ancestral land?

The answer is *yes*. Israel's ancient Jubilee of return and the nation's prophetic return to the land are joined together in a mystery, a Jubilean mystery. It is what I opened up in the book called *The Oracle*. For the purposes of the present mystery, I will here give a brief overview. Though no one knows when the ancient Israelites observed the Jubilean year, what we are about to see is how the return of Israel followed the amazingly precise fifty-year cycle of a prophetic Jubilee.

The Beginning

The Ottoman Turks had taken the land of Israel in the year 1517. In the year of Jubilee the land is to be released from those who occupy it and given back to those to whom it belongs. Counting seven cycles of fifty years, from the Ottoman conquest of the land to the seventh Jubilee, brings us to the year 1867. It was that year that a change began and the seeds of restoration were sown. In 1867 the Ottoman sultan issued a law that would, in effect, allow for and begin the release of the land from those who occupied it back to the Jewish people.[2]

In that same year, another restoration began. In 1867 the British archaeologist Charles Warren accidentally stumbled upon the hidden ruins of the City of David.[3] The City of David was the original city of Jerusalem. Another of Israel's ancient possessions now returned to the modern world.

In the years following 1867, Jewish refugees began returning to their ancestral land. It would be known as the *First Aliyah*,[4] the beginning of Israel's modern resurrection. It was in that same period that the sultan's releasing of the land led to its repurchasing, its reclamation, its redemption, its replanting, and ultimately to its full restoration to those who had lost it in ancient times.

The Homeland

The return had begun, but the land was still under Ottoman control. But in the year of Jubilee those who occupy the land must depart from it. Counting fifty years from 1867 takes us to the year 1917—the first Jubilee from the first release and the eighth Jubilee from the beginning of Ottoman rule.

In that Jubilean year, as the First World War raged in the Middle East, the armies of the British Empire, under the command of General Edmund Allenby, entered the land of Israel. In the face of their advance the Ottoman troops fled. And so in the year of Jubilee those who occupied the land began departing from it. And in that same year the British government issued the Balfour Declaration. The declaration, in effect, promised the return of the land to the Jewish people—the second restoration.[5]

The Holy City

One thing was missing—Jerusalem. Jerusalem was Israel's center, its eternal capital. Even at Israel's rebirth as a nation-state in 1948, the holy city of Jerusalem eluded it, having been seized by Jordan.[6] But if the Jubilee ordains that one must return to one's lost possession, then it must also mean the return of the Jewish people to Jerusalem. And the ancient prophecies of Scripture foretold it.

Counting fifty years from the Jubilee of 1917 brings us to the year 1967. In

June of 1967 the Six-Day War broke out. On the third day of that war Israeli soldiers entered the gates of the ancient city. They made their way to the Western Wall, where they wept and prayed.[7] After nearly two thousand years the people of Israel returned to their most holy city. And so in the year of Jubilee, "when each of you shall return to his possession," the Jewish people returned to their most sacred possession, Jerusalem.

The Declaration

In the year of Jubilee not only does one return to one's ancestral land, but one is given the legal right and recognition to possess it. But when Israel returned to its ancient capital, the world refused to give it recognition. And yet no nation could so claim the right to any city as Israel could to Jerusalem. Its title deed was the Bible itself.

Counting fifty years from the Jubilee of 1967 brings us to the year 2017. And so it was in 2017, the Jubilee of Israel's return to Jerusalem, that the legal recognition withheld for fifty years would finally be granted. It would begin on June 5 of that year as the United States Senate passed a resolution recognizing Jerusalem as the capital of Israel and called on the president to do likewise.[8] June 5, 2017, was fifty years, one Jubilee, from the start of the Six-Day War—*to the exact day.*

Later that year, the president would issue the Jerusalem Declaration, in which, for the first time ever, the United States would officially recognize Jerusalem as the capital of Israel and authorize the moving of the American embassy there.[9] It was an unprecedented moment not only for America but for the world. It was the first time that any major world leader or power had recognized Jerusalem as the capital of the Jewish nation since ancient times.

The Jubilean Desecration

And as the Enemy wars against the return and restoration of Israel, so he would war against Israel's sacred vessel of return and restoration, the Jubilee. He would therefore seek its desecration.

How, then, would he desecrate it? He would invert it. He would give to Israel a Jubilee, not of freedom but captivity, not of restoration but destruction; he would give them a Devil's Jubilee.

------■■■------

Could there be an event that took place decades before October 7 that contained the mystery of what would happen on that day—and when?

Chapter 50

THE DEVIL'S JUBILEE

WHEN WOULD THE Devil's Jubilee take place?

The Fifty-Year Cycle

As Israel's restoration followed the fifty-year template and timing of the Jubilean ordinance, so the Enemy would follow the same template and timing—but for destruction. As the fiftieth year was ordained for Israel's blessing, the Enemy would repurpose it for calamity. But when would the fifty-year cycle begin? In the case of Israel's restoration, each Jubilean restoration had taken place fifty years after the previous restoration and blessing. The Devil's Jubilean countdown would begin not with an event of blessing and restoration but of calamity.

The Yom Kippur Calamity

It was, by far, the most demoralizing war Israel had ever fought since its rebirth. It would be called "the most traumatic event in Israel's history."[1] It would shake the nation's confidence for years to come. It would cause its prime minister to consider suicide and later resign from office.[2] And it would lead its highest defense minister to contemplate that the destruction of the Jewish nation was at hand. It was called the *Yom Kippur War*.

It began with a mass invasion of Egyptian forces from the Sinai and Syrian forces from the Golan Heights. Israel was caught by surprise and was overwhelmed by the massive numbers involved. Egypt came in with two hundred thousand soldiers and over two thousand tanks. On the Israeli side were eighteen thousand soldiers and three hundred tanks. The Egyptian army smashed through Israel's Bar-Lev defensive line in a matter of hours. The Syrian army outnumbered the Israeli troops by ten to one. Israel would suffer three times more fatalities per capita in that one war than Americans had suffered in over ten years of the war in Vietnam. The nation would ultimately survive the onslaught and turn it around to the point of victory.[3] But the trauma of that invasion and war would stay in its national consciousness into the next century.

The Appointed Year

In the spiritual realm it was the closest the Dragon had come in modern times to destroying the state of Israel. And so it was from this event that he would begin his Jubilean countdown. And so Israel's greatest calamity in modern times would lead to a Jubilee of darkness and destruction.

The Yom Kippur War took place in 1973. Counting fifty years forward brings us to the year 2023. This would be the year of the Devil's Jubilee. The Yom Kippur War began as an invasion of Israel. Thus we could expect that in 2023 another invasion would come to the land of Israel.

In the year of Jubilee the people of Israel were to return to their possession, their homes, and their inheritance. But in the Dragon's Jubilee, it would all be reversed. The people of Israel would be *uprooted from their homes, taken away from their possessions,* and *separated from their inheritance.* In the year of Jubilee those who were enslaved would be set free. But in the Dragon's Jubilee those who were free would be enslaved, taken away as captives.

The Jubilean Invasion

Before the Yom Kippur War there were signs of a coming invasion. But the Israeli government didn't take them seriously—for which a great price would be paid. Fifty years later it would replay with warning signs in the days leading up to October 7. But the government agencies that received those warnings did not take them seriously—for which, likewise, a great price would be paid.

The war of 1973 began as a massive ground invasion. Its Jubilee of 2023 would see another massive ground invasion of Israel, the first such ground invasion of Israel in *fifty years.*

The Yom Kippur invasion caught Israel by surprise, unaware, and unprepared. In the Jubilee of 2023 Israel would again be caught by surprise, unaware, and unprepared in the face of a massive calamity.

In the invasion of 1973 Egypt and Syria employed rapid speed and massive numbers and overwhelmed the small numbers of Israeli soldiers stationed on the border and in the line of attack. Fifty years later Hamas would likewise employ rapid speed and massive numbers to invade Israel. It would begin with the firing of massive numbers of rockets and then a deadly onslaught of armed invaders. It would, as in the Yom Kippur War, overwhelm the small numbers of soldiers stationed on the border and in the line of attack.[4]

The Jubilean Sabbath

The Yom Kippur War was launched on the Sabbath. Israel's enemies knew that by attacking the Jewish nation on its day of rest, when much of the nation's functions were shut down, they would gain a massive strategic advantage.[5] Fifty years later, on the Dragon's Jubilee, another enemy would invade the land on the Sabbath, Israel's day of rest.

On that Saturday of 1973 the quiet calm of the Sabbath was broken by the wails of sirens to warn the nation of the attack and to desperately call its reserve soldiers to come to the nation's defense.[6] In its year of Jubilee, on that Saturday of 2023, the invasion would again take place on the Sabbath. On that day the quiet calm of the Israeli Sabbath would again be broken by the wails of sirens and desperate calls for its reserves to come to the nation's defense.

The Jubilean Holy Day

After the War of Independence in 1948, the Yom Kippur War stands as the bloodiest of Israel's wars. October 7 would stand as the bloodiest of all its days.

The invasion of 1973 took place not only on the Sabbath but on a Hebrew holy day—Yom Kippur, the Day of Atonement. The invasion of 2023 took place not only on the Sabbath but on a Hebrew holy day—Shemini Atzeret and Simchat Torah.

The invasion of 1973 would bring Israel into war. The Dragon's Jubilee of 2023 would, likewise, bring Israel into war.

———————— ∎∎∎ ————————

And yet there was more…

Chapter 51

THE 18,263rd DAY

THE MYSTERY WOULD go further, beyond the realm of years and into that mystery of days.

The October Mystery

It was a Friday night worship service at Beth Israel. *The Josiah Manifesto*, my latest book, had just been released thirty days earlier. For the night's message I was led to do something different, to open up one of the mysteries contained in the book. Before the end of that Friday night in America the calamity that would shock the world had begun in the Gaza Strip. Thousands of rockets would begin raining down into Israeli cities and towns, and then came the invaders.

Those who had been at the service that Friday night and awoke on Saturday to hear the news from across the world sent word to the ministry that the mystery I had shared the night before had foretold what was now unfolding across the world.

The Foretelling of a Plague

The mystery was that of the fifty-year Jubilean cycle and its manifestations in modern times. The mystery had foretold some of the most critical of world events. The mystery was precise, pinpointing those events down to their exact dates. It had foretold the coming of a plague, the exact day that COVID-19 would officially arrive on American soil. It had foretold what the media called "the day that everything changed," when the outbreak officially became a pandemic, when the United States was placed under quarantine, and when, for most Americans, the reality of the virus came crashing down on their lives. The mystery had foretold these and other major events down to their exact dates and based on a mystery that had preceded them by thousands of years.

On that Friday night in October, I shared of the mystery's fulfillments up to the start of 2023. But the mystery wasn't finished. The Friday night on which I spoke of *the fifty-year* Jubilean cycle was *the fifty-year* anniversary of one of the most significant events of 1973. It was fifty years to the day that started the Yom Kippur War.

The Pinpointing of October 7

The mystery had foretold not only the calamity that would come upon Israel but exactly when it would come.

The Yom Kippur invasion took place in *October 1973*. So the invasion would take place in *October of 2023*.

Since the Yom Kippur War took place on a Sabbath, if that was to hold in its Jubilean parallel, it would mean that the coming calamity had to take place on *one of the Sabbaths of October of 2023*. That would narrow it down to only one of *four days*.

One of the four Saturdays in October of 2023 would also have to fall on a Hebrew holy day, one of the sacred *moedeem*, the appointed times of God given in Leviticus 23, as had the Yom Kippur War.

There would only be one date that would fall in the year 2023, in the month of October, on a Sabbath day, on a Hebrew holy day, and on one of the sacred moedeem given in Leviticus 23. *That date was October 7, 2023—the day of the calamity.*

The First Sabbath of October

Even if we had not possessed any of these keys, we would still have another. The Yom Kippur War was launched on the *first Sabbath* and the *first Saturday* of October 1973. Thus the mystery would foretell a calamitous invasion of Israel that would happen on the first Sabbath and first Saturday of that month and year. Only one day would meet these criteria. The first Saturday of the October of that year was *October 7, 2023*.

The Yom Kippur War began on October 6, 1973.[1] In 2023, October 6 fell on a Friday. In America, it would still be October 6 when the Hamas invasion of Israel began. But in Israel it was Saturday, October 7. Had the invasion taken place during the day, as it had fifty years before, but on October 6, it would not have corresponded to the Sabbath day of the Yom Kippur invasion. From the Yom Kippur invasion of 1973 to the Simchat Torah invasion of 2023 was one Jubilee, fifty years, from Sabbath to Sabbath.

And yet the difference of that one day, October 6 and October 7, is going to open up yet another mystery.

The Dragon's Counterattack

In the vision of Revelation 12 a number of patterns emerge. The Dragon seeks to devour the woman's child, the Messiah. He fails. He then wages war against the woman who gave birth to the child. The woman is given the wings of an eagle to escape. The Dragon then sends a flood against the woman. The earth swallows the flood. The Dragon then burns with rage against the woman and makes war against her other children.

The Dragon tries to destroy the woman but ultimately fails. So the Enemy has tried to destroy the Jewish people for ages and has failed. When the Dragon fails to destroy the woman, he tries again with a different strategy. He retaliates; he strikes back, he launches a counterattack.

The Prophetic Counterattack

When Israel emerged from the Six-Day War, it had achieved one of the greatest military victories in history. But it was also the fulfillment of biblical prophecy. It had regained Jerusalem. What would the Dragon's response be? He would be enraged, he would seek to reverse his loss, he would retaliate. He would strike back. How would it come?

It would come in the form of the Yom Kippur War. Without understanding the significance of the Six-Day War, one cannot understand the Yom Kippur War. The Yom Kippur invasion was a direct response to the Six-Day War, both militarily and politically. It was the striking back of Israel's enemies in an attempt to undo Israel's victory in the Six-Day War.

But beyond the political and military realms is the spiritual realm. End-time prophecy, the return of the Messiah, and the coming of God's kingdom all require the Jewish people to return to Jerusalem. For nearly two thousand years the Dragon had largely kept the Jewish people away from Jerusalem. Now it was all undone. And so in 1973 the Dragon would launch a war so sudden, intense, and massive that it threatened Israel's very existence.

The 2,315th Day

So how long would it be from the war by which God's prophetic purposes were fulfilled to the war in which the Enemy struck back to undo those purposes—how long from the Six-Day War to the Yom Kippur War? The Six-Day War began on June 5, 1967.[2] The Yom Kippur War began on October 6, 1973. From the day that started the Six-Day War to the day that started the Yom Kippur War were 2,315 days.

The physical restoration of Jerusalem to the Jewish people in 1967 was followed fifty years later by a legal restoration in 2017. If one counts fifty years, exactly fifty years, from the day the Six-Day War began, the countdown ends on June 5, 2017—the exact day that the United States Senate passed the resolution recognizing Jerusalem as the capital of Israel—another victory and progression in Israel's restoration. Therefore, it would follow that the Dragon would strike back against that victory and restoration. When?

If the Six-Day War and the Yom Kippur War were separated by 2,315 days, then what about their two Jubilees, their two fifty-year anniversaries? If we start from the fifty-year anniversary of Jerusalem's restoration, the day of the Jerusalem Resolution in the United States Senate on June 5, 2017, and count forward 2,315 days, on what day does the countdown end?

Because of the variation in leap years between the two periods, the count-down *does not end* on Friday, October 6. *The 2,315th day* falls on *October 7, 2023, the exact date of the invasion.*

The 18,263rd Day

One more mystery of days—from Jubilee to Jubilee—from the start of the Six-Day War, on June 5, 1967, to its Jubilee, on June 5, 2017, the day of the Jerusalem Resolution—from the one restoration to the other—how long was it? How many days are in the Jubilean cycle of Jerusalem's restoration? It comes out to 18,263 days.

As the Enemy is an imitator, what if he imitated the Jerusalem Jubilean cycle? What if he took the exact number of days in the cycle of Jerusalem's restoration and started the countdown not from a day of victory but a day of calamity, not to restore but to strike back and undo? Starting from the invasion that began the Yom Kippur War on October 6, 1973, and counting forward the 18,263 days of the Jerusalem cycle, what does it lead to? Because of the variation of leap years in the two cycles, it *does not lead to* October 6, 2023. When is the 18,263rd day?

The 18,263rd day is October 7, 2023. It falls on the exact day of the calamity— the day of the Dragon's counterattack.

---------------■■■---------------

Could what happened on that October morning and what followed in its wake be a shadow of things yet to come? We now open up the end of days.

Part XII

THE END OF DAYS

Chapter 52

THE END OF DAYS

WHAT IS THE *end of days?* The words are as ancient as the Torah, the very start of Scripture. In Hebrew it reads *the akharit hayamim.*

The Akharit Hayamim

The phrase may also be translated as *the later days, the last of days, the latter days, the remnant of days, the latter end of the days,* and *the last days.* The words refer not to the "end of the world" but the end of the age, the days leading up to and ushering in the coming of Messiah and the kingdom of God. One of the earliest appearances of the term is found in Moses' last words to Israel:

> When you are in *distress*, and all these things come
> upon you in *the end of days, when you turn* to the
> LORD your God and obey His voice...[1]

The word translated here as *turn* is the Hebrew word *shuv. Shuv* can also be rendered as *return.* The end of days will thus be marked by return. It will witness the return of the Jewish people to their homeland and their ultimate return to God.

Days of the Enemy

The word rendered as *distress* is the Hebrew *tsar. Tsar* can also be translated as *tribulation, adversity, affliction,* and *sorrow.* Biblical prophecy consistently speaks of the end of days as a time of great tribulation for the nation of Israel and the world, a time of war, calamity, and unprecedented destruction.

The word *tsar* can also be translated as *enemy* or *adversary.* The end of days will, likewise, be marked by the empowerment of God's enemies and the enemies of Israel, with war being waged against both.

The end of days will also be marked by another *tsar*, another enemy, *the* Enemy, the Dragon. It is no accident that the Dragon plays a key role in the Book of Revelation. The last days will be marked by evil and apostasy, when immorality will increase and "the love of many will grow cold."[2]

Putting together the pieces, the end of days will be marked by return, adversity, evil, war against God and Israel, persecution, tribulation, calamity, and the Dragon.

The Shepherd's Prophecy

Imagine being a shepherd in the ancient Middle East. Your technology does not exceed that of a shepherd's staff or the stones of an olive press. But you have the Scriptures and, within them, the prophecies of the last days. Having only that, the Word of God, what could you know of the future? What would it tell you?

It would tell you of a future in which the Jewish people have returned from a global dispersion to their ancient land, and in which the nation of Israel would be resurrected. It would tell you that in that future the focus of the entire world would be fixed on Israel. It would tell you that Israel would be viewed by the nations as the source of controversy and conflict, and that wars would be waged concerning it. It would tell you that the world at that time would be marked by apostasy, a departure from God, from faith, and from what had long been accepted as morality, a world that advanced an anti-biblical morality, a world over which the shadow of destruction loomed.

Thus with no technology greater than that of our shepherd's rods, you could do what no scientist, no think tank, and no supercomputer of the present day could begin to do. You could describe the modern world ages before its coming.

In other words, if there is an age that corresponds with what biblical prophecy foretells of the end of days—we are already there.

Sign of the End

It is no accident that October 7, 2023, the worst day in the history of the Jewish state, embodied the central dynamics prophesied of the end days—a resurrected Israel, an Israel at the center of global controversy, and a campaign that would seek to eradicate it. October 7 was saturated with end-time markers. As it was the day of the Enemy's works and power, so the end times will be marked by many days of the Enemy's works and powers. And so what took place that day will give us a glimpse into the days ahead, the end-time tactics, plans, and strategies of the Dragon.

On October 7 the Enemy came against Israel with a massive onslaught designed to overwhelm all defenses, resistance, and hedges of protection. That is the Enemy's strategy. As his influence increases in the last days, he will seek to break down all resistance, all defenses, and all hedges of protection by coming against the works and purposes of God in a massive and overwhelming onslaught. As the operation that came against Israel bore the name *Flood*, so in the end times the Enemy will come upon the world as an overwhelming flood. The flood will come through culture, government, media, law, technology, indoctrination, propaganda, economics, religion, and every means at his disposal, including literal and physical war. Those who oppose his agenda he will seek to sweep away.

The Days of Desecration

October 7, as we have seen, was marked by desecration. So the last days will be marked by desecration, sacrilege, and defilement. The Dragon will seek to defile the creation of God, twist the works of God, and subvert, invert, and pervert the image of God wherever it appears. And thus will come the desecration of man, of woman, of child, of sexuality, of marriage, of faith, of worship, of life, of all things. And as the desecration of October 7 imitated the appointed times of God, so the end times will, likewise, be marked by imitation, a false god, and a false messiah.

The Days of Mania

As October 7 was a manifestation of the Dragon's orgidzo, his rage, so the last days will be driven by the Dragon's orgidzo, ruled and possessed by it. It will manifest in a growing animosity toward the things of God in every realm of culture and life and an all-out war to destroy them. As the acts committed on that day were demonic, impelled by the Dragon's spirit, so at the end of the age the spirit of the Enemy will take possession of world culture. Nations will be impelled by it, governments ruled by it, and cultures transformed by it. It will lead many to embrace what they once knew to be evil, to practice, rejoice in, and celebrate it. Under its sway the pure will be defiled, the good condemned, and, as on October 7, the blood of the innocent shed. It will give birth to movements of irrationality, a satanic mania.

Could a prominent symbol in the war of Palestine against Israel be connected to a vision in the Book of Revelation?

Chapter 53

COLORS OF THE APOCALYPSE

I N REVELATION 6 a scroll bound with seven seals is opened. As each seal is removed, an apocalyptic event takes place on earth connected to judgment on earth. The first four seals are linked to four horses and four riders.

The Four Horsemen

Of the first horseman it is written:

> He who sat on it had a bow; and a crown was given to him, and he went out conquering and to conquer.[1]

And thus the first apocalyptic event is linked to conquest. Of the second horseman it is written:

> And it was granted to the one who sat on it to take peace from the earth, and that people should kill one another; and there was given to him a great sword.[2]

The second apocalyptic event is thus connected to conflict and war. Of the third rider it is written:

> He who sat on it had a pair of scales in his hand. And I heard a voice in the midst of the four living creatures saying, "A quart of wheat for a denarius, and three quarts of barley for a denarius; and do not harm the oil and the wine."[3]

The third apocalyptic event is linked to hunger, want, or famine. And of the fourth rider it is written:

> And the name of him who sat on it was Death, and Hades followed with him.[4]

The fourth event is embodied by death.

The four riders have become known as the *Four Horsemen of the Apocalypse*. To them was given power to "kill with sword, with hunger, with death, and by the beasts of the earth."[5] Together they constitute an ominous image of coming judgment.

The Blue and White

The Jewish prayer shawl, the *tallit*, is to be made of white cloth framed with stripes, ideally of blue. The Israeli flag was officially adopted during the first Zionist Congresses at the end of the nineteenth century, fifty years before the nation's resurrection. It consisted of a white cloth with a blue Star of David framed with two stripes of blue. It resembled the Jewish prayer cloth. That was no accident. Israel's national flag was created after the pattern of the Hebrew tallit. So the colors and patterns represented on Israel's flag are connected to prayer, worship, and God.

The Palestine Flag

The word *Palestine* has already become the lightning rod of anti-Israel hatred throughout the world. Is it possible that the issue of Palestine could be used to plant seeds that will come to fruition in the apocalypse? The flag of Palestine was adopted by the Palestine Liberation Organization in 1964. It was based on an earlier flag representing Arab revolt. That flag was created in the latter part of the First World War, at the same time that the Balfour Declaration, promising the Jewish people a homeland in Israel, was birthed.[6]

The White Horse

The flag of Palestine consists of a triangle, three stripes, and four colors linked to four Arab dynasties. But beyond the dynasties the four colors of the flag match up with something else that no one intended.

The first of the four horses of the apocalypse is called, in Greek, *huppos leukos*. The word *leukos* comes from the Greek word for *light*. It means *white*.

> *I looked, and behold, a white horse.*[7]

The first color of the flag of Palestine is *white*.

The Red Horse

The second of the four horses is called, in Greek, a *huppos purrhos*. *Purrhos* comes from the Greek word for *fire*. It means red or bright red.

> *Another horse, fiery red, went out.*[8]

The second color of the flag of Palestine is *red*.

The Black Horse

The third of the four horses is called, in Greek, *huppos melos*. The word *melos* means *black*.

> *So I looked, and behold, a black horse.*[9]

The third color of the flag of Palestine is *black*.

The Green Horse

The last of the four horses is called, in Greek, *huppos khloros*. The word *khloros* is commonly translated here as *pale*. But *khloros* means something other than pale. In fact, every other time it appears in the New Testament, it is translated otherwise. It is used three times to describe the color of grass. It means *green*.

> *So I looked, and behold, a green horse.*[10]

The last color of the flag of Palestine is *green*.

The Flag of Apocalyptic Colors

So the Palestinian flag, the flag that was created to nullify the nation of Israel, the flag that is waved around the world in rage against the nation of Israel, just happens to bear the four colors of the four horses of the four horsemen of the apocalypse. Not only that, but the nations of the world that fly these four colors on their flags are almost exclusively the same that have opposed the Jewish nation, that have actively waged war against it, or that are prophesied to do so at the end of the age—white, red, black, and green, the colors of Palestine, the colors of October 7, and—the apocalypse.

Could the wave of hatred and rage that swept the world in the wake of October 7 give us a clue into the last days?

Chapter 54

THE FROGS

And I saw three unclean spirits like frogs coming out of the mouth of the Dragon, out of the mouth of the Beast, and out of the mouth of the false prophet.[1]

"Spirits Like Frogs"

Most of what is revealed in the vision of Revelation 12 concerns the end of the age. It is then that the Dragon's war against the woman will reach its greatest intensity. Though the war is manifested on earth, it is ultimately spiritual. According to biblical prophecy, it will ultimately engulf the entire world. So as that day approaches, we would expect to see eruptions of the Dragon's orgidzo, outbreaks of rage and hatred against the Jewish people and the nation of Israel—and we would expect those eruptions and outbreaks to span the globe.

Revelation 16 depicts unclean spirits "like frogs" emerging from the mouth of the Dragon and his vessels. They go forth to "the kings of the earth."[2] The goal of the spirits is to draw the world into the Dragon's will and into waging war against Israel. Can we see shadows of that coming day even now?

The Global Fury

Though, in the immediate wake of October 6, there were statements of sympathy issued from around the world, the most striking response to the calamity was not compassion or sympathy—but celebration. The Dragon's orgidzo that had possessed the invaders of October 7 would now break out of the borders of Philistia and explode across the world.

The celebrations and demonstrations that originated with the Palestinians now exploded across the Islamic world from Egypt to Iraq, from Lebanon to Iran. But they would not stop there. They would break out, as well, across Europe, from Germany to the United Kingdom. They would even break out in the most pro-Israel of world powers, America.[3]

Blood Frenzy

Celebration is not a normal response to atrocities and mass murder of any people. Nor is it normal that those who commit atrocity and murder against innocent civilians should be hailed as heroes. But the victims in this case were not *any people*—they were Jews. And so the normal laws did not apply, nor did the guardrails of rational thought hold up. The phenomenon was not normal or natural but driven by the entity whose nature was both unnatural and abnormal.

Why did that happen? The Dragon's nature is predatorial. For many predators the scent of blood triggers them to hunt down and devour their prey. In some species the scent of blood sends them into killing frenzies. In the wake of October 7 it was as if the killing of Jewish people had triggered a blood frenzy in the spiritual realm that manifested in eruptions of rage and celebrations of murder throughout the world. And it was not even that the rage was rooted in Israel's response to October 7 in seeking to protect its people from future calamities. The frenzies of rage began immediately after it became known that Jewish blood was shed.

Spirit of the Predator

The predator of Revelation 12, the Dragon, pursues, hunts for the woman. In the wake of October 7 the world was given a glimpse of that hunt as the spirit of the Dragon triggered the stalking of the woman's children. In Western cities Orthodox Jews were pursued and attacked on the streets. Jewish people now hid their Stars of David under their shirts and their yarmulkes under baseball caps. In New York City, Jewish students had to be locked inside the school library in order to save them from the violence of the roving anti-Israel mob raging outside. In the two months following October 7, anti-Jewish hate crimes multiplied nearly five times what they had been a year earlier. And all across the world the children of Israel were vilified, attacked, pursued, terrorized, and abused. And the faces of Israelis being held hostage by Hamas were ripped down from the walls on which they were posted or else defaced.[4]

Swastikas Over the Woke

And in the world of wokeness, where perceived microaggression and offended sensibilities were invariably met with the severest of condemnations and retribution, the murder of Jewish people was met instead with silence or applause. It was then that Jewish people throughout the world awoke to the realization that the new Left that had trumpeted the virtues of tolerance and inclusion was actually filled with a virulent strain of Jew hatred.

Groups dedicated to countering the mistreatment of women, including those operating within the United Nations, when it came to the raping and murdering of Israeli women, grew strangely silent. Organizations dedicated to the protection of children, likewise, found that when it came to the killing of Jewish children, they had nothing to say. An American chapter of Black

Lives Matter celebrated October 7 by posting images of Hamas gunmen paragliding into the land to slaughter the Israeli villagers. The images depicted the gunmen as heroes. And demonstrations throughout the world featured Nazi-style anti-Semitic caricatures, chants of "Gas the Jews," and the waving of swastikas.[5]

October 7 was far from the first such explosion of the Dragon's rage against the Jewish people since Israel's rebirth. It would not be the last. But it was unique in the immense scope and scale of global rage against the Jewish people it ignited. It served as a vessel through which the Dragon's fury against Israel exploded across the world—a precursor to the going forth of the unclean spirits of Revelation that will, likewise, take hold of the earth.

Philistine World

The Philistine virus had now infected the world. Whereas the ancient Philistines celebrated Jewish calamity and bloodshed in the streets of Philistia— the dark celebrations had metastasized and spread across the world. They could now be seen in the streets of London, in the courts of Harvard,[6] and in the televised reports of cable news channels. The seeds of ancient Philistia were being sown into the nations. Its deep hatred of Israel was becoming a central part of global culture. The world was increasingly taking on the attributes, the nature, and the hatred of Israel's ancient enemies. It was becoming a global Philistia.

Could one of the most controversial of end-time biblical prophecies be connected to the events of October 7?

Chapter 55

EZEKIEL'S RAIDERS

N THE BOOK of Ezekiel is a unique prophecy that has evoked much attention and controversy among students of the end times. Many believe it foretells the next major prophetic event.

"After Many Days"

The prophecy is given in Ezekiel 38 and 39. Though the language includes the imagery of swords and shields, it is believed that these correspond to their modern counterparts and are the only language that could have been employed and understood by the prophet and his age. But there are many other elements of Ezekiel's prophecy that place its fulfillment firmly at the end of the age.

First, there is no evidence of what was foretold having been fulfilled in ancient times. And since it concerns Israel, the only other age in which it could be fulfilled is that of the modern Jewish nation. Further, it exclusively concerns nations that do *not* border the land of Israel, several of which are considerably distant from the others. It is for that reason that various Bible commentaries in past ages have taken the prophecy as figurative rather than literal. They didn't believe that nations so geographically distant from each other could play a part in a coordinated military invasion. But such a scenario is more than possible in the modern world. Beyond all this is the context given in the prophecy itself:

> *After many days* you will be visited. In the *latter years* you will come into the land of those *brought back from the sword and gathered from many people* on the mountains of Israel, which had *long been desolate*; they were *brought out of the nations*, and now all of them dwell safely.[1]

The prophecy is for *many days*, a biblical way of denoting ages.[2] It is appointed for *the latter years*, a phrase that specifically denotes the end of the age. The land of Israel is referred to as that which has been "*brought back from the sword*" and "*gathered from many people*." That was never as true of Israel as it is in the present time. Further, it speaks of the land having "*long been desolate*." That too has never been so fulfilled as in modern times, when the land of Israel had lain desolate for nearly two thousand years.

The End-Time Invasion

So what does the prophecy foretell? It describes a coordinated attack of enemy nations against the resurrected Israel, a mass invasion. The invading nations will say,

> I will go up against a land of unwalled villages; I
> will go to a peaceful people, who dwell safely, all
> of them dwelling without walls…against the waste
> places that are again inhabited, and against a
> people gathered from the nations.[3]

The description given of the invaded nation, again, matches modern Israel after its twentieth-century resurrection. According to the prophecy, the attack will overwhelm the Jewish nation and engulf the land. It will be then that God will intervene and bring judgment on the invaders.[4] The event appears to serve as both a prelude and bridge to the global conflict foretold in Revelation.

Identifying the Players

October 7 was the first mass invasion of Israel in half a century. If the nations cited in Ezekiel's prophecy are to launch a future mass invasion of Israel, is it possible that they could be, in some way, connected to the invasion of October? And thus is it possible that the October invasion was a precursor to the fulfillment of Ezekiel's prophecy?

Which nations? Their names as given in the prophecy are *Gog, Magog, Meshekh, Tubal, Paras, Kush, Phut, Gomer,* and *Togarmah*. The word *Rosh* also appears,[5] but since we cannot be sure if this is a proper name denoting a nation or simply the Hebrew word signifying *head* or *chief*, we will focus on those we can be sure of. Leaving, for now, the question, the controversy, and the possibility that the prophecy contains a connection to modern-day Russia, we will begin identifying the ancient and prophesied invaders—and reveal a secret they all have in common.

The Mystery of Kush

Who is Kush? The Kushites were an ancient people who lived on the north-eastern coast of Africa by the Red Sea. Much of their history was played out in the shadow of Egypt. The kingdoms of Kush and Egypt alternately invaded and subjugated one another. The word *Kush* has often been trans-lated as *Ethiopia* in the Bible. But this is not to be confused with the nation that now bears that name. So what modern nation comprises the land and corresponds to the ancient nation of Kush? The answer is *Sudan*.[6]

The Kush Connection to October 7

If, then, Sudan is to be part of a coming invasion of Israel, could it have played a part in the invasion of Israel on October 7? The answer is *yes*. Sudan, the biblical Kush of Ezekiel's prophecy, actually played a central part in the October 7 invasion. Sudan served as a conduit to supply Hamas with massive amounts of weaponry that would be used against Israel on that day. From a news article on the modern-day Kush:

> *Sudan* had…allowed Hamas to turn its territory into a major smuggling route for weapons…to the Gaza Strip.[7]

Hamas was able to wreak havoc on Israel because terrorist organizations

> *smuggled weapons to Hamas* overland through Sinai via *Sudan*…as well as by sea.[8]

> …Sinai-based Bedouin smugglers brought items *to Gaza via Sudan.*[9]

Sudan's role in arming Hamas was so great that Israel repeatedly and publicly exposed it. Sudan would also enable Hamas to access millions of dollars in funding to support its war against Israel.[10]

And even though a recent Sudanese coup had curtailed Hamas support in that land,[11] a coup that could be reversed at any time, the nation prophesied to invade Israel in future days had played a major role in helping to make October 7 possible. On October 7 Kush had invaded Israel by proxy.

The Mystery of Phut

Who is *Phut*? The Neo-Babylonians called the land of Phut, *Puta*. The Persians knew it as *Putaya*. In the Book of Nahum they are linked to the Lubim people.[12] The collective witness of ancient writings places Phut on the north African coast to the west of Egypt.[13]

So what nation in the modern world comprises the land or corresponds with the ancient nation of *Phut*? The correspondence may include Algeria and Tunisia, but it is most centrally identified with one nation above all. It bears the same name that was connected to Phut from ancient times. The ancient Jewish historian Josephus writes of a river in north Africa called *Phut* and notes that its name was changed to *Lybyos*—as in Libya.[14] *Phut* corresponds with modern *Libya*.

The Phut Connection to October 7

If, then, Libya is a player in the end-time invasion of Israel, could it have also been a player in the invasion of October 7? The answer is, again, *yes*. Libya, the biblical Phut, served as one of the most important suppliers of weapons to Hamas in the Gaza Strip. From a news article on the Libyan connection to Hamas:

> *Libyan* militias...*are helping armed Palestinian group Hamas circumvent Israel's blockade of the Gaza Strip.*[15]

From another:

> Israeli officials warned that *Hamas was working with Libyan weapons smugglers.*...Egyptian security forces confiscated 138 Grad rockets brought in *from Libya* and *destined for Gaza.*[16]

And:

> "All the missiles you might see in *Gaza*"...includes transfers by sea and apparent *deliveries from Libya.*[17]

Libya made possible the thousands of rockets that rained down on Israel from Gaza on October 7.

Thus both of these prophesied invaders of Israel—Kush, in the form of Sudan, and Phut, in the form of Libya—played a critical role in the invasion of Israel in October 2023.

Gog and Its Hordes

Who, then, are *Gog, Magog, Meshekh*, and *Tubal*? From the writings of ancient historians and chroniclers, we know that they inhabited the land known as *Anatolia*. The names of *Gomer* and *Togarmah* are also identified as having dwelt in that same region. The region was a crossroads of culture and populations, and so with the migration of peoples it is possible that additional nations may be included in Ezekiel's prophecy. But the strongest clues we have are that they were the ancient inhabitants of Anatolia, also known as Asia Minor. What nation in the modern world corresponds with Asia Minor? It can only be *Turkey*.[18]

The Gog Connection to October 7

Could Turkey also have been a player in the October 7 invasion?

The answer is *yes*, and in a big way. Turkey was critical in providing the funds Hamas needed to arm itself and invade Israel. From a *New York Times* article exposing the financial network funding Hamas, a network that traced back to Turkey:

> Though the investment portfolio spanned many countries, *Turkey was key.*[19]

The support of Turkey for Hamas was so central that the US Treasury Department pressed the Turkish government to stop sheltering funds earmarked for the terrorist group. Turkey was even behind the Libyan operation of transporting arms to Hamas.[20] One headline read:

> *Turkish-backed group in Libya smuggling arms to Hamas.*[21]

So Turkey, or *Gog, Magog, Meshekh*, and *Tubal*, worked with Libya, *Phut*, to attack and foster an invasion of the land of Israel.

The Mystery of Paras

There remains only one more invader cited in Ezekiel's prophecy: the nation of *Paras*. As to its identity, there can be no question. Paras would play a key role in ancient Jewish history and a very different one in modern times. In Arabic it was known as *Faris*. The Greeks referred to it as *Persis*. It called itself *Parsa* after one of its tribes. In Latin it became *Persia*, the name by which the West would long identify it. *Paras* is *Iran.*[22]

The Paras Connection to October 7

Could Iran have also played a part in the October 7 invasion of Israel? The answer is *yes*, and more so than any other nation. Iran's part in sponsoring and arming Hamas cannot be overstated. In many ways it was the shadow power behind it all. The following are from a variety of articles on Iran, Hamas, or October 7:

> *Hamas...relied principally on Iran to fund* its military wing...[23]

> *U.S. officials assert that Iran gives funds, weapons, and training to Hamas...*[24]

> *Hamas fights with a patchwork of weapons built by Iran...*[25]

> *Iran has since supplied materiel and know-how for Hamas to build a sizable rocket arsenal*, with more than 10,000 rockets and mortar shells fired in the current conflict.[26]

> *Iranian sponsorship played a major role in enabling Hamas to start last month's fighting in Gaza.*[27]

Without Iran, the *Paras* prophesied of in Ezekiel 38, the invasion of October 7 could never have taken place.

Untranslating the Mystery

What happens if we take such news reports, articles, and headlines and replace their modern names with their ancient names? This is what happens:

> *Gog*-backed groups in *Phut* smuggling arms to Hamas...

> *Yisrael* repeatedly accused *Paras, Persia*, of transshipping weapons to Hamas via *Kush*...

> *Paras* and Hezbollah have smuggled weapons to Hamas overland through Sinai via *Kush* and *Phut*...

> Militias of *Phut* funded by *Paras, Persia*...and *Gog, Meshekh*, and *Tubal* are helping armed *Filastin* group Hamas circumvent *Yisrael's* blockade of *Philistia*...

What happens is that the words of the news reports begin morphing into the likeness of the ancient prophecy of Ezekiel 38 and 39.

The Unprecedented

When Ezekiel's prophecy was first committed to parchment, the majority of the peoples and nations it named not only were *not* at war with Israel but had little, if anything, to do with it.[28] For ages the prophecy puzzled the Bible commentators who studied it. And yet two and a half thousand years later, against all odds, all of the peoples or nations spoken of in the prophecy have become and have actively functioned as enemies of the Jewish state.

The same nations prophesied of in Ezekiel to wage war against a resurrected Israel have, as of October 7, 2023, through their proxies, waged war against that very nation. The same nations that the prophecy foretold would all be part of the invasion of Israel have now all had a part in that very thing—an invasion of Israel.

The prophecy's fulfillment is still to come. The road that leads there may be filled with turns, reversals, and departures. And the timing is in God's hands. But on October 7, 2023, *for the first time ever*, the nations cited in Ezekiel's prophecy to be involved in a future mass invasion of Israel were all involved in a mass invasion of Israel. The signs of October 7 would thus indicate we are closer to the day of the prophecy's fulfillment than we might have imagined.

The Shadow Powers

How did Hamas manage to obtain weapons despite a blockade set up to prevent that very thing from happening? It happened because of the shadow powers that funded and armed the terrorist organization for the express purpose of waging war against Israel. And of all the nations and powers that could have played that role, those that did just happened to be the same as foretold in Ezekiel's ancient prophecy. Without them Hamas could never have launched its invasion. So October 7 was made possible by the players specifically cited in Ezekiel 38 and 39, two and a half thousand years earlier—*Gog, Magog, Meshekh, Tubal, Gomer, Togarmah, Kush, Phut, and Persia.*

The Storm

Ezekiel's prophecy describes the invasion of Israel this way:

> You will ascend, coming like a *storm*...you and all
> your troops and many peoples with you.[29]

The invasion would come upon the land as a storm, suddenly, massively, and ferociously. So too the invasion of Israel on October 7 came upon the land suddenly, massively, and ferociously, as a storm. But it was not just that the invasion shared those attributes. The official name of the invasion, *Tufan*, meaning *Flood*, had an alternate translation. It could also be rendered as *Storm*. And thus, according to this translation, the invasion bore the same name as the word given in Ezekiel's prophecy.

The actual Hebrew word for *storm* in Ezekiel's prophecy is *shoah*. *Shoah* can be translated as *storm, devastation, destruction, desolation,* or *sudden catastrophe.* As the worst day in Jewish history since the Holocaust, October 7 was likened to that calamity. But in Hebrew the Holocaust is not called *the*

Holocaust. It is called *the Shoah.* Thus the Arabic code name for October 7 matched the Hebrew name for the Holocaust.

And for the first time ever the nations that were prophesied in Ezekiel 38 and 39 to take part in an invasion of Israel that will come upon the land as a storm actually took part in an invasion of Israel that actually bore the name *Storm.* And the same Arabic word by which that invasion was named, *Tufan,* also happened to match the Greek word that appears in Revelation 12 to speak of the Dragon's flood against the woman, *Potamon*—while at the same time matching the Hebrew word given to name the Dragon's deadliest campaign ever launched against the Jewish people, the Holocaust, or *Shoah.*

It is one of the most mysterious of entities identified in Scripture. Is it possible that it still exists and is at work in our day—even directing the course of world events?

Chapter 56

THE SAR PARAS

And war broke out in heaven.[1]

IN THE MIDST of Revelation 12 a war breaks out in the heavenly realms. On one side are the angelic forces of God, and on the other, the Dragon and his angels. One of the realities of the spiritual realm is war. What we are about to see will concern that war and its convergence with world events. To uncover it, we must go back to ancient times and to the court of a pagan king.

The Man by the Tigris

The prophet Daniel was taken captive from Israel into Babylon.[2] There, in the royal court, he would receive prophecies from God concerning the end of days. While standing by the Tigris River he saw a "man," an angel, who had been sent to him with a prophetic revelation.[3] The angel said:

> Do not fear, Daniel, for from the first day that you set your heart to understand, and to humble yourself before your God, your words were heard; and I have come because of your words. But the [*Sar Malkhut Paras*] withstood me twenty-one days.[4]

The angel tells Daniel that he would have come earlier but was prevented from doing so by another entity. The entity is identified in Hebrew as the *Sar Malkhut Paras*. The word *sar* can be translated as *prince, head, chief, ruler, captain, keeper, steward, lord,* or *master*. The word *malkhut* means *kingdom*. And the word *Paras*, as it appeared in Ezekiel 38, means *Persia*. Persia, at that time, was at the height of its power, having just established its empire across the Middle Eastern world.[5]

What kind of entity was the *Sar Paras*? It had battled against an angel. That would make it a spiritual entity. That which engages in battle against an angel of God is evil. It was an angel of darkness. The Sar Paras is a demonic entity.

A Dark Angel

Why did it seek to hinder the angel sent to Daniel? The angel had a mission:

> Now I have come to make you understand what
> will happen to your people in the latter days, for
> the vision refers to many days yet to come.[6]

The Sar Paras was fighting to stop the transmission of a revelation concerning God's purposes for Israel in the latter days. The revelation would concern the city of Jerusalem, the restored Temple of Jerusalem, the Book of Revelation, the Antichrist, the end of the age, and the return of the Messiah. It was this that the demonic entity was trying to prevent. At the time of the prophecy, most of the Jewish people were in exile from the land. The prophecy required their return to the land, to Jerusalem, and the rebuilding of God's Temple. Upon departing from the prophet, the angel would resume his battle with the demonic entity.

So the Sar Paras wars against the purposes of God. It seeks to stop them before their fulfillment. More specifically, it wars against and seeks to thwart the purposes of God concerning Israel. And still more specifically, it wars against God's purposes for Israel in the latter days, the end of the age.

Prince of Persia

This unique demonic entity is linked to a particular nation—Persia. The title *Sar Paras* may be translated as *Prince of Persia*, or the *Persian Lord and Master of Persia*. As Persia became Iran, the entity may be called the *Ruler of Iran*, the *Iranian Lord*, or the *Lord and Master of Iran*. Thus it seeks to control the nation of Persia, Iran, to lead it, impel it, drive it, and use it as the instrument of its purposes.

Spirits do not die. Thus the Sar Paras did not perish in ancient times—it still exists. And since it specifically wars against the nation of Israel and God's end-time purposes for that nation, what would we expect to happen with the return of Israel to the modern world and the Jewish people to Jerusalem? We would expect that it would trigger and reactivate the Sar Paras and his ancient war.

The Paras Transformation

Under Shah Reza Pahlavi, Iran and Israel enjoyed friendly relations. But in the late 1970s the Shah was overthrown. A new and radical Iran was unleashed on the world stage. As the Sar Paras seeks to stop the end-time purposes of God concerning Israel, so the new Iran became obsessed with the nation of Israel. It established itself as Israel's nemesis, its archenemy among the nations. It would engage in an unrelenting campaign of opposing, thwarting, and warring against the Jewish nation. As the Sar Paras ultimately seeks Israel's destruction, so the new radical Iran would do likewise.[7]

As demonic spirits possess and use others as their vessels, agents, and proxies, so the Sar Paras–driven Iran would, likewise, use others as its instruments, agents, and proxies. And as demonic spirits use others to inspire terror and fear, so the radical Iran would become a terror state, sponsoring terrorism around the world. It would subsidize and facilitate terrorism, radicalism, and anti-Israel hatred in Iraq, Lebanon, Bahrain, Yemen, Pakistan, and Syria, among other nations. It would fund, train, and support the terrorist organization Hezbollah in its relentless war against the Jewish nation.[8]

Spirits of Destruction

It would reach into Gaza. There, Iran would become the chief sponsor of the terrorist organization Hamas.[9] Behind the empowering of Hamas in Gaza was the Sar Paras. Behind the smuggling of arms, the transferring of funds, and the training of troops to attack Israel was the ancient demonic Persian spirit. It was the Sar Paras that caused thousands of rockets to be launched into Israeli dwellings. And in the madness of those who invaded Israel on October 7 was the madness of the Sar Paras.

Demonic spirits seek death and destruction. So indwelt by the ancient spirit, Iran sought death and destruction and thus became a threat to the world order. It became obsessed with attaining nuclear capabilities with which it could strike other nations—particularly Israel.[10] Massive efforts were undertaken on the part of nations in an attempt to reduce the danger Iran posed to the world. The problem was that they believed they were dealing with a nation. They were dealing with a spirit. Iran had become a unique power among the nations just as the entity that possessed it was a unique power among the spirits.

The Sar Yisrael

The angel sent to give Daniel the prophecy was not alone in his fight against the demonic entity. He recounted to the prophet:

> And behold, Michael, one of the chief princes,
> came to help me.[11]

Michael, pronounced, *Me-kha-el*, is here referred to as a *chief prince*. The angel also calls him *"the great prince who stands for the children of your people."*[12] Behind the word *prince* is the Hebrew word *sar*, the same Hebrew word in *Sar Paras*. So as the Sar Paras is connected to Persia, or Iran, Michael is connected to and fights for the children of Israel. He is their prince, their general, their keeper. He is the *Sar Yisrael*.

And so behind Iran is the Sar Paras, the Prince of Persia. And behind Israel is Michael, the Sar Yisrael, the Prince of Israel. So what would we expect of these two nations in the last days? If the two entities that stand for the two nations are battling in the spiritual realm, what, then, would we expect of the two nations? We would expect the two nations to become mortal enemies. And that is exactly what has happened. For behind the earthly realm and the events of that realm are spiritual realities, forces, and agents. And behind the conflict of Israel and Iran is the conflict of two entities, each one identified thousands of years earlier, each waging war in the angelic realm.

Michael and the Dragon

The appearances of Michael in Scripture are rare. Outside of Daniel his most prominent appearance is found in the Book of Revelation. And it occurs in the midst of the vision of the Dragon:

> And war broke out in heaven: Michael and his
> angels fought with the Dragon; and the Dragon
> and his angels fought.[13]

In Daniel, Michael wars against the Sar Paras. In Revelation he wars against the Dragon and his angels. Thus the Dragon and the Sar Paras war against and are warred against by the same opponent. They are on the same side of the same war. They are of the same army. The Sar Paras is one of the Dragon's angels. Each will especially wage war against Israel and the Jewish people in the last days. Each waged war against Israel on October 7. And those who actually carried out the invasion, the agents of Hamas, were, likewise, serving in the same army, the ground troops of the Dragon and his angels.

And yet there was more. The mystery would continue to unfold and explode onto the world stage. At one point it would even lead to the possibility of regional and world war. And it would happen while I was in the midst of writing these pages. Thus the following two chapters were not originally planned to be written—but were written because the mystery has not stopped its unfolding.

THE PERSIAN GENERAL

WHEN I BEGAN writing the chapter on Ezekiel's prophecy of the invasion of Israel in the end times, one of the most significant events in line with the fulfillment of that prophecy had never taken place—and then it did.

General Zahedi

Mohammad Reza Zahedi was the Iranian general in command of the *Quds Force* in Syria and Lebanon, a senior military figure of the *Islamic Revolutionary Guard Corps*. The United States had designated both groups as terrorist organizations. Zahedi was critical in giving aid, counsel, and military support to anti-Israel forces in the region. He was instrumental in strengthening such terrorist groups as Hezbollah on Israel's northern border.[1]

In the wake of October 7, Hezbollah began launching missile attacks into Israel, forcing the mass evacuation of Israel's northern region.[2] An all-out war between Israel and Hezbollah became a very real prospect. Making the situation more dangerous, Hezbollah's ability to inflict destruction in the land of Israel was far greater than that of Hamas. Zahedi was a key agent behind Hezbollah's power and actions. Israel knew it. This would lead to a chain of events that would bring the Middle East to the brink of war, all overflowing from October 7.

The Strike

On April 1, 2024, the Israeli Air Force struck an annex building of the Iranian consulate in Syria. Zahedi was conducting a meeting inside the annex. He and those with him were immediately killed. The Iranian government condemned the attack and vowed to retaliate.[3] The Israeli-Iranian conflict was about to enter a new and much more dangerous realm.

Two days after his death the Iranian Coalition Council of Islamic Revolutionary Forces, an organization affiliated with Ayatollah Khamenei, Iran's supreme leader, sent forth a communication praising Zahedi. MEMRI, the US-based Middle East Media Research Institute, translated the communication into English. It read:

> The strategic role of the martyr Zahedi in consolidating and strengthening the resistance

front, and in the planning and execution of
Al-Aqsa Flood...[4]

It was praising General Zahedi for having played an instrumental part in
the October 7 invasion of Israel.

To the Brink

For over a week the world watched anxiously and on edge for the retaliation
of Iran against Israel, fearing it would set off a regional war, if not something even greater and more dangerous. And then it came. On April 13 Iran,
together with the Islamic Resistance in Iraq, the Houthis in Yemen, and Hezbollah in Lebanon, launched over 120 ballistic missiles, 170 drones, and over
30 cruise missiles into the land of Israel. It was the largest missile attack ever
launched by Iran and the largest drone strike in military history.[5] It was
intended to overwhelm Israel's defensive capabilities.[6]

The attack marked a watershed moment. Up to that date Iran had attacked
Israel only indirectly and covertly, using agents and proxies. But this was
the first time it had ever launched a direct attack.[7] With Israel allied with
America and the West, and Iran with Russia and China, the danger was not
only that it could set off a major war in the Middle East but that it could
escalate into a world war. And it was all emanating from October 7. The
Dragon's Operation Flood had brought the world to the brink of calamity.

Uncharted Territory

Israel, with its allies, shot down an estimated 99 percent of the incoming
missiles. Less than a week later Israel responded. It chose to do so with a
highly restrained strike on varied Iranian, Syrian, and Iraqi military sites
to demonstrate its capabilities of de-escalating the situation.[8] Though the
immediate crisis de-escalated, a formerly unbreached line had been broken.
Iran had attacked the land of Israel, and Israel, the land of Iran. The Middle
East and world had entered an uncharted and dangerous territory.

According to the Prophecy

It was a historic watershed, and more than that. It was a prophetic milestone.
Ezekiel had foretold that, in the last days, Persia, or Iran, would launch an
attack against an Israel that had been "gathered from the nations." That had
never happened. And it had not happened when I began writing the chapter
on that very prophecy and its connection to Iran. But on April 13, 2024, for
the first time ever, Persia, Iran, had launched a direct attack on the resurrected nation of Israel. It was not yet the fullness of what was prophesied but

was the most definitive step ever taken toward its fulfillment. A prophetic line had been crossed.

October 7 had marked the first time that virtually every identifiable people or nation cited in Ezekiel's prophecy had played a part in an invasion of Israel. April 13 would mark the first time that any of those prophesied nations had *actually attacked* the resurrected nation of Israel.

In the Ouranos, the Heavenlies

The war of Michael and his angels against the Dragon and his angels is described in the Book of Revelation as taking place in *heaven*. The word translated as *heaven* is the Greek word *ouranos*. Its primary meaning is *sky*. The heavens, the place of spiritual warfare, is represented in the physical realm by the sky. The war of Iran and Israel took place in *ouranos*, the sky, in the heavens, above each land.

That 99 percent of the missiles fired into the Israeli skies were struck down before hitting their targets was seen as a miracle. The one who fights in the heavenlies on behalf of Israel is the Sar Yisrael, Michael. Is it possible that the miracle of Israel's protection in the *heavenlies* involved more than high-tech defense systems? Could it have involved a spiritual entity entrusted with Israel's protection and who wars in the heavenly places?

The Iranian General

Iran's attack on Israel centered on General Zahedi. As Zahedi specialized in empowering and mobilizing terrorists, militias, and radical factions against Israel, he could be seen as a vessel, an instrument, if not an embodiment, of the Sar Paras. In 1 Chronicles 27 it is written:

> And the *general* of the king's army was Joab.[9]

The word *general* stands for the Hebrew word *sar*. And so the *Sar Paras* can be translated as the *Persian General* or the *Iranian General*.

Not only was Zahedi an agent of Israel's destruction—he was the *Iranian General* over which the Middle East was brought to the brink of war. In Hebrew he was a *Sar Paras*. Therefore, in view of the spiritual realities behind the conflict, it should not be surprising that Israel would strike down a *Sar Paras*, the Iranian general, or that when the *Sar Paras* was struck down, all hell should break loose.

But there was another player, even more central to Iran's war against Israel, one who would touch an ancient covenant that would end up destroying him.

Chapter 58

AGAINST THE MOUNTAINS

HE WAS THE power behind General Zahedi. He presided over the arming and strengthening of Hamas leading up to the October 7 invasion. His name was Ebrahim Raisi.

The Butcher of Teheran

Raisi was the president of Iran under Ayatollah Khamenei.[1] Thus he was even more critical than Zahedi as an agent of chaos in the region and in the leading of factions and proxies working for Israel's destruction. He too was an instrument of the Sar Paras.

As the Sar Paras is an entity bent on death, Raisi was infamous among his own people as a minister of death. They called him the "Butcher of Teheran."[2] He was responsible for the brutal repression of Iranian dissidents. He served as a judge in the Iranian Death Commission. He would be accused of sentencing without a trial thousands of innocent Iranians to their deaths. He would be cited for committing crimes against humanity. And he was the president of Iran when Iran launched its missile attack on the land of Israel.[3]

The Other Sar Paras

The word *sar* can be rendered as *chief, ruler,* or *leader.* Thus *Sar Paras* can be translated as *Ruler of Iran* or the *Iranian Leader.* Under the Ayatollah, Raisi was ruler and leader of Iran—a Sar Paras. But there was more to it. *Raisi,* a shortened form of a longer surname, is a Persian word based on an Arabic title. *Sar* is the Hebrew word for *chief* or *ruler. Raisi* means *chief* and *ruler.* And as his name corresponds with the *Persian* name for *chief* or *ruler,* it equates to *Persian Ruler* or *Sar Paras.* So Raisi not only served as an instrument and embodied the Sar Paras; his very name spoke of it.

Ebrahim

Raisi was at the height of his powers and presumed by many to be the Ayatollah's successor. But that was not to be. On May 19, 2024, the helicopter in which he was flying over Iran's East Azerbaijan province crashed into a mountain. One of the world's most powerful rulers was no more.

What about Raisi's first name, Ebrahim? *Ebrahim* is the Persian form of *Abraham.* Abraham is the father of the Jewish people, the grandfather of

Israel from whom the Jewish nation is named. So Raisi was named after the father of the nation he warred against. Abraham was given the promise that his children would inherit the land of God. Raisi, bearing the name of the man who received that promise, empowered and armed those who sought to remove the children of Abraham from the land God had given them.

The Covenant

The name *Ebrahim* also pointed back to the man with whom God made a unique covenant, the *Abrahamic Covenant*. It consisted of these words:

> I will bless those who bless you, and I will curse
> him who curses you.[4]

In other words, those who bless the children of Abraham, the Jewish people, the nation of Israel, will be blessed. Those who curse them will be cursed. It implies, as well, the dynamic of reciprocity—what you do to Israel, for good or evil, will, in turn, be done to you. It is, for those who bless the Jewish people, a word of encouragement, and for those who rage against them, for the anti-Semites of the world, a word of warning.

The Eye of God

Raisi had cursed the nation of Israel. But he did more than that. He waged war against them. He was unique in being the only president in Iranian history to actually launch an attack against the nation of Israel, to send missiles into the land of Israel. It is written in the Book of Zechariah, concerning those who *touch* Israel:

> He who touches you touches the apple of His eye.[5]

In other words, to touch Israel is to touch the eye of God. Raisi oversaw the firing of missiles into Israel on April 13. He touched the eye of God. One month and six days later he was dead.

Through the Skies

In his death was the working of reciprocity. Raisi had sought to bring death and destruction to Israel. And so death and destruction would be brought to him. More specifically, he had sought to bring destruction to Israel *through the skies*. So it was that destruction would come to Raisi *through the sky*. He had sent airborne objects into the skies of Israel to bring destruction upon their crashing into the land. So it would be an airborne object, that which carried him through the skies of Iran, that would bring him destruction, upon its crashing into the land. As he had done to Israel, so it was done to him.

And yet he had done more than that.

The Threat

It was just a few days after he had sent the missiles into Israel that Raisi sealed his actions—and his fate. Soon after Israel sought to de-escalate the crisis with a muted response, Raisi issued a public statement. It was a threat. He said that if Israel took any future action against Iran, Israel would very possibly be annihilated. There would be nothing left of it. The statement made headlines around the world.

> Iranian President Threatens Israel's Annihilation...[6]
>
> Nothing Will Be Left of Israel...[7]

Raisi was threatening the Jewish state with total destruction, a total destruction that would come through Iran and thus under his leadership.[8] Raisi, in other words, would be the one to destroy it.

It was reportedly the last public statement he would ever make.[9] Not only had he attacked Israel; he had sealed his actions with a curse and threat of total destruction. To threaten and plan for Israel's destruction is a most dangerous thing. One month later, Israel was still there—Raisi was not. He was struck down. And there was nothing left of his life.

An Unseen Hand

We have seen the connection in the Greek *ouranos* between the "heavens" of the spiritual realm—the realm of angelic warfare, of the Sar Paras and the Sar Yisrael—and the skies above the earth, the heavens of the physical realm. Raisi had sent death through the ouranos, the heavens, the skies, of Israel. Now death would come to him, likewise, through the ouranos, through the skies of Iran. There were three helicopters flying as a convoy over East Azerbaijan that day. Two made it to their destination—only one did not. Michael is the Sar Yisrael, the angelic entity in charge of protecting Israel. That charge would include preventing threats of destruction from being fulfilled. He fights in the ouranos, the heavenlies. There was no human hand believed to have been involved in the crash of Raisi's helicopter. Is it possible there was another hand in the sky that day, the hand of the Sar Yisrael?

"Against the Mountains"

In Ezekiel's prophecy of Israel's end-time invasion, God gives this word to the invaders:

> I will...bring you against the mountains....You
> shall fall upon the mountains...[10]

Those who attack Israel will be brought to judgment *on the mountains*. Raisi was the first leader of a nation cited in the prophecy to actually launch an attack on Israel. And what was his fate? He was brought to the mountains—he was brought *against* the mountains. His fate was that of those who will, at the appointed time, attack the land. Just one month after the first of Ezekiel's nations attacked the land of Israel, its leader would literally "fall upon the mountains."

When the prophecy comes to its fulfillment, the invaders will fall upon the mountains of Israel. But as Iran's attack was a shadow of that coming attack, Raisi's fall can be taken as a shadow of its coming judgment *on the mountains*.

The Day of Pharaoh's Breaking

The first kingdom, or power, to come against the nation of Israel was Egypt. The day that broke the power of Egypt and its ruler, the Pharaoh, was Passover. Passover commemorates the deliverance of Israel from the power of the Pharaoh and the bondage of Egypt. President Raisi was the leader of a modern nation that sought Israel's destruction. He issued his threat to annihilate Israel on April 23, 2024.[11] Could the timing of that threat be significant? It was.

He issued his threat on Passover. An evil ruler threatened the destruction of Israel on the day that God gave victory to Israel over an evil ruler. Israel's enemy had threatened it with annihilation on the day the power of Israel's enemy was broken. Could the fact that Raisi issued his threat to destroy Israel on that day of all days have constituted a sign portending the destruction of his power and his life?

On the day that Raisi threatened to destroy Israel, the people of Israel were celebrating Passover, the commemoration of the day God delivered them from the power of an evil leader. God would deliver them again.

The Act of Blasphemy

What Raisi did on that Passover day was more than a threat. He was threatening the annihilation of God's eternal nation—to destroy the work of God, nullify the promise of God, and eradicate the purposes of God. It was an act of blasphemy. The fact that he committed it on a Hebrew holy day, Passover, was a double blasphemy. And the fact that he had done so after actually attempting to bring destruction to that nation and striking "the apple of God's eye" was a triple blasphemy. He had no idea what he was doing or what he was invoking.

The Appointed Word

Every Sabbath day there is a passage of Scripture appointed from ages past to be read on that particular Sabbath. Raisi would be killed on the day after the Sabbath. So on the day before he died, there was an appointed scripture. It would be read, recited, and chanted by the Jewish people throughout Israel and throughout the world. What was the appointed word?

The appointed word came from the Book of Leviticus and spoke of the holy days of Israel, starting with Passover, the day on which Raisi had committed his blasphemy. But it would conclude with a unique account and then a command. It spoke of a man who had committed an act of blasphemy. So Raisi had committed an act of blasphemy. Raisi's acts were unique in the history of the Iranian-Israeli conflict. He had both struck the land of Israel and then followed it up with an act of blasphemy. It would not end well. And the appointed scripture had foretold it.

"He Shall Be Put to Death"

The scripture goes on to proclaim this command:

> Whoever blasphemes the name of the LORD shall
> surely be put to death.[12]

This is the law concerning blasphemy. It does not apply to the Jewish people only. The appointed scripture clarifies that it applies to "the stranger as well as him who is born in the land."[13]

Raisi had blasphemed the name of the Lord. The very last of the last words of the scripture be proclaimed the day before his death record that the man who committed blasphemy was taken outside the camp and put to death.[14] So Raisi would be taken outside the camp of his people, to the mountainous outskirts of Iran, and there, he who had blasphemed the Lord was put to death. He had spoken the blasphemy on April 23. The following month, on May 23, exactly thirty days after he spoke it, they laid his body in a tomb.

The Fall of Monsters

Raisi was at the pinnacle of his powers. But he had not bargained for the fact that by waging war against Israel, the God of Israel would wage war against him. Nor had he bargained for the covenant made with the man whose name he bore, and that by that covenant what he had done and planned to do to Israel would be done to him. Nor had he considered that when he attacked the land of Israel, he had touched the apple of God's eye and that by then threatening Israel's annihilation, he had committed an act of blasphemy. And then he was gone.

And so he joined a long list of fallen tyrants, evildoers, anti-Semites, blasphemers, and assorted monsters of history who learned the hard way that the God of the universe also happens to be the God of Israel, and the God of Israel happens also to be the Almighty.

Behind All Things

What does this all tell us?

Though the world is unaware, the course of history is ultimately determined not by what we see but by what we don't. There is another realm and other agents moving behind the events of our time.

> Behind October 7 were the militants and terrorists of Gaza.

> And behind the militants and terrorists of Gaza was Hamas.

> But behind Hamas were the nations prophesied two and a half thousand years earlier in Ezekiel 38 and 39.

> And behind one of those nations was the ancient entity called the *Sar Paras.*

> And behind the Sar Paras was the Dragon.

> But behind Israel is the Sar Yisrael, Michael.

> And behind the Sar Yisrael is Messiah.

> And behind all things is God.

It all began with the Dragon's strike on that October Sabbath. It would all end, ultimately, in the Book of Revelation.

We now move to the most controversial human figure of biblical prophecy. Could that which manifested to the world on Israel's day of tragedy and in the days that followed give us a glimpse into that figure—*into the nature of the Beast?*

Chapter 59

THE BEAST

And I saw a beast rising up out of the sea....The
Dragon gave him his power.[1]

The Therion

The vision of the Dragon's war leads into that of a beast that rises from the
sea. The word translated as *beast* is the Greek *therion*. *Therion* denotes a
dangerous animal, wild and venomous, a predator. Thus the Beast shares the
nature of the Serpent and the Dragon, and with good reason. It is the Dragon
that gives to the Beast his power, his authority, and his reign.

As a spiritual entity, the Dragon needs vessels of flesh and blood by which
to act and wage war on earth. Throughout history it is through such vessels that he has brought calamity and destruction to the Jewish people. On
October 7 it was the Gazan invaders who served as his vessels. The Dragon's
ultimate vessel will come at the end of the age—the Beast. So as the vision of
the Dragon's war reveals the spiritual forces in play at the end of the age, the
vision of the Beast reveals how those forces will manifest.

The Dragon's Child

The Beast will exist as the Dragon's personification and manifestation on
earth. We would thus expect him to embody the Dragon's nature. As the
name *Satan* and *Diabolo* speak of the one who opposes and wars against, so
the nature of the Beast will be to oppose and war against all that is of God.
So the apostle Paul writes that the end will not come unless the Beast, the
man of lawlessness,

> is revealed, the son of destruction, *who opposes...*[2]

His nature is to defy. As the Dragon sought to exalt himself in the place
of and in defiance of God, so the Beast will seek to do likewise. He is the one
who

> exalts himself above all that is called God or that
> is worshiped.[3]

As the Dragon's nature is pride and blasphemy, so too the nature of the
Beast. Thus in Revelation it is written:

Then he opened his mouth in blasphemy against
God, to blaspheme His name, His tabernacle, and
those who dwell in heaven.[4]

The Twister

The Dragon is the twister, twisting reality, bending the fabric of existence, turning the creation away from its state of being. So the Beast will likewise twist, bend, and turn that which is. So it is written he will

attempt to change times and law.[5]

The Latin root word for *to turn* is *vert*. So the Beast will invert, revert, convert, divert, pervert, and subvert. He will war against the Creator by inverting, perverting, and subverting the created order. His will be an unnatural kingdom, a kingdom that wages war against the order of creation.

He will thus seek to twist the nature of humanity so that it becomes that which is other than human, more than human, less than human, and inhuman. He will seek to twist the nature of man, of woman, of gender, of family, of society, of civilization. And as the Dragon wars against existence, so the Beast will war against life, its essence, and its sanctity. He will alter values, definitions, and perception. He will twist and bend the image of God that he might destroy it.

The Anti-Messiah

As the nature of evil is to take the place of the good, and the nature of the Dragon to take the place of God, so the nature of the Beast will be to take the place of the Messiah. He will thus be the substitute Messiah, the Anti-Messiah, the Antichrist. As the Dragon seeks to imitate God in order to replace Him, the Beast will come in the imitation of the Messiah. As Messiah is the Savior, the Beast will be the false savior. As Messiah will bring peace on earth, the Beast will bring a false peace. As Messiah will reign over a kingdom that will cover the earth, the Beast will rule over a one-world civilization and state. And as the world has venerated the Messiah, the world will venerate the Beast.

The Arch-Predator

Though the Beast comes in the appearance of the Messiah, he is His opposite and antithesis. Messiah is the redemption of life, so the Beast is its negation. Messiah personifies humility; the Beast, arrogance. Messiah is the healer, the restorer of the broken; the Beast is the wounder and the Destroyer. Messiah reconciles the world to God; the Beast turns the world away from God.

Messiah is the shepherd; the Beast is the predator. Messiah is the Lamb; the Beast is the wolf.

The Grand Desecrator

On October 7 we witnessed the Dragon's desecration of the Sabbath, the holy days, and the Jubilee. So the Beast, as the Dragon's offspring, will usher in a kingdom of desecration. He will defile the pure, debase the creation, pervert the holy, and satanize the godly. It is no accident the Scriptures prophesy his coming to the holy city, Jerusalem. It is the most holy place that can be most desecrated. There he will sit

> as God seated in the Temple of God, showing himself that he is God.[6]

His desecration of the Temple will epitomize his desecration of man.

The Anti-Semite Beast

Finally, as the Dragon wages war against the woman, the Beast will wage war against Israel. He will be the culmination of all the dark leaders of history whose evil and brutality were matched only by their deadly obsession with the Jewish people. But he will excel them all. Demonic figures such as Hitler and Himmler will pale in comparison. As the Dragon is the father of anti-Semitism, the Beast will be its incarnation. He will implement the Dragon's plans for the children of Israel and the final attempt at their annihilation.

Signs of the Beast

As the days of the Beast grow nearer, it would follow that the signs of his coming would become more and more visible. We would expect that his nature and characteristics would increasingly mark, indwell, and characterize modern culture. The Scriptures speak of the *spirit of the Antichrist* as present in the world.[7] So as the time of his coming grows closer, we would expect the spirit of the Beast to become increasingly manifest, brazen, and dominant. We would expect to see the rise of a civilization that manifests the Beast's attributes.

We would thus expect to see

> An unprecedented turning away from God, from His Word, His ways, from Messiah, a mass movement of apostasy.

The overturning of standards and foundations that have stood since ancient times, the changing of values, laws, morality, and perception.

An unprecedented war against nature, against creation, against manhood, womanhood, children, sexuality, marriage, family, and life.

A growing animosity against God and His ways and the prevailing of this animosity over the leading institutions of culture.

The emergence of a virulent anti-Israel, anti-Jewish spirit. What erupted on October 7 in Israel and then in its wake across the world was a glimpse of that emergence. We would expect that spirit to increasingly possess the emerging generation and the mainstream of world culture.

———————■■■———————

In short, the signs of the Beast are already manifesting, and the spirit of the Beast is already moving, transforming, possessing, and preparing the world for that day.

———————■■■———————

Could there be more to the matter of Palestine than we have imagined? Could it reveal a dynamic and a strategy behind what is transforming Western civilization and national cultures? Could it even now be altering human nature, man, woman, marriage, family, and our lives? To reveal this other side, we now move to the heart of the matter to open up the mystery of Palestine.

THE PALESTINE MYSTERY AND STRATAGEM

THE ISSUE OF Palestine involves Israel, the Middle East, and, increasingly, all nations. It lies behind acts of terrorism, UN resolutions, uprisings, global conflicts, and even the possibility of world war. But could the issue be even larger? Could it reveal a master plan that touches virtually every realm of life? Could it expose the Enemy's strategy and agenda for the end times? We now come to the essence, the heart of the matter—the Palestine mystery and stratagem.

The Palestine Stratagem

What is the essence of the Enemy's strategy as touching the Promised Land?

It is to take the land that especially belongs to God, the land given to a specific people, Israel, and for a specific purpose, redemption, and separate it from that people and purpose. It is to erase the land's identity, expunge its history, and divorce it from the calling it was given. It is to then replace the erased identity with an alternate identity, an invented identity, and a conflicting identity born of the land's ancient enemies. That is the meaning of Palestine—it is that which wars against and replaces that which was purposed by God. It is to remove *Israel* from the land of Israel and the *promise* from the Promised Land, and, by this, to destroy the purposes of God.

But the stratagem goes far beyond the Promised Land. It is the Enemy's master stratagem for every realm—to take that which belongs to God and separate it from God, from its identity and purpose, and then give it an alternate and fabricated identity and a purpose that wars against the reason for its existence.

The Palestinization of Culture

The stratagem can be seen in all realms of the Enemy's works and will become increasingly evident in the end times. It is, even now, transforming Western civilization. It is the Enemy's agenda to take a civilization birthed on a biblical foundation and imbued with a Christian identity and purpose, and separate it from that foundation, that identity, and that purpose. As the land of Israel was severed from Israel, so Western civilization is now being progressively severed from the Christian and biblical foundation on which it has stood since ancient times.

As the land of Israel was renamed *Palestine* and thus given an identity that was anti-God, anti-biblical, and pagan, so we are now witnessing the same transformation of Western civilization, the emergence of a new and alternate identity that is, likewise, anti-biblical, anti-God, and pagan. We are witnessing the Palestinization of Western civilization.

This same process and transformation can be seen at work in virtually every nation and culture within Western civilization as each is progressively divorced from its biblical foundation and its Judeo-Christian identity and as each assumes an alternate and anti-biblical identity. And as the Palestine stratagem is to ultimately erase the memory of Israel, so there is at work, throughout Western civilization, a massive erasure, a rewriting of history, and an altering of collective memory, in which its Christian and biblical underpinnings are suppressed, condemned, or wiped away altogether.

The Palestinization of Human Nature

But the stratagem goes deeper. It is now touching human nature itself. And so humanity is redefined and separated from its natural state of being, severed from its connection to God and its created purpose. Men are progressively severed from fatherhood, marriage, family—from manhood—then given alternate, unnatural, and demasculinized identities, identities that war against their created nature. So too women are progressively severed from motherhood, marriage, family—from womanhood—and, likewise, given alternate, unnatural, and defeminized identities that war against their created nature. And as the land of Israel bore a name that warred against its essence, *Palestine*, so men are called *she* and *they*, and women, *he* and *them*. The stratagem severs all things, redefines all things, and alters all things—marriage, family, life, existence.

And so it is no accident that the same world that wars against God's promise and purpose concerning Israel, likewise, rages against God's purposes and plan concerning man, woman, children, marriage, family, society, and humanity. And it is no accident that the same world that celebrates Palestine, the alternate identity given to the Promised Land, likewise celebrates the alternate identities given to man. And by the same token, it is no accident that those in the world who most strongly uphold God's purposes for the created order are overwhelmingly the same who, likewise, most strongly uphold God's purposes for Israel. It is no accident, because the two realms are intrinsically bound.

The Palestinization of Life

We cannot conclude the Palestine stratagem without bringing it to its most personal application and realm. Just as the Enemy applies the strategy to Israel and the world, to civilization and human nature, so he applies it to each life. It is his strategy to separate each life from God and from the identity and purpose for which it was created. He then gives to each an alternate and fallen identity, an alternate and fallen purpose, and an alternate and fallen life. The alternate identity wars against the true identity, the alternate purpose replaces the true purpose, and the alternate life keeps each away from the life for which each was created.

And yet even when the Promised Land was called *Palestine*, even when it languished in its fallen state, even under its ruins and the trappings of a foreign identity, it was still the land of Israel. Underneath it all it was still the Promised Land, the land God had promised and given to the children of Israel. And the promises of God were still upon it. So too even in our alternate and fallen identities, even in our sins, and the ruins of life, underneath it all is that which God created in His image and a God-shaped void that can only be filled by His presence. Underneath it all is still a promise, a calling, and the hope of redemption. And underneath it all is a heart that cries out for redemption. And only in the receiving of God's presence can that redemption come into that life, and its brokenness be healed, and its deserts bloom, and its promise be fulfilled, as in the resurrection of a promised land.

It is the destination of world history, its final cataclysm. Is it possible that the events of October 7 and that which followed in their wakes are connected to what is known as *Armageddon*?

Chapter 61

ARMAGEDDON AND THE DRAGON'S MADNESS

THE THREE UNCLEAN spirits that proceed "like frogs" from the Dragon, the Beast, and the false prophet—what is their purpose and mission? They go out

> to the kings of the earth and of the whole world....
> And they gathered them together to the place
> called in Hebrew, Armageddon.[1]

Armageddon

The word *Armageddon* has come to mean the *final war*, or the last war before the coming of Messiah. But it is first the name of a place, a valley in northern Israel. It is only in this verse that the word *Armageddon* appears. It is thus significant that its appearance is linked to the Dragon.

Armageddon is the ground on which the world's armies will gather to fight the final war. What will be the purpose of that war? The scenario given in Revelation coalesces with similar prophecies given in the Hebrew Scriptures in which the nations of the world converge in a war against Israel. The idea of the entire world waging war against a tiny Middle Eastern nation might appear preposterous, if not impossible. But it is no more preposterous or impossible than the prophecies of a nation rising from the dead after two thousand years. And yet what the Bible foretold has come to pass.

Under the Influence

From what is revealed in the Book of Zechariah, the nations will come against Israel in a war that threatens its existence. Why? Why would the entire world seek to destroy the Jewish nation? It would appear totally irrational. The answer is given in Revelation. They will do so under the influence of the Dragon, just as, under the same influence, the Third Reich, just as irrationally and demonically, sought to wipe the Jewish nation off the face of the earth.

When the Jewish people were scattered throughout the earth, so too was the Enemy's war against them scattered throughout the earth. But with their regathering and concentration in the land of Israel, so too will his war be concentrated there. Thus will come Armageddon. Under the influence of the Dragon, the nations will seek to annihilate the Jewish people.

A Time of Possession

The prophecy's implication is that the spirits that go forth to the kings of the earth will, in some way, possess them to execute the Dragon's will. According to biblical prophecy, the civilization of the end times will be one that has turned from God and emptied itself of His presence. Such a civilization is most vulnerable to the Enemy's possession. In this, as well, October 7 provides us with a glimpse of things to come.

The deadly satanic rage of that day was a foreshadowing of an even deadlier and more satanic rage that will, in the last days, possess the nations. The spreading of that rage and the explosion of anti-Israel and anti-Jewish hatred throughout the world in the wake of October 7 give us another glimpse of that which will drive the nations to Armageddon.

The Chess Game

It is a chess game played by the Dragon. The fury that erupted across the world against Israel did so in the name of *Palestine*. For the Filastin resurrection was always about more than the Palestinians. The Enemy knew they would not, on their own, be able to destroy the nation of Israel. But if he could make them the cause, the lightning rod, the trigger, and the catalyst to impel the world to rage against Israel and seek its destruction, he could accomplish his end.

The name *Palestine* has always been about Israel's existence, or rather about the erasing of its existence. The Enemy used October 7 to revive the issue of Palestine, to ignite anti-Israel hatred across the world. Thus what happened on that October morning and what it triggered throughout the world may give us a glimpse into the dynamics of Armageddon. The issue of Palestine may not only foreshadow that end-of-days event—it may actually be one of the seeds used to bring about its coming.

The Dragon Goes to College

As I write these words, events are once more unfolding in the world according to the mysteries and prophecies opened in these chapters. It was after I began writing of Armageddon and the Dragon's madness that a wave of the Dragon's madness, a torrent of anti-Israel, anti-Jewish, anti-Semitic hatred and fury, exploded across American colleges. The chants of *"Long live Hamas!"* and *"Death to Jews!"* could be heard in the nation's most prominent and elite universities.

What was equally striking was *where* it was happening. It was not happening in a Muslim or Arab nation, or a nation at war with Israel. It was happening in America, Israel's closest ally. It is that fact that is especially significant with regard to end-time prophecy.

The Ancient Contagion on American Soil

In view of the mystery and the war waged from ancient times until now, we should not be surprised that Israel has now become the chief target and scapegoat of the woke, just as it had been the chief target and scapegoat of countless movements and hatreds throughout the ages. Nor should we be surprised that even Israel's staunchest ally, America, should be infected by the Dragon's orgidzo. The contagion is far more ancient than America.

The Bible prophesies that, in the end, *all nations* will come against the nation of Israel. *All nations* would have to include America. The idea that America, Israel's greatest ally, could one day declare war against Israel would seem an impossibility, but the fact that those leading the anti-Israel demonstrations across the nation represent America's future speaks otherwise. And the demonstrations were only the symptom of an ominous change taking place among the American young against the Jewish nation, a change that happens to align with biblical prophecy. In other words, the turning of America against Israel equals Armageddon.

Strange Planet

In view of the prophecy of Armageddon one must consider the fact that one is already living in a world in which the nations regularly gather together to condemn not its dictatorships, not its brutal totalitarian regimes, not those nations that have slaughtered millions of their own citizens, but rather a tiny Middle Eastern democracy—for the crime of existing. It has been noted in recent times that the United Nations has condemned Israel more than it has condemned *all other nations put together*. They have raged against the same nation that rose out of the ashes of the Holocaust and that, on the day of its birth, had to fight for its very existence as the surrounding nations sought to annihilate it—the same nation whose birth the majority of the world's nations commemorate as a *nakba*, a calamity, a holocaust.

A Form of Madness

If visitors from another world observed such things, they would conclude not only that something very strange and more than natural was going on—but that they had arrived on a planet suffering from an acute form of madness. And they would be right. But the madness involved is an ancient one, the same madness that required the birth of an Israel in the first place that the Jewish people might be protected from annihilation. It is the same madness that once spewed forth out of the mouth of Adolf Hitler at Nuremberg, the same madness that operated the gas chambers at Auschwitz, the same madness that led to the slaughter of October 7, and the same madness that will lead the world to Armageddon. It is a satanic insanity, an apocalyptic mania. It is the madness of the Dragon.

Now that we have opened up the end of days, we can uncover one final mystery behind Israel's day of calamity, one that is directly connected to the apocalypse, the Book of Revelation, and the most holy of grounds.

Part XIII

SECRET ON THE MOUNT

Chapter 62

THE GROUND ZERO OF PROPHECY

COULD AN EVENT foretold in end-time prophecy and the Book of Revelation actually be the hidden cause and secret behind October 7?

> Now when the Dragon saw that he had been cast to the earth, he persecuted the woman who gave birth to the male Child. But the woman was given two wings of a great eagle, that she might fly into the wilderness to her place, where she is nourished for *a time and times and half a time*, from the presence of the Serpent.[1]

In the vision of the Dragon's war the woman is taken into the wilderness to find safety. The duration of her hiding is given in a mysterious phrase: "*a time and times and half a time*." What does it mean?

"When All These Things Shall Be Finished"

In the closing chapters of Daniel an angel gives the prophet a glimpse of Israel's future in the coming centuries and the last days. The glimpse includes war, persecution, and the ruler referred to in Revelation as the *Beast*. At the very end of the prophecy a second angel asks how long it will be until all is fulfilled. The answer given is this:

> It shall be for *a time, times, and half a time;* and when the power of the holy people has been completely shattered, all these things shall be finished.[2]

It is the same phrase given to describe the time of the woman's hiding from the Dragon. Earlier in the Book of Daniel an angel gives the prophet another revelation concerning the Beast and the end of days:

> He shall speak words against the Most High, shall persecute the holy ones of the Most High, and shall intend to change times and law. And they will be given into his hand for *a time and times and half a time.*[3]

From Daniel to the Book of Revelation, the consistency of the Scriptures is striking, as is the reappearance of the phrase *"a time, times, and half a time."* Each appearance refers to a time of persecution. The persecution is orchestrated by the Dragon and carried out by the Beast.

The Beast's Dominion

The prophecy of the Beast in Revelation 13 matches precisely that given in Daniel:

> And he was given a mouth speaking great things and blasphemies, and he was given authority to continue for *forty-two months.*[4]

In Daniel it is for *a time and times and half a time.* In Revelation it is for *forty-two months.* Forty-two months is three and a half years. Thus *a time* is one year, *times* is two years, and *half a time* is half a year—three and a half years. This is the time of the Beast's dominion.

The Refuge

The meaning of the phrase is further confirmed in another verse from Revelation 12 where the woman's time of refuge from the Dragon is given in terms of days:

> Then the woman fled into the wilderness, where she has a place prepared by God, that they should feed her there *one thousand two hundred and sixty days.*[5]

One thousand two hundred and sixty days is another version of three and a half years. So three and a half years are given for the reign of the Beast, the power of the Dragon, and the demonic persecution of the woman, Israel.

The Temple Mount

But the Scriptures give us even more specific revelation as to what will happen in that time. It all centers on the Temple Mount. In Revelation 11 an angel tells the disciple to measure the Temple Mount with one exception:

> But leave out the court which is outside the temple, and do not measure it, for it has been given to the Gentiles. And they will tread the holy city underfoot for *forty-two months.*[6]

Again, we have the span of forty-two months. In that time the Temple courts and the city of Jerusalem will be given to God's enemies and the enemies of Israel. The foremost of those enemies will be the Beast. So the reign of the Antichrist at the end of the age is connected to the Temple Mount.

Shikutzim—the Abominations

Daniel 9 gives us one more clue as to what will happen on the Temple Mount:

> Then he shall confirm a covenant with many for
> *one week*; but *in the middle of the week* he shall
> bring an end to sacrifice.[7]

The word translated here as *week* is the Hebrew *shavuah*. It speaks of a span of time marked by the number seven—in this case, seven years. This has become known as the *Tribulation Period*, the last seven years leading up to Messiah's return. *The middle of the week,* or seven divided by two, comes out to, again, three and a half years, a time, times, and half a time. What will then happen? The Antichrist will abolish the offerings and sacrifices of the Temple. The prophecy continues:

> And on the wing of abominations shall be one who
> makes desolate.[8]

The word translated as *abominations* is the Hebrew *shikutzim*. The same word is used in the Hebrew Scriptures to speak of idols. This is what Messiah referred to as the "abomination of desolation." It is commonly understood as the Antichrist's setting up of an idol on the Temple Mount in the last three and a half years of the Tribulation Period—thus causing the desecration of the holy place.

The Ground Zero of Prophecy

So it all centers on the piece of earth known as the *Temple Mount*. The Beast's possession of that mount will constitute his ultimate conquest. Its desecration will represent his ultimate act. Why the Temple Mount? The Temple Mount is the center of Jerusalem, the center of Israel, the center of God's purposes on earth. It is the most holy of grounds. It was there that the people of Israel ascended to worship the Lord, observed His appointed holy days, and celebrated His appointed feasts. It was there that the house of God stood and His presence rested.

So if the Temple Mount is the central ground of God's purposes, it will also become the central ground of the Enemy's purposes. And if the Temple Mount is the nearest thing on earth to God's throne, and the Enemy seeks to sit on God's throne, then it is inevitable that he will seek to take possession of it.

Further, if the Temple Mount is the place from which Messiah will reign, and the Enemy seeks to stop the purposes of God, then he will seek to establish on that Mount his own reign. Lastly, if the Temple Mount is God's most holy of grounds, then it must become the ground of the Enemy's most unholy of desecrations.

So it was inevitable that the Temple Mount should become the most fought-over ground on earth, the central space in the war of God and the Enemy, the woman and the Dragon, the Lamb and the Beast.

The Creature's Territory

The Dragon is a territorial creature. He never gives up ground without a fight. For the land of Israel to be given back to the Jewish people—it took the First World War. For the land to actually become the nation of Israel, it took the War of Independence. For Jerusalem to be restored to the Jewish people, it took the Six-Day War. In each case the focus narrowed, from the land to the nation to the city. In each case it came through war and bloodshed. The final narrowing of focus must concern the Temple Mount. And so the slightest movement with regard to that ground can ignite a firestorm. What we are about to see is that it actually already did—and we all witnessed it.

-------------■■■-------------

If the Temple Mount is the central ground in the war of the Dragon and the woman, could it have played a part in the calamity of October 7? Could it, in fact, be the prophetic mystery that lay behind it all?

Chapter 63

THE RED COWS

I N THE SECOND chapter of Isaiah we are given a prophetic glimpse into the kingdom of God on earth:

> Now it shall come to pass in the latter days that the
> mountain of the LORD's house shall be established
> on the top of the mountains, and shall be exalted
> above the hills; and all nations shall flow to it.[1]

The mountain of the Lord is, most specifically, the Temple Mount. It is from that mount that the word of God will go forth to the world, the knowledge of God to the nations, and the kingdom of God to the ends of the earth. And from there Messiah will reign.

The Dragon on the Mount

In view of the importance of the Temple Mount to the kingdom of God, we would expect the Enemy to seek its possession. Having possession, it would follow that he would seek to prevent, at all costs, a possession or place for any Jewish person within it. By doing so, he would stop the prophecies from being fulfilled there, the Temple from being built there, the festivals and holy days of Israel from being observed there, and Messiah from reigning there. We might even expect him to go so far as to stop the prayers of the Jewish people from being prayed there.

The Most Dangerous Ground

How would the Enemy do all this? By using those who would act as his unwitting pawns, those who would fight to keep the Jewish people or any manifestation of Jewish worship and observance off the Mount.

What we would expect the Dragon to do, he has already done. At the time of this writing no Jewish Temple or house of worship is allowed to stand on the Temple Mount. No Jewish festival is permitted to be celebrated there, and no Jewish holy day can be observed there. Even the utterance of Jewish prayers has long been banned from being offered there.[2] Any breaking of these bans threatens to cause an explosion. And so the Temple Mount has become the most dangerous plot of land on earth.

Losing Control

Having driven the Jewish people off of their holy mountain and having banned their return to worship there, what then would happen if there was a risk that the Dragon could lose, in any degree, his control or possession of the Mount? What if there was a possibility of Jewish worship or observance returning in any way to the Temple Mount? What would happen if there was any report, rumor, or slightest movement concerning the return of Jewish people to the Mount, to pray or to observe one of God's appointed holy days?

We would expect it to be a threat to the Dragon. We would expect an explosion of his rage and madness. That explosion would actually come—on October 7. But what does October 7 have to do with the Temple Mount? Everything. The strange truth is that one cannot understand what happened that day without understanding its connection to the Temple Mount.

"Playing With Fire"

In the spring of 2023, amid reports of Jewish people seeking to observe a Jewish holy day on the Temple Mount, a clash broke out on top of the Mount in the Al-Aqsa Mosque between Palestinians and Israeli police. The Palestinians attacked the police with rocks and fireworks. The police responded with rubber bullets and stun grenades. At least a dozen people were injured, and hundreds were arrested. The next night, another clash broke out in the same place.[3]

In the wake of that conflict on the Temple Mount, rockets were fired into Israel from Gaza as well as from Lebanon.[4] Afterward, Hamas issued a warning to Israel that it was "playing with fire."[5] Six months later, on October 7, the fire broke out.

The Secret Origins of October 7

In the immediate wake of the October 7 invasion, Hamas leader Ismail Haniyeh gave an address in which he told the world the reason for the day of slaughter and atrocities. It was, he said, the answer to what had happened on the Temple Mount the previous spring. He claimed that Israel had seen fit to

> sow corruption in the holy *Al-Aqsa Mosque* [*the Temple Mount*] in *Al-Quds* [*Jerusalem*]. We told them, "Don't play with fire"...they have invaded *Al-Aqsa Mosque.*[6]

It is not a matter of debate. In the words of those who masterminded it, October 7 was the response to what had taken place on the Mount. Haniyeh continued:

> And when *Al-Aqsa Mosque* finds itself in imminent danger…this [*Israeli*] government is preparing to impose its sovereignty and authority over blessed *Al-Aqsa Mosque.*[7]

Even the rumor of Jewish sovereignty returning in any way and to any degree to the Temple Mount was enough to trigger the bloodshed and calamity of October 7. It all began with the Al-Aqsa Mosque, and according to Haniyeh, it would all end there:

> With a crushing defeat that will expel it [Israel] from our lands, our holy city of *Al-Quds,* our *Al-Aqsa Mosque.*[8]

A statement released by Fatah called October 7 a day of victory, joy, and pride, in

> waging the battle of defending its honor and *its holy sites,* and *foremost among them the blessed Al-Aqsa Mosque.*[9]

What took place on October 7 was intrinsically bound to the Temple Mount.

The Temple Mount, the Dragon, and 9/11

October 7 was not the first time that the issue of the Dragon and the Temple Mount would lead to calamity. One of those calamities was directed against America, New York and Washington, DC. It would be known as *9/11.* Though most people had no idea, the tragedy that struck America on September 11, 2001, and brought the death of three thousand Americans was linked to God's holy mountain in Jerusalem, the Temple Mount.

When Osama Bin Laden wrote his letter to America giving his reasons for masterminding the calamity of 9/11, foremost among them was the issue of Palestine. America was Israel's most important ally and supporter. So it had to be struck and punished. As Bin Laden railed against the Jews of Israel, he wrote this:

> With your help and under your protection, *the Israelis are planning to destroy the Al-Aqsa Mosque.*[10]

Compare Bin Laden's words in the aftermath of 9/11 to the words of those who masterminded October 7:

> *This [Israeli] government is preparing to impose its sovereignty and authority over blessed Al-Aqsa Mosque.*[11]

The charges are virtually identical, as is the wording. And yet they were made by two different people in two different statements separated by over twenty years. One was the rationale given for the calamity of October 7; the other for September 11. Yet both traced back to the same charge and the same plot of land—the Temple Mount. Their parallels, their common causes, and the fact that they each resulted in a deluge of death and destruction bear witness to the more-than-natural reality that lay behind them.

So as Americans watched the Pentagon go up in flames and the World Trade Center go down in ruins, they had no idea that behind their national calamity lay an ancient ground and an ancient entity. Behind the calamity of 9/11, just as behind the calamity of October 7, was a dragon on the Temple Mount.

"The Bringing of Red Cows"

One hundred days into the war that began with Israel's calamity, Abu Obeida, spokesperson for the Al-Qassam Brigades, the military wing of Hamas, issued a statement in which he attributed the day of slaughter to

> an aggression that reached its peak against our path (*Al Quds*) and *Al-Aqsa*, with the start of its actual temporal and spatial division.[12]

As with the masterminds of October 7, Obeida reaffirmed the connection to Al-Aqsa and the Temple Mount. But his statement also contained a mysterious reference that bewildered most who heard it. The bloodshed also had to do with *cows*, or as he put it,

> the bringing of *red cows* as an application of a detestable religious myth...[13]

What were the red cows? And how was October 7 a response to bringing them in? The *red cows* were red heifers. According to an ancient ordinance, red heifers were a required part in one of the Temple functions. In the autumn of 2022 five red heifers arrived in Israel from America.[14] How would that cause the satanic rampage of October 7? It would not make sense in the natural realm. But we are, again, not dealing with that realm.

Red Heifer, Red Dragon

The rite of the red heifer is connected to the Temple. It implies the Temple's rebuilding. Those who brought the cows to Israel did so in the hope of being part of the Temple's future restoration on the Mount.[15] In the eyes of the Dragon the presence of red heifers in the land of Israel would constitute a threat to his dominion over the Mount. The presence of Israeli troops on the Mount would constitute another. In view of the Dragon's mission to keep the Temple Mount away from the people of Israel and the Temple of God from the Mount, what would we expect to happen? Exactly what did happen; it would set off a satanic explosion—October 7. The mystery had ordained it.

Operation *Al-Aqsa* Flood

The connection between the Temple Mount and October 7 was so central and so strong that it could even be seen in the name given to the invasion by Hamas. It was named *the Flood*. But its full name was *Amaliyyat Tufan Al-Aqsa*, or the *Al-Aqsa Flood*.[16] It was all about the Temple Mount. It was all about the Temple Mount. It was all about the Dragon's possession of that Mount and the war waged there over the purposes of God.

So the invasion of October 7 bore the name of a flood and the mosque that sat on the Temple Mount. On that day a flood of fury poured down from the Mount and onto the people of Israel from the mouth of the Dragon.

———————— ∎∎∎ ————————

Could Israel's most calamitous event since the Holocaust be connected to its first and last of days?

THE FIRST AND LAST OF DAYS

THE HOLY DAYS of Israel were meant to be kept on the holy ground—the Temple Mount. The Mount was appointed for the days, and the days for the Mount. We have already witnessed how the Dragon's war involved the desecration of Israel's holy days. But the prospect of *the holy days* coming to the Temple Mount would present to the Dragon a double threat. Could such a connection and such a threat have played a part in what happened on October 7?

The First of Days

The sacred Hebrew year begins in the springtime. The first of its festivals, Passover, falls in the first of Hebrew months, *Nisan*, the name signifying *the beginning*. So it is ordained,

> On the fourteenth day of the first month at twilight
> is the LORD's Passover.[1]

It was the Passover sacrifice that ushered in the sacred year. In ancient times, it was offered up on the Temple Courts on the fourteenth day of Nisan. So the year of sacred times began with the celebration of Passover on the Temple Mount.

Israel's year of calamity would also begin with Passover and the Temple Mount. October 7 was ushered in by the same holy day that ushers in Israel's sacred year. The conflict erupted on the night of April 4. The Hebrew day begins at sundown, and the night of April 4 was *Nisan 14*. Nisan 14 is the day that ushers in the Passover and Israel's sacred year. But in 2023, the Dragon would observe his own Passover and usher in a year of dark and unholy days. As God used Passover to bring redemption and freedom to Israel, so the Dragon would use the holiday to bring to Israel calamity and terror. The mere idea of Passover being observed on the Temple Mount was enough to ignite the explosion.

It was in the spring of 2023 that a number of observant Israelis hoped to observe Passover on the Temple Mount and to offer up the sacrifice of the Passover lamb.[2] It was the closest the Passover had come to the Temple Mount in ages—too close for the Enemy. No sacrifice would be offered that day, but the possibility of it happening was all that was needed. The sacrifices, the shedding of blood, would come later.

"Their Sinister Religious Festivals"

When the Hamas spokesman explained to the world the reason for the October 7 massacre, he made specific mention of a biblical festival. He said:

> …during *their sinister religious festivals* they have invaded Al-Aqsa Mosque. They *desecrated* and *defiled* it.[3]

What the Hamas spokesman is referring to as "*their sinister religious festivals*" are the sacred holy days given by God to Israel at Mount Sinai. It was an amazing inversion. The Temple Mount, from its inception, was to serve as the ground on which the holy days of Israel would be observed. But to Hamas the sacred appointed days of God, the holy days of Israel, were *sinister religious festivals*. It begs the question: "Who would view the holy day of God as desecrations and sinister?" The inverter. It is the Dragon, for whom the holy is a desecration and desecration is holy, and for all his children.

The Last of Days

If Passover is the inaugural and opening day of the sacred biblical year, then what is its end, its consummation day? The last of all holy days given by God is the twenty-second day of Tishri. It is that which culminates all the appointed times of God and closes the sacred year. So the sacred calendar begins in the springtime on the fourteenth day of Nisan and closes in the autumn on the twenty-second day of Tishri.

And so if the day appointed to usher in the sacred Hebrew year, Passover, ushered in Israel's year and day of calamity, what about the day appointed to close that sacred Hebrew year? In other words, when in the year 2023 did the last and closing day of Israel's sacred calendar, the twenty-second of Tishri, fall?

It fell on *October 7*.

It all converged on the last and closing day of Israel's appointed times, Shemini Atzeret.

From Nisan 14 to Tishri 22

The two holy days, Passover and Shemini Atzeret, Nisan 14 and Tishri 22, the first and the last, of God's appointed times are joined together in framing the sacred year. In 2023 they were again joined together but, this time, by the Dragon. His calendar of calamity was birthed on the opening day of God's sacred calendar, Nisan 14, and would come to its finale on the culmination day of that calendar. The great imitator had mimicked the entire sacred calendar of God that he might desecrate it.

A Mystery of Desecrations

It was a Hebrew holy day, Nisan 14, that threatened the Dragon's control of the Temple Mount, so he would choose a Hebrew holy day as his day of revenge—October 7. And as it was the first of God's holy days, Passover, that threatened to "desecrate" his possession of the Mount, so he would desecrate the last of God's holy days, Shemini Atzeret. It all began on the first of the ancient days, and it would all come home on the last.

————————■■■————————

There was one more secret to Israel's most calamitous day. To uncover it, we must go back to a gathering on the Temple Mount led by one of the most famous of the nation's ancient leaders—King Solomon.

Chapter 65

THE KING SOLOMON SECRET

WE HAVE SEEN what was *not* intended for the Temple Mount. What about that which *was*?

The Temple Dedication

It all began three thousand years ago, with King Solomon standing before the people of Israel on the Temple Mount. They had gathered there for a most holy purpose, to dedicate the newly built Temple of God. So it was written:

> ...when Solomon had finished praying all this prayer and supplication to the LORD, that he arose from before the altar of the LORD, from kneeling on his knees with his hands spread up to heaven. Then he stood and blessed all the assembly of Israel.[1]

And so with prayer, thanksgiving, and sacrifice, the Temple of God was dedicated:

> So the king and all the children of Israel dedicated the house of the LORD.[2]

The Eighth-Day Sealing

Then the people celebrated a festival to the Lord. So it was recorded:

> At that time Solomon held a feast, and all Israel with him, a great assembly...seven more days.[3]

On the eighth day the dedication was sealed:

> On the eighth day he sent the people away; and they blessed the king.[4]

The festival that sealed the Temple's dedication was the Feast of Tabernacles, Sukkot. It is celebrated by the Jewish people every autumn. A festival connected to the building of God's Temple on the Temple Mount would represent a challenge to the Dragon's possession of that Mount—all the more, the eighth and final day that sealed the Temple's dedication.

In 2023 the holy day that sealed the dedication of the Temple on the Temple Mount fell on *October 7*. That would be the day of the Dragon's vengeance. It was not only that he attacked Israel on a Hebrew holy day—it was that he attacked Israel on the *one specific Hebrew holy day that sealed the dedication of the Temple on the Temple Mount.*

The Chanting

It is appointed that on the gathering of the eighth day, Shemini Atzeret, the scrolls of God's Word be opened and a passage of Scripture, especially appointed for that day, is to be recited and chanted. What is the scripture appointed for that day? *It is the account of the Temple's dedication.* So October 7 was not only the day that commemorated the sealing of the Temple's dedication—it was the day on which the words of the account of that dedication were publicly recited and chanted in synagogues and homes throughout the Jewish world.[5]

In fact, every scripture quoted in this chapter concerning the Temple's dedication was taken from the specific passage appointed to be read and chanted on Shemini Atzeret. Thus they were the words proclaimed on October 7, 2023. And they all focus on the Temple of God on the Temple Mount.

The Most Fitting of Days

There is only one day of the entire Jewish year on which those words are to be so proclaimed. In 2023 it fell on October 7. And so on the morning of October 7, 2023, across the land of Israel and throughout the world the words declaring the consecration of the Temple on the Temple Mount were proclaimed. To the Dragon the proclaiming of such words would represent a challenge to his possession of the Mount. And so it would be the most fitting of days on which to strike Israel in an attack concerning the possession of the Mount.

And so on October 7 Hamas began its Operation Al-Aqsa Flood, referring to the Temple Mount, while the people of Israel prepared to recite the scripture that likewise spoke of the Temple Mount. Each spoke of the same Mount, one in Hebrew, the other in Arabic; one, from the lips of the Jewish rabbi and cantor, the other from the lips of Hamas, the overflow of a flood pouring out from the mouth of the Dragon.

The Mastermind

The true mastermind of October 7 was not Hamas. They couldn't have known of all the details, intricacies, and convergences involved in the sacred Hebrew. The mastermind was the Dragon. It was he who planned that the attack would fall on the day that sealed the building and dedication of the Temple on the Temple Mount. He had now done in the realm of time as he had already done in the realm of space. He had already taken possession of God's holy ground—now he took possession of His holy day. As the one who seeks to seize and possess the things of God, it was his nature to do so.

As with 9/11, the world could not have imagined what lay behind what happened on October 7. In this case it was a mystery stretching back to the days of King Solomon and ultimately forward to the Book of Revelation, to the Lamb, the Beast, the kingdom of God, and a raging Dragon on the mountain of the Lord.

There is one more dimension to the Dragon's war, one that is joined to the nation of Israel and yet beyond it.

Part XIV

THE
OTHERS

Chapter 66

THE REST OF HER CHILDREN

> And the Dragon was enraged with the woman, and
> he went to wage war with the *rest of her children,*
> who keep the commandments of God and hold the
> testimony of Yeshua, Jesus, the Messiah.[1]

THWARTED IN HIS pursuit of the woman, the Dragon makes war with the "rest of her children." Who, then, are *the rest of her children?*

The Others

If the woman is Israel, they must in some way be children of Israel. So then, who are the rest of her children? There are two possible answers, one more specific, the other more universal. The more specific is that "the rest of her children" are the flesh-and-blood children of Israel, the Jewish people who follow the Messiah, as in the apostles, disciples, and believers who, at the beginning of the age, made up the majority of the faith and gave to the world the gospel.

The more universal answer is that "the rest of her children" refers to all believers, those who follow the Messiah of every nation, tribe, and tongue. But if they are not born of Israel, how could they be called "her children"? The answer, according to the New Testament, is that they *are* her children—that every true follower of Messiah is, by the Spirit, a child of Abraham, adopted into God's household, and spiritually Jewish. Likewise, the faith known to the world as *Christianity* was born of a Jewish womb, of the matrix of Israel.

Emperors and Chieftains

Then what does the Dragon's war against the "rest of her children" mean? It means that just as he has waged war against Israel, he will wage war, as well, against her spiritual children. It means that the people of Messiah, believers of all nations, those whom the Bible declares to be children of Israel by virtue of the new birth, will, likewise, be the object of the Dragon's wrath. So it was the Dragon who caused the emperors of Rome to wage war against the early Christians, to demonize them, imprison them, have them crucified and torn apart by wild animals. It was the Dragon who caused the rulers and chieftains of other kingdoms and other lands to wage war against those who brought them the gospel or who, of their own people, embraced it. But the "*rest of her children*" has an even more specific focus.

"To Make War With the Holy Ones"

The Dragon's pursuit of the woman's children in Revelation 12 comes in the context of his pursuit of the woman in the last days, when Israel will have returned to the world. So the Dragon's war against the woman's children will especially center on and reach its most intense state at *the end of the age*. This goes hand in hand with what is revealed of the Beast in the next chapter:

> It was granted to him *to make war with the holy ones* and to overcome them.[2]

This, in turn, matches the words given in the Book of Daniel concerning the Beast and God's people:

> *And the holy ones will be handed over to him.*[3]

So what does this all mean for the believer, for the true Christian, for those who keep the commands of God and the testimony of the Messiah?

"The Falling Away Comes First"

Piecing together the prophetic keys, we are given a picture. The end of the age will see a great persecution waged against the followers of Messiah. That persecution will not come out of the blue. The Antichrist's rule will come in the context of a culture and world prepared for and conducive to it. So too with the persecution of God's people, the signs of its coming will appear before its full manifestation.

When the apostle Paul speaks of the Antichrist and Messiah's second coming, he says this:

> That day will not come unless the *falling away* comes first, and the man of sin is revealed.[4]

So there must first come a great *falling away*. The Greek word behind "falling away" is *apostasia*. It means *to leave, to depart from one's former stand*, as in *a defection from truth, a falling away from faith*. So before the great persecution there will first come a great falling away from the faith. It is that falling away from faith that will open the door for everything else that is to come.

The Antichristianization

There is only one civilization that can fall away from the Christian faith—a "Christian" or "Judeo-Christian" one, a civilization that has known the Christian faith. So according to the prophecy, we would expect to see a once Christian civilization departing from Christianity. We would expect to see a metamorphosis in which it transforms into a non-Christian, secular, or neutral civilization, and, after that, into an anti-Christian civilization.

It is this that we are now witnessing. We have seen the secularization and the dechristianization of Western civilization. We are now witnessing the next stage—the antichristianization. A civilization that once upheld and revered biblical values now increasingly wages war against them.

The Eve of Persecution

The Antichrist will rule over every "tribe, tongue, and nation" and, at the same time, "make war with the holy ones." Therefore, he will war against those *under his rule*. And so the war against believers will be waged through governmental and governing institutions—persecution. It is no accident that even now governments that once upheld the gospel are increasingly targeting, prosecuting, and persecuting those who uphold the gospel within their jurisdictions. When nations, many of which were once considered Christian and many which are still Christian in name, persecute Christians for upholding basic Christian and biblical values and views, the days of apostasy have come. And when the governments of such treat believers as aliens, obstacles, problems, agitators, and dangers—just as they were once viewed by the government of Rome and just as they are always viewed by the Dragon—one is living on the eve of a great persecution.

The Beast Civilization

Another sign of what is coming is that what had once been associated with communist and fascist dictatorships is increasingly manifesting as an emerging characteristic of Western civilization. We are witnessing a creeping progressive totalitarianism in which government, economics, and culture are being weaponized against biblical and traditional values and those who uphold them. Though it masks itself in progressive terminology, it is nevertheless a manifestation of totalitarianism, one that even now seeks to cancel, to ban, to deplatform, to defund, to fire, to expel, to prosecute, to punish, and to imprison those who will not affirm it. It even seeks to decree which words and thoughts are acceptable and which must be eliminated. It is the preparation for the coming civilization and government of the Beast.

This Present Darkness

In both the East and the West, in the never Christian and the once Christian world, Christians are, even now, living under persecution. In the most advanced and sophisticated of ages Christians are persecuted not less so than in past ages—but more so. In fact, the persecution of Christians is greater now than it was in the days of Rome and, in fact, worse than at any other time in human history. And yet this is exactly what we would expect of a world increasingly turned from God and progressively impelled by the Dragon's spirit. And it is exactly what the prophecies of Scripture and the vision of the Dragon foretell would come.

Turning From the Lamb to the Beast

What happens to a civilization that has known of God but then departs from Him? One need look no further than the case of the Soviet Union or that of Nazi Germany. When God is driven out, the Dragon enters in. It is no accident that in both cases a war of persecution was launched against those who upheld the ways of God. Nor is it an accident that each case produced a shadow of the Beast, one in the form of Joseph Stalin and the other in the form of Adolf Hitler. Each also produced a shadow of the Beast's kingdom, on the one hand, the Soviet Union, and on the other, the Third Reich.

As the Christian civilization we have once known proceeded *from* the Christ, the Messiah, so the anti-Christian civilization we are coming to know will proceed *toward* the Antichrist, the Beast. If one turns away from the Lamb, one will inevitably find oneself turning to the Beast.

■■■

And so the people of God must prepare for persecution and for greater persecution. For the Beast will war against the saints, and the Dragon, against the rest of her children.

■■■

That which was separated in the beginning, must, in the end, be joined together again. It is a mystery that concerns every child of Israel and every follower of Messiah—even the entire world.

Chapter 67

THE END-OF-DAYS REUNION

WHAT DOES ISRAEL, and what happens to Israel, have to do with the follower of Jesus, Yeshua?

Everything.

The Physical and the Spiritual

First, as we have noted, the two are intrinsically bound. The one was born of the other. Christianity, in its essence, was, is, and will always be a Jewish faith, and, at the same time, universal to all peoples. True Christians are spiritually joined to the nation of Israel, as revealed in the New Testament, *grafted in* to Israel's olive tree. Their Savior is Israel's Messiah, and their hope of God's kingdom comes only in Israel's redemption. As Israel is the physical, flesh-and-blood nation of God, that which is called the "church" is the spiritual nation, an Israel of spirit, a spiritual Israel. The one corresponds to the other, and the other, to the one.

But in the vision of Revelation 12 the two are joined for another reason. The Dragon wars against both the woman and her children, Israel and "those who have the testimony of Yeshua, Jesus." So the two are bound together as well in that they are both the object of the Dragon's wrath and focal points of his war. And since the Dragon's war will, in the last days, intensify against each, the two, Israel and those who follow Messiah, must and will be increasingly and effectively joined together.

Two Kingdoms, One Lamb, and One Dragon

In Revelation the Dragon and the Beast wage war against the Lamb. There are two entities on earth that are joined to the Lamb—the church and Israel. The church is joined to the Lamb in spirit and as He is its Savior and Redeemer. Israel is joined to Him in flesh and blood and as He is the Messiah of Israel, King of the Jews. One represents Him in spirit, and the other in flesh and blood. And so the Dragon wages war against them both. They are two sides of the same war, the Dragon and the Lamb.

Both Israel and the church are essential for the coming of God's kingdom on earth. If the church fulfills its mission in the world, and Israel its purposes in the land, the kingdom will come. So the Dragon will war to keep the church from its mission and Israel from its purposes. He will seek to marginalize and alienate Israel from the nations and the church from society. He will seek the delegitimization of each. He will challenge their right to exist. He will stir up hostility against the church and rage against Israel. He will attempt the spiritual destruction of the church and the physical destruction of Israel. The nations will, in turn, persecute the followers of Messiah and seek Israel's annihilation.

The End-of-Days Reunion

The closer we come to the end of days, the more important it will be for the two peoples of Messiah to stand as one. The coming together has already begun. That Israel's greatest friends are those who follow the Messiah, Yeshua, and who are known as *Christians* is more evident now than it has ever been. As for the church, it has increasingly been moving to the reclamation of its biblical roots and its Jewish heritage as it turns increasingly from Rome to Jerusalem. The Dragon's rage against each will accelerate their reunion. For each was destined in the end to be rejoined to the other—just as each will be joined as the focal point of the Dragon's fury—in his rage against the woman and his war against the rest of her children.

———— ■■■ ————

Could there be yet another return and another resurrection, not of the earthly but of the Spirit?

Chapter 68

THE RETURN TO THE BEGINNING

THERE *IS* ANOTHER return and another resurrection. To find it, we must go back to the beginning.

The Book of Acts Exemplar

If Israel and the church are intrinsically joined, if one corresponds to the other, then would not the return and resurrection of Israel point to a corresponding return and resurrection of the church? If, at the end of the age, the Jewish people have returned to where they were at the beginning of the age, to Israel, then would it not also be the time for the followers of Messiah to return to where they were at the beginning of the age? And where were they at the beginning of the age? They were in the Book of Acts. It is time to return to the Book of Acts.

From the Revolutionary to the Status Quo

In the beginning of the age the church was not established or part of the status quo. It was not comfortable in the world or endowed with worldly power. It was not favored or supported by institutional power or mainstream culture, but rather was, by these, opposed. And yet in the ensuing centuries it would become increasingly joined to the world and worldly power. And by so being, it would lose the spiritual power it once had. It would move from being a revolutionary entity to one of the status quo. And yet it was never so pure, so powerful, so life-changing, so world-changing as it was in the Book of Acts, at the beginning of the age. It was then, when its worldly power was at its least, that its spiritual power was at its greatest. And it was then, when it was least part of the status quo, that it possessed its greatest power to change the status quo. And it was then that it was its most radical. It was not cultural as much as it was countercultural, not of the established order but revolutionary.

From the Status Quo to the Revolutionary

For the Jewish people to return to Israel meant laying aside an identity they had acquired in their two thousand years of statelessness and wandering. It meant the taking up and restoring of the identity from which they had been long separated. The church, the followers of Messiah, must do likewise.

They must lay aside the identity they had acquired in ages of being joined to the world and to the status quo. They must take up the identity they had possessed at the beginning. The force of persecution will not hinder that process—it will accelerate it. As the Jewish people had to repossess their ancient inheritance, the church must likewise repossess its ancient inheritance in the Book of Acts.

In other words, the Christian faith must move away from its union with the world and become once again a radical entity. It must once again don its revolutionary and world-changing mantle.

The Forgotten Calling

Just as the Jewish people who returned to Israel were charged with reviving a long-dead land, so too each end-time believer is to revive the long-lost life and power of the Book of Acts. Each must walk the long-unwalked ways of those who, at the dawn of the age, transformed the world.

The believers of the end must take up the mantle of the beginning. They must choose to live as they lived, not of worldly power, but by the power of the Spirit. They must stand as did the first believers, in faith, hope, courage, and victory, and not be overcome by the world but, by the power of God, overcome it.

———————■■■———————

And as the first believers stood and prevailed in the face of the Dragon's war against them, so too must the end-time believer. And for that we must unlock one more secret, a critical key to the prevailing of God's people.

Chapter 69

THE MYSTERY OF THE SECRET ISRAELIS

WE ARE NOW led to a critical key. In the Book of Ephesians a word is given to those not born of the nations but who then came to faith in Messiah:

> You were without the Messiah, excluded from the *citizenship of Israel*, and foreigners to the covenants of the promise....So then you are no longer foreigners and strangers, but *fellow citizens*.[1]

The End-Time Secret

The believer in Messiah, the true Christian, is, by virtue of the new birth, not only joined to the Jewish people but a *fellow citizen* in the *commonwealth* or *polity of Israel*—a spiritual Israelite. It is another long-forgotten or long-missed truth among most of those called *Christians*. But even among those in past ages who realized that they were spiritual Israelites, they did so when there was no actual nation in the world called *Israel*. But there now is. So is there a connection between the spiritual Israelites and the resurrected state of Israel?

Most see the word *Israeli* as modern, bound to the twentieth- and twenty-first-century world and the reborn state of Israel. But it is not so. The word *Israelite* is an English rendering of a Latin rendering of a Greek rendering of a Hebrew word. The actual word that appears in the Hebrew Scriptures is *Israeli*. So the believer in Jesus is not only spiritually Jewish, a spiritual Israelite; he or she is a *spiritual Israeli*. And since there actually exists a nation of Israel in the world as there was when the Book of Ephesians was written, and since the citizens of the modern nation of Israel are called *Israelis*, could this open up a revelation for the end-time believer?

The Israeli and the Dragon

This is where two mysteries come together—that of the Dragon and that of the Israeli. The Israeli has come into existence not only because of God but because of the Dragon or, rather, in response to the Dragon.

In the realm of the natural the nation of Israel came back into the world because of nearly two thousand years of persecution and calamity. The first waves of Jewish refugees returning to the land were triggered by the anti-Jewish persecutions and pogroms of Tsarist Russia. Behind those calamities and bloodshed was the Dragon. The next waves of return happened as a result of the rise of anti-Semitism in Europe, the rise of Hitler, and then the Holocaust. Behind those calamities was, again, the Dragon.

So the Israeli came into existence in defiance of two thousand years of persecution, in defiance of the Dragon and his war against them. For most of that time, they had been victims of that war. But from the moment of their national resurrection, they would be fighters. They would fight back.

"An Exceedingly Great Army"

> And breath came into them, and they lived, and
> stood upon their feet, *an exceedingly great army.*[2]

In the ages of their wandering the earth, the Jewish people were not seen as fighters. But with Israel's resurrection all that changed. Born in the ashes of the Holocaust and surrounded by a sea of nations seeking their destruction, they realized that unless they learned to fight, they would not survive.

And so a people who had long and largely been averse to fighting, to waging war, quickly learned how to do so. In 1948, as the armies of multiple nations converged on the newborn nation, Israel's existence hung in the balance. Those who had never fought in a war before and armed with secondhand weapons smuggled in from other countries were charged with defending the nation against destruction.[3] By a miracle they won.

The Israel Defense Forces, the IDF, made up of refugees and survivors of the Holocaust, would become one of the most powerful military forces on earth, an army feared by its enemies and revered around the world. Had they not, Israel would have long ago ceased to exist.

The Other Israelis

If the Israelis of the spirit are connected to the Israelis of flesh and blood, then, as the Jewish people, as Israelis, had to learn to fight, so too those who follow the Messiah must in the last days, likewise, learn to fight. As the nation of Israel is made up of soldiers, so too must the church of the end times be made of soldiers. As the Israelis of flesh and blood had to become fighters in the earthly realm, the Israelis of spirit must become fighters in the spiritual.

For the same reason that the Israelis had to become warriors in the world, the people of Messiah must become warriors in the Spirit—because of the Dragon. In the last days the Dragon will war against both Israels and both Israelis. The Israeli must fight. In an age increasingly hostile to their faith, their ways, and their existence, the people of Messiah will have no more choice than did the Israelis but to become especially strong in fighting, in warfare, in this case in the Spirit. In such an age it is not enough to maintain one's stand—one must resist the darkness. One must counter it. One must take up the stand of a warrior, of godly defiance, of divine resistance, of spiritual war, and fight.

And None Shall Make Him Afraid

It is of note that Ezekiel's vision of the valley of dry bones foretells not only the resurrection of an Israelite nation but an Israeli army. The prophet Jeremiah foretold that after God had regathered Israel back to the land, *none shall make him afraid*.[4] The world's picture of Jewish victimhood in the face of persecution was, in the Israeli soldier, changed into one of strength. The Jewish fighter had returned to the world, and none would make him afraid. That is the stance that must also be taken up by the spiritual Israelis, the people of God in the last days. They must rise in boldness, courage, confidence in the will and power of God, that none should make them afraid.

Footsteps of the Ancients

It was not that the Jews had never known what it was to fight and wage war as children of Israel. They had once. But it was thousands of years in the past. The world had forgotten. And they had forgotten. But in ancient times the Jewish people were known as fighters. They had once stood with shield and sword on countless battlefields and against countless enemies. Now they had to step back into the sandals of their ancient forerunners. They had to take up, as a new identity, their ancient identity. It was for that reason that the soldiers of the resurrected Israel took their oath of service on top of Masada, where the soldiers of Israel, in ancient times, had made their last stand.[5]

The Jewish warrior had returned and would again fight for his people.

In the same way, the believers of the end times, the spiritual Israelis, must take up as their new identity their ancient identity. They must take up the spiritual armor of their ancient forerunners, the believers, the disciples, the apostles, the messengers of Messiah, who took their stand at the beginning of the age, who waged war in the spiritual realms, who withstood and fought against the darkness and overcame the world. They must walk in their footsteps, take up their spiritual swords, and, again, overcome the world.

As Those Who War Against Him

As the Israelis must stand alone in the world, apart in the world, and against the flow of the world, so too must the spiritual Israelis be willing to stand alone in the world, apart in the world, and against the spiritual flow of their world and their age. In a day marked by the Dragon's rule, if one is to follow

God, one must defy the defiance, resist the resistance, and stand and fight against the darkness. One must wage that war in one's surrounding world and one's own life. In such an age it is not enough to have faith and hope and righteousness—one now must take up a fighting faith, a fighting hope, a fighting holiness, a fighting love, and a fighting joy. The people of God are to become a victorious people, a heavenly army, a spiritual IDF. They are no longer to be counted as victims of the Dragon—but as those who war against him.

———————■■■———————

As we bring this home, we must turn to that which involves and will involve everyone reading these words. For we must all deal with the Dragon. And so we will now set our focus on the ultimate and final overcoming of the Dragon.

Part XV

THE
DRAGON
SLAYERS

Chapter 70

THE DRAGON SLAYER

And the Dragon stood before the woman who was
ready to give birth, to devour her Child as soon as
it was born.[1]

The Dragon's Antithesis

Messiah is the epitome of Israel and Jewish existence—and the antithesis of
the Dragon. Therefore, Messiah is the focal point of the Enemy's war and
wrath. In the vision of Revelation 12 the first object of the Dragon's fury is
the child, Messiah. Only after that does he pursue the woman, Israel, and
her children. In this is a mystery; the Dragon's war against the woman is
connected to his war against the child. And so the Enemy's persecution of
the Jewish people is connected to his war against Messiah. And the sufferings of Messiah are connected to the sufferings of Israel. The one is the
microcosm of the other, and the other, the macrocosm of the one.

Messiah the Lamb

The Lamb is the antithesis of the Dragon, and the Dragon of the Lamb. The
war between the two comes to its head on the cross. It is there that the forces
of hell converge against the incarnation of good and there that the darkness
crucifies the Light. There the Dragon strikes his blow against the Lamb. It is
the most evil of things, the crucifixion of the good. And yet it is, at the same
time, the most beautiful, the love of God giving of itself as a sacrifice to bring
redemption and life. It is the pinnacle of good and evil.

Nailed to the cross over Messiah's head were the words *King of the Jews*.
For the cross is, as well, the epitome of the Dragon's war against the Jewish
people. And so too the Jewish people have been crucified, and so too they
have risen.

Lastly, the cross is the epitome of the Dragon's war against all who follow
and belong to God, and all who bear His image. It is a shadow of the end
of that war—as it is through the cross that the love of God overcomes all
judgment and hatred, the light prevails against the darkness, and life overcomes death. For the Dragon, with all his powers, could not overcome, but
the Lamb overcomes the Dragon.

Messiah the Shepherd

Messiah is also called the *Shepherd of Israel*. What then happens if a flock is separated from its shepherd? That flock will be scattered and become defenseless against its predators. And so if Yeshua, Jesus, is the Messiah, He is the Shepherd of Israel. And if the children of Israel are separated from Him, they will become as sheep without a shepherd. They will scatter and wander the earth and become defenseless, as prey to the predators of the world.

And that is exactly what has happened. The two thousand years of Jewish history that followed the appearance of Yeshua bear witness that He is their Messiah, their Shepherd. For two thousand years they wandered the earth as sheep without their Shepherd. For two thousand years they became prey to their predators and to their arch-predator, *the Dragon*. So their Shepherd wept for them as He foresaw it. As He approached Jerusalem,

> He saw the city and wept over it, saying, "If you
> had known, even you, especially in this your day,
> the things that make for your peace! But now they
> are hidden from your eyes."[2]

It was the tears of the Shepherd weeping at the fate of His flock. And for two thousand years their peace has indeed been hidden from them—even to this day.

The King Messiah

In the last two thousand years, when one nation or power has come against the Jewish people, there was always another refuge, nation, or hope on the horizon. But in the end, when all nations come against them, there will be no such refuge or hope. And so it will be then that He will come. Messiah will return. The flock of Israel will return to their Shepherd and will be saved by His hand. And the kingdom will come, and its name will be Israel, and its King will be Messiah. In that day, all the servants of the Dragon, the Hitlers, the terrorists, and the Antichrists, will fade into the realm of memory. And the wolf will lie down with the lamb, and the child of Israel and the child of the Palestinian will walk together as one.

———————■■■———————

What happens if we now take the mystery of the Dragon's war to the most personal of realms?

Chapter 71

THE MYSTERY'S ANSWER

WE HAVE SEEN the reality of evil and the war of the Dragon. We have seen the war that underlies world history. But that war takes place not only on the world stage and on a global scale—but on a much more personal level.

The Enemy of All

As the Enemy opposes all of God's works, so he opposes *each* of God's works. As the Enemy of God, he is the Enemy of each life created in God's image. He wages wars against each. He wills and seeks the breaking of every life, every soul, every relationship, every marriage, every home, every hope and dream, every heart. And so he bruises, debases, oppresses, intimidates, terrorizes, paralyzes, cripples, crushes, and discards.

To some he wars through bondage, addiction, and slaveries. To others, through the wrath of man, rejection, abandonment, and abuse. Others he cripples through guilt, defilement, failure, regret, shame, and the hauntings of the past. And to others, he wars more slowly, through the continual hardening of heart, the gradual darkening of soul and the deadening of spirit. Through one means or another he seeks the destruction of every soul and life.

The Dragon's Antidote

What is the antidote to the Dragon and the answer to his war against our lives? It is the same answer to his war against Israel—Messiah. For the Shepherd of Israel is also the Shepherd of souls, Yeshua, Jesus, whose very name signifies not only the salvation of all—but the salvation of each. And as the power of the Enemy lies in the separating of all and each from God, so the power of Messiah is manifest in the ending of that separation and the bringing back of each and all to God. That separation can be ended only in the ending of evil, the nullifying of sin. And it is only in the Lamb, in His sacrifice, that evil can be ended and sins wiped away. Only in the Lamb can our separation from God be undone and the works of the Dragon be destroyed. So it is written:

> For this purpose the Son of God was manifested,
> that He might destroy the works of the Devil.[1]

The Double-Negative Redemption

In the atonement of Messiah the separation is separated, the condemnation is condemned, the breach is broken, and the end is brought to its ending. It is the double negative of redemption. Only in this can we be made new—born again. So it is written that for all who are in Messiah the old life has passed away and a new life begun. They are freed from the Dragon's power and have passed out of darkness to light, from death to life and the kingdom of heaven.

Good and evil are freely chosen. So it must also be with salvation. It is the choice of each. It can be chosen at any time and begin in any place—in a prayer, in the opening of one's heart, in the turning away from darkness and to the light, in the receiving of forgiveness, cleansing, God's love, God's peace, and God's Spirit, a new beginning, Yeshua, Jesus, salvation, a new birth, and the beginning of a new life.

The Mystery's Answer

We began with the problem and mystery of evil—that which should not exist but does. It is for that very reason, because it exists and should not, that we cannot solve it. It can only be solved by ceasing to exist. And only He who can bring into existence that which is not can bring out of existence that which is. And so the problem of evil can only be answered by the One who is the Answer—and only by receiving the Answer into one's life. For it is only the good that can overcome evil, and only the Lamb that can overcome the Dragon, on the earth, in the cosmos, and in our lives.

Being that there is no one in the image of God who is not the focus of the Dragon, how do we fight? How do we overcome?

Chapter 72

NIKAO

IT IS ONE of the most important encouragements given to the end-time believer. And it is found in Revelation 12, in the vision of the Dragon and the woman. It is this:

> And they overcame him by the blood of the Lamb
> and by the word of their testimony, and they did
> not love their lives to the death.[1]

The Dragon Fighters

They refers to believers in Messiah. *Him* refers to the Dragon. What do *they* do with regard to *him*? They *overcome*. This is the other side of the story. And for the believer it is the most critical side of the story. It is not conditioned by time or circumstance. It doesn't matter what age or circumstance the believer is in. For the Dragon wages war on every believer in all times and places. And the promise holds true regardless. So between now and the ultimate victory of Messiah's coming, believers will be at war. How, then, must we live?

We must live as Dragon fighters. The prospect of fighting dragons conjures up images from ancient mythology, medieval tales, or the sagas of modern fantasy and science fiction. But this is the one instance in which dragon fighting is not of mythology, fantasy, or fiction. The fight is, of course, of the spiritual realm, and the Dragon is the embodiment of evil. But it is a dragon nonetheless, and so the call of every believer—man, woman, and child, in Messiah—is to fight the Dragon. For though the vision focuses on the one side of the war, this one verse is enough to establish the other. The Dragon wages war against every believer—and every believer must, likewise, become a dragon fighter and wage war against him.

They Overcame Him, Past Tense and Yet to Come

With all that has been revealed from the vision of the Dragon and the rest of the Book of Revelation, how can we stand in light of it, much less fight against it?

The word here rendered as *overcame* is rooted in the Greek word *nikao*. *Nikao* means not only to *overcome* but *to conquer, to subdue, to triumph, to win the victory*. And though the word appears in Revelation 12 to speak of things to come, it does so in the past tense. The victory is sure and absolute and as good as done. And so that is to be the stand, the strategy, the attitude, and the life of the believer in the days to come—*nikao*, in the *past tense and yet to come.*

The End of Evil

Why is it that the people of God are bound for victory, and the Dragon for defeat? It goes back to the beginning—the nature of evil is parasitic. Therefore, it cannot exist on its own but only in relation to the good against which it wars. Unlike the good, evil is not primary but secondary and contingent. And so the more that evil wars against the good, the more it cuts itself off from the reality by which it exists. Therefore, it cannot, in the end, remain. And in its war against the good, it cannot, in the end, prevail.

The Serpentine and Reptilian Nature

It is of note that the one called *Dragon* and *Serpent* is named after two creatures that share a common nature. Serpentine and reptilian creatures lack endurance. Though some can move fast, they cannot move for long. So as both serpentine and reptilian, the Enemy also lacks the ability to endure. The power of the Dragon, the power of evil, lies in the temporary and momentary. Its dominion is ephemeral. It cannot last. It cannot endure.

In the vision of the Dragon's war it is written:

> For the Devil has come down to you, having great
> wrath, because he knows that *he has a short time.*[2]

Though this applies ultimately to the future, it is, in another sense, always true—the Dragon has only a short time. In that time, he will rage and wreak havoc and terror, but his days are numbered. So with evil—its days are finite; its time is limited. Though it can appear overwhelming and relentless in its war against the good, it can only do so for a time. And even then, the appearance is false. For evil exists in the realm of falsehood and illusion—and then is gone.

Evil, by nature, leads to destruction, even its own. It is no accident that the most evil of world figures, Adolf Hitler, died by his own hand. Nor is it an accident that those closest to him and most complicit in his acts likewise died by their own hands.[3] Evil, of inversion by nature, contains its own inversion, its own undoing, the seeds of its end. It will not last—because it cannot last. And it will not prevail, because its prevailing is its own destruction.

The Foreverness of Good

But with the good, it is the opposite. Unlike evil, the good is not secondary or contingent but primary and absolute. It cannot be cut off from existence, as it is from the good that existence is born. It *is* existence. And so unlike evil, the good is not passing or temporary. Unlike the Dragon and unlike evil, the Lamb and the good are warm-blooded. The good will endure forever because it must. It is, by nature, eternal. And so while the days of the Dragon's evil are numbered and cannot last, the days of God's love and goodness are without number and will not end, as it is written, "His steadfast love endures forever."[4]

And so heaven is forever, because forever is how long it takes to contain the goodness of God.

Little Lambs and Dragons

The final conflict as revealed in the Book of Revelation is between the Dragon and the Lamb. A lamb is innocent and harmless, an animal of prey, defenseless. A dragon is a predator, fierce, and deadly. An encounter of the two would seem not so much a conflict as a slaughter. And yet it is the Lamb who overcomes the Dragon. For the Lamb is the incarnation of the good, and the Dragon, of evil. And in the end the good will always overcome, prevail, and remain.

The battle of the Dragon and the Lamb can be seen throughout history. When the Roman Empire launched its persecutions against the first Christians and threw them to the lions,[5] it was the warring of the Dragon against the Lamb. The Christians were innocent and appeared defenseless. And yet they prevailed. The Lamb overcame the Dragon. When the Soviet Union sought to stamp out faith and persecuted the followers of Messiah,[6] it was again the warring of the Dragon against the Lamb. Again it had seemed a one-sided and hopeless battle. But the Soviet Union crumbled into history. The Dragon was overcome, and the Lamb prevailed.

The Power of Nikao

In the battle of good and evil, the evil will often take the form of a dragon and the good will often assume the form of a lamb. The evil will often appear strong, colossal, unstoppable, fierce, and deadly—as a dragon—and the good, weak, defenseless, and without hope of prevailing—as a lamb. But in the end the good will prevail, the evil will crumble, and the Lamb will overcome the Dragon.

It is only the Lamb that can overcome the Dragon. Without the Lamb we are subject to the Dragon's rule and cannot overcome the power of evil, of darkness, or sin. But in the Lamb we are given the power to overcome the Dragon.

The *nikao* is with the Lamb. It is the Lamb who will be victorious, and those who follow the Lamb who will, in the end, be victorious.

———■■■———

Could there be, in this world and in the midst of human history, a witness, a confirmation, a sign that evil cannot, in the end, prevail, and that the good will not cease, that the Word of God is true, that His promises will be fulfilled, and that His purposes will overcome all things?

Chapter 73

THE UNCONQUERED

THERE IS ONE more fact that must be noted. With regard to the Dragon's war, it is the most important of facts, the overarching fact and the ultimate context. And as with so much else of what we have witnessed, it is contained as well in the vision of Revelation 12.

The Weakest of All Peoples

The Dragon's war against the children of Israel has been waged across the globe and in every generation from ancient times until now. And so the Jewish people have become the most persecuted, oppressed, attacked, besieged, barraged, struck-down, slaughtered, and warred-against people in world history. And at the same time, they were in the weakest of possible positions to withstand such an onslaught, having been shattered as a nation, scattered across the earth, with no king, no leadership, no government, no army, no weapons, no effectual unity, no land, no rights, no defense, and no hope. They were as defenseless as lambs, lambs without a shepherd, a lamb nation. And their enemies towered over them, as fierce and deadly as dragons.

Against All Odds

By the laws of human history they should have long ago perished from the earth. Stronger and more formidable nations have collapsed in the face of no such opposition, no such predicament, and no such odds. No other nation has existed in such a state and for so long a time, with so many and colossal forces set against it, and so great the odds against its survival and in favor of its annihilation. The children of Israel should have gone the way of the Hittites, the Hurrians, and the Babylonians ages and ages ago. They should have long ago been consigned to the pages of ancient history and the archaeological displays of museum walls.

The Great Contradiction

The greatest and most powerful of the world empires, Egypt, Assyria, Babylon, and Rome, to name just a few, all sought to eradicate the children of Israel from the face of the earth and the name of Israel from history.

But...

The Pharaohs are gone.

Assyria lies in ruins.

Babylon has fallen.

Rome has crumbled.

The Third Reich has been wiped off the earth.

The Soviet Union has collapsed.

All the enemies of Israel have fallen and have perished from the earth and will be no more.

But…

The nation of Israel lives.

Because the God of Israel lives.

The Savior of Israel lives.

The Messiah of Israel lives.

The weakest and most vulnerable have, in the end, prevailed, and have proved the strongest of peoples.

The most warred-against, embattled of nations has, in the end, proved the most enduring.

And the most hopeless of nations has, in the end, become the epitome of hope.

The nation that once dwelt among the ancient Egyptians, Assyrians, and Babylonians is, after the passing of ages, still as young and as full of life as it has ever been. It still defies the laws of nations. It still flouts the laws of history. And it still disobeys the laws of decay and death.

Why?

Because He Is

God brought the nation of Israel into existence to bear witness of His existence. They are because He is. They exist because He exists. And they continue to exist because He yet still exists. They would survive despite the attempts of all hell to destroy them—because more real than any other reality is the reality of God, and more powerful than any power is the power of God. That they have survived against all odds and all hell is a cause for rejoicing. For the Jew is the microcosm of man. And so if the children of Israel rise, then all can rise. And if they rise again from death, then all can, from death, rise again.

The One Left Standing

In Revelation 12 the Dragon pursues the woman in order to destroy her—but cannot. He cannot destroy her because he cannot overcome the will and purposes of God. And so for all that the Enemy has done and sought to do to annihilate the Jewish people throughout the ages, for all the calamities, the oppressions, the destructions, the exterminations, and for all the dark powers of the Dragon's rage—no matter what he does, he cannot destroy them. Why? Because the power of God is stronger and the reality of God, more real. And so they have not ceased to exist. For they bear witness of the Eternal, of whom there is no end.

And so the Jewish people have wandered the earth in between heaven and hell, life and death, and death and resurrection. They have stood in the center of God's promises and the Dragon's fury. And so theirs has been the most dramatic of histories. It could not have been any other way.

They stand as a witness on the stage of human history to testify of that which underlies all human history and every human life, two realities, a transcendent good and a transcendent evil, the reality of the Dragon and the very much greater reality of God. And so to them is, as well, the most miraculous of histories—a history that bears witness to the fact that after all is said and done, only one of those two realities, in the end, will be left standing.

The Promise

It was all there in ancient times. Thousands of years before the modern world, it was all foretold. The word of the Lord came to the prophet Jeremiah and said,

> Thus says the LORD, who gives the sun for a light by day, the ordinances of the moon and the stars for a light by night, who stirs up the sea that its waves roar—the LORD of Hosts *is* His name: "If these ordinances should depart from before Me," says the LORD, "only then will the children of Israel cease from being a nation before Me forever."[1]

In other words, as long as the sun and moon and stars give light to the earth and the laws of nature are upheld, so the children of Israel, the Jewish people, will not cease from existing. They will survive. From the ancient world, to the medieval world, to the modern world, and beyond, from age to age, they will endure; they will survive; they will exist.

Why?

Because God is real. And because God, the God of the universe, is the God of Israel.

And the Word of God is true.

And the promises of God are good.

His faithfulness never ends.

And His love endures forever.

And, finally, what does the mystery have to do with you?

Chapter 74

YOU

WHAT WE HAVE opened up and seen must be applied to the most important of realms—*your life*.

Your Life and the Dragon's War

This is to you who are reading these words. The war of the Dragon is waged not only against a world, nations, peoples, and other people. It is waged against *you*. You bear the image of God, and so to the Dragon you are the enemy. And if you know and follow God and uphold His ways, you are all the more his enemy.

He has waged war against you from the very beginning of your life. It was God who called you into existence. And so it is the Dragon who seeks to bring you out of existence.

It is God who speaks over your life the words "Let there be." And it is the Dragon who speaks over your life the words "Let there cease to be."

God brought you into existence for a high and sacred purpose. The Dragon has sought to keep you away from that purpose, to turn you away from life, from God.

The Dragon has sought to wound and scar you, defile and degrade you, enslave and oppress you, hinder and thwart you, break your spirit, to cripple and paralyze you, to defeat, crush you—and destroy you. He is waging war against your life—even this very moment.

Your Life and the Power of Nikao

But if you are of the Lamb, of the Messiah, then the word given for your life and your battle with the Dragon is *nikao*—victory. God did not call you to be defeated, but to *nikao*, to triumph, to win, to overcome.

Overcoming requires that which must be overcome. Victory requires a fight. Therefore, you cannot fear the fight, the adversity, the attacks, or the battle. For they are the very things that make it possible for you to become victorious.

Your Life and the Calling

In this book we have witnessed the reality of the longest and most colossal of wars ever fought in this world, a war that continues to this day. And yet we have seen that against all odds the people of God, the children of Israel, have survived and prevailed.

In this is a message for all who will follow in the ways and footsteps of God.

If God has kept His word and promise to Israel, He will keep His word and promise to you.

And if God has been faithful to Israel, He will be faithful to you.

And if after all that was set against it Israel has overcome, then so too will you overcome all things.

Your Life and the Power to Overcome

And as the Lamb will prevail against the Dragon, so you who walk in the footsteps of the Lamb will, likewise, prevail against the Dragon. Whatever the darkness, whatever the evil, and whatever the attack, whether of your world, of your circumstance, or of your life, it will not, in the end, prevail.

Whatever the darkness, whatever the evil, if you follow the Lamb, if you walk in His will, you will prevail. No matter how great the evil, it will, in the end, be vanquished. And no matter how dark its night, the darkness will, in the end, fade into the light of dawn.

By the power of the Lamb, you can overcome all things. Therefore, be not overcome by evil, but by the good overcome it. Therefore, be not overcome by fear, not by hate, not by despair, or sorrow, but overcome evil with good, fear with faith, hate with love, despair with hope, and sorrow with joy. By the power of life, overcome the power of death. By the power of God, overcome the impossible. And by the power of heaven, overcome the world.

To All Who Press On

Press on in confidence, in courage, in love, in the true, the right, the heavenly, and the good.

No matter what, press on.

For the good will prevail and the love of God will not give up.

And all who keep running will win the race.

And all who keep fighting will win the battle.

And all who press on in the power of the Lamb will be victorious.

------------ ■■■ ------------

And what of the end?

Chapter 75

THE DAYS OF DRAGONLESSNESS

A T THE VERY end of the Bible, in the very last pages of the Book of Revelation, the Dragon's war is finally brought to its final end. The inverted angel, the Devil, Satan, the Enemy, the Dragon, will then be vanquished. The power of evil will be gone. The good will prevail and will never end.

The kingdom of God will then be manifested in its glory. Messiah, the Lamb, will reign upon the throne. And the will and purposes of God will be fulfilled. And then, that of which the apostle Paul wrote will be revealed:

> Eye has not seen, nor ear heard, nor have entered
> into the heart of man the things which God has
> prepared for those who love Him.[1]

And all of God's people will then see it and know. There will then be no more darkness. For the Lord God will be their light, and the Lamb, their illumination. And all things will be made new.

And there will be no more Dragon then to rage against the children of Israel, the people of God, and the creation of His hands. No more will he terrorize the nations; no more will he wound, or scar, or mar, or destroy. The darkness of the Dragon will no longer obscure the light, nor will his evil ever again hide the face of God.

There will be then…

no more wars,

no more prisons,

no more hatred,

no more violence,

no more invasions,

no more terrorists,

no more slaughters,

no more holocausts,

no more fear,

no more pain,

no more graveyards,

no more sorrow,

no more death,

no more mourning,

no more weeping,

and no more pain.

———————■■■———————

The days of the Dragon will have passed away. His footprints will have long been washed away from the shores of memory, and his works from the memory of God's children.

And God will wipe away every tear from our eyes.

And He will then dwell among us. And we will be His people. And He will be our God.

The Dragon's war will be over.

And heaven will have begun.

———————■■■———————

Until then, be strong in the Lord.

And in the power of His might.

Fight the good fight.

Finish the course.

Never give in.

And never give up.

Press on to the victory.

And overcome the Dragon!

NOTES

Chapter 4

1. John 8:44, ESV.
2. Isaiah 14:14.
3. John 8:44.

Chapter 5

1. Numbers 23:9.
2. Exodus 19:6.
3. Genesis 12:3.
4. Isaiah 43:10.

Chapter 6

1. Revelation 12:10.
2. Ephesians 6:11.

Chapter 7

1. Revelation 12:1.
2. Genesis 37:9.
3. Revelation 12:3.
4. Revelation 12:9, author's translation.
5. Revelation 12:2.
6. Revelation 12:5.
7. Revelation 12:4, author's translation.
8. Revelation 12:13, author's translation.
9. Revelation 12:15, author's translation.
10. Revelation 12:17, author's translation.

Chapter 8

1. Luke 21:20, 24, emphasis added.
2. Deuteronomy 28:64, emphasis added.
3. Deuteronomy 28:66.
4. Deuteronomy 30:3, 5, emphasis added.
5. Hosea 3:4.
6. Jeremiah 31:8–9.
7. Jeremiah 31:10.
8. Hosea 3:5, NASB, emphasis added.

Chapter 9

1. Ezekiel 37:7–8.
2. Ezekiel 37:10.
3. Ezekiel 37:11–12.
4. John 19:19.
5. Ezekiel 37:3.
6. Thomas Hockenhull, "The Shekel: A Modern-Day Coin With 5,000 Years of History," *Coin World*, November 14, 2014, https://www.coinworld.com/news/world-coins/coin-world-shekel-history-numismatics-israel-world-coins-ancient-collecting-hobby.html; "The Arch of Titus Project," Center for Israel Studies, Yeshiva University, accessed June 10, 2024, https://www.yu.edu/cis/activities/arch-of-titus.
7. *Encyclopaedia Britannica*, s.v. "David Ben-Gurion," accessed May 28, 2024, https://www.britannica.com/biography/David-Ben-Gurion.
8. Jeremiah 31:4, ESV.

Chapter 10

1. 2 Corinthians 11:14, emphasis added.
2. Isaiah 14:13–14.

Chapter 11

1. Revelation 13:4.
2. Jeremiah 51:34, MEV, emphasis added.
3. Ezekiel 29:3, MEV, emphasis added.
4. Revelation 12:9, emphasis added.

Chapter 12

1. Julia Fridman, "Riddle of the Ages Solved: Where Did the Philistines Come From?," *Haaretz*, September 21, 2015, https://www.haaretz.com/archaeology/2015-09-21/ ty-article/philistine-homeland-found-and-surprise/0000017f-e10f-d568-ad7f- f36f8bb00000; Assaf Yasur-Landau, *The Philistines and Aegean Migration at the End of the Late Bronze Age* (New York: Cambridge University Press, 2010), 328–34.
2. *Encyclopaedia Britannica*, s.v. "Sea People," accessed May 13, 2024, https://www. britannica.com/topic/Sea-People; "The Philistines in Canaan and Palestine," Luwian Studies, accessed May 8, 2024, https://luwianstudies.org/the-philistines-in-canaan-and- palestine/; Ann E. Killebrew, *Biblical Peoples and Ethnicity: An Archaeological Study of Egyptians, Canaanites, Philistines, and Early Israel, 1300–1100 B.C.E.* (Atlanta: SBL Press, 2005), 83.
3. Kenton L. Sparks, *Ethnicity and Identity in Ancient Israel* (University Park, PA: Eisenbrauns, 1998), 96–97, emphasis added.
4. Ilan Ben Zion, "The Philistine Age," *Archaeology*, July/August 2022, https://www. archaeology.org/issues/473-2207/features/10600-levant-philistine-#art_page2; Don Knebel, "Medinet Habu: Philistines in Egypt," Biblical Archaeology Society, September 3, 2019, https://www.biblicalarchaeology.org/daily/medinet-habu-philistines-in-egypt/.
5. James Henry Breasted, *Ancient Records of Egypt*, vol. 4, *The Twentieth to the Twenty- Sixth Dynasties* (Chicago: Chicago University Press, 1906), 201, emphasis added.
6. Ben Zion, "The Philistine Age."
7. Owen Jarus, "Who Were the Philistines?," Live Science, July 16, 2016, https://www. livescience.com/55429-philistines.html.

Chapter 13

1. "Josephus Describes the Romans' Sack of Jerusalem," PBS, accessed May 28, 2024, https:// www.pbs.org/wgbh/pages/frontline/shows/religion/maps/primary/josephussack.html; Abraham Malamat, *A History of the Jewish People* (United Kingdom: Harvard University Press, 1976), 308, 332–33.
2. Peter Schäfer, *The History of the Jews in the Greco-Roman World: The Jews of Palestine From Alexander the Great to the Arab Conquest* (United Kingdom: Routledge, 2003), 163.
3. *Oxford Classical Dictionary*, s.v. "Judaea-Palaestina," updated May 29, 2020, https://doi. org/10.1093/acrefore/9780199381135.013.3500.

Chapter 14

1. Jonathan Laden, "Jews and Arabs Descended From Canaanites," *Bible History Daily*, November 25, 2023, https://www.biblicalarchaeology.org/daily/ancient-cultures/ancient- near-eastern-world/jews-and-arabs-descended-from-canaanites/.
2. Megan Gannon, "Ancient DNA Sheds New Light on the Biblical Philistines," *Smithsonian Magazine*, July 3, 2019, https://www.smithsonianmag.com/science-nature/ ancient-dna-sheds-new-light-biblical-philistines-180972561/.
3. Laden, "Jews and Arabs Descended From Canaanites."
4. *Encyclopaedia Britannica*, s.v. "Theodor Herzl," updated April 30, 2024, https://www. britannica.com/biography/Theodor-Herzl.
5. Perwez Anwer, *Palestine, Part 1* (IBTN Publications, June 21, 2022), preface.
6. "For the Record: Palestine: From Partition to Independence 1947–1988," *The Palestine Yearbook of International Law Online* 4, no. 1 (1987): 247, https://doi. org/10.1163/221161488X00089; *Encyclopedia of the Modern Middle East and North Africa*, s.v. "All-Palestine Government," accessed May 23, 2024, https://www.encyclopedia. com/humanities/encyclopedias-almanacs-transcripts-and-maps/all-palestine- government.

7. Douglas J. Feith, "The Forgotten History of the Term 'Palestine,'" *Mosaic,* December 13, 2021, https://www.hudson.org/node/44363.

Chapter 15

1. The Learning Network, "Nov. 29, 1947: U.N. Partitions Palestine, Allowing for Creation of Israel," *New York Times,* accessed May 13, 2024, https://archive.nytimes.com/learning. blogs.nytimes.com/2011/11/29/nov-29-1947-united-nations-partitions-palestine-allowing-for-creation-of-israel/; Benny Morris, *1948: A History of the First Arab-Israeli War* (New Haven, CT: Yale University Press, 2008), 72.
2. Mordechai Nisan, "The Conundrum of Israeli-Arab Citizenship," *Middle East Quarterly,* Summer 2020, https://www.meforum.org/61033/the-conundrum-of-israeli-arab-citizenship; "A Brief History of Gaza's Centuries of War," Reuters, accessed May 10, 2024, https://www.reuters.com/world/middle-east/brief-history-gazas-centuries-war-2023-10-13/; "The Tragedy of Palestine," The Hashemite Kingdom of Jordan, accessed May 10, 2024, http://www.kinghussein.gov.jo/his_palestine.html.
3. Mazen Masri, "The PLO and the Crisis of Representation," *Muftah,* October 15, 2010, https://web.archive.org/web/20160322193612/http://muftah.org/the-plo-and-the-crisis-of-representation-by-mazen-masri/#.VvGernbei3B; Encyclopedia.com, s.v. "Palestine Liberation Army," accessed May 13, 2024, https://www.encyclopedia.com/politics/dictionaries-thesauruses-pictures-and-press-releases/palestine-liberation-army.
4. "The Six-Day War: Israel Launches Preemptive Strike," Jewish Virtual Library, accessed May 10, 2024, https://www.jewishvirtuallibrary.org/background-and-overview-six-day-war#pre.
5. "The Six-Day War: The Liberation of the Temple Mount and Western Wall," Jewish Virtual Library, accessed May 10, 2024, https://www.jewishvirtuallibrary.org/the-liberation-of-the-temple-mount-and-western-wall-june-1967.
6. "Fatah," Palestinian Academic Society for the Study of International Affairs, accessed May 13, 2024, http://passia.org/media/filer_public/b8/db/b8db1845-9729-4802-8e34-6d6b46884cfb/factsheet_fateh.pdf.
7. *Interactive Encyclopedia of the Palestine Question,* s.v. "The Palestinian National Liberation Movement—Fatah (1) 1957–1990," accessed May 13, 2024, https://www.palquest.org/en/highlight/23292/palestinian-national-liberation-movement-%E2%80%93-fatah-i.
8. Patrick Martin, "At Six Years Old, Yasser Arafat Dreamed of the Conquest of Palestine, a Dream That Would Become His," *Globe and Mail,* November 6, 2004, https://www.theglobeandmail.com/news/world/at-six-years-old-yasser-arafat-dreamed-of-the-conquest-of-palestine-a-dream-that-would-become-his/article4091466/; Tass Saada, *Once an Arafat Man* (Carol Stream, IL: Tyndale House Publishers, 2008), 4; David N. Bossie and Christopher M. Gray, "Yasser Arafat: Architect of Terror," Citizens United Foundation, accessed May 14, 2024, https://www.citizensunitedfoundation.org/yasser-arafat-architect-of-terror/; "19 Years Since the Martyrdom of the Leader and Symbol Yasser Arafat," Alquds, November 11, 2023, https://www.alquds.com/en/posts/100326.
9. Exodus 23:31, MEV, emphasis added.
10. Laurie Kellman, "'From the River to the Sea': Why These 6 Words Spark Fury and Passion Over the Israel-Hamas War," Associated Press, November 10, 2023, https://apnews.com/article/river-sea-israel-gaza-hamas-protests-d7abbd756f481fe50b6fa5c0b907cd49, emphasis added.
11. Rick Gladstone, "An Annual Day of Palestinian Grievance Comes Amid the Upheaval," *New York Times,* May 15, 2021, https://www.nytimes.com/2021/05/15/world/middleeast/nakba-day.html.

Chapter 16

1. Carl S. Ehrlich, *The Philistines in Transition: A History From ca. 1000–730 BCE* (Germany: E.J. Brill, 1996), 7–8; "Canaan and Ancient Israel," University of Pennsylvania Museum of Archaeology and Anthropology, accessed May 28, 2024, https://www.penn.museum/sites/Canaan/IronAgeI.html; Roger Atwood, "Egypt's Final Redoubt in Canaan," *Archaeology,* July/August 2017, https://www.archaeology.org/issues/262-1707/features/5627-jaffa-egypt-canaan-colony.

2. *Encyclopaedia Britannica*, s.v. "1948 Arab-Israeli War," accessed May 10, 2024, https://www.britannica.com/event/1948-Arab-Israeli-War; Julia Frankel, "Gaza Has Long Been a Powder Keg. Here's a Look at the History of the Embattled Region," Associated Press, October 20, 2023, https://apnews.com/article/gaza-history-israel-palestinians-hamas-egypt-688d202c53c0cc72bf2242dccb47fcd5; "A Brief History of Gaza's 75 Years of Woe," Reuters, October 11, 2023, https://www.reuters.com/world/middle-east/brief-history-gazas-75-years-woe-2023-10-10/; *Encyclopaedia Britannica*, s.v. "Palestine and the Palestinians (1948–67)," accessed May 28, 2024, https://www.britannica.com/place/Palestine/Palestine-and-the-Palestinians-1948-67; Beryl Cheal, "Refugees in the Gaza Strip, December 1948–May 1950," *Journal of Palestine Studies* 18, no. 1 (October 1988): 138, https://www.researchgate.net/publication/249978298_Refugees_in_the_Gaza_Strip_DeDecemb_1948May_1950.
3. Genesis 10:19.
4. Ben Zion, "The Philistine Age."
5. Ken Feisel, "The Philistine Age," image, *Archaeology*, July/August 2022, https://www.archaeology.org/images/JA2022/Philistines/Philistines-Map.jpg; *Encyclopaedia Britannica*, s.v. "Gaza Strip," image, accessed May 10, 2024, https://www.britannica.com/place/Gaza-Strip#/media/1/227456/100799.

Chapter 17

1. Exodus 13:17, emphasis added.
2. S. R. Driver, *The Book of Exodus in the Revised Version* (England: Cambridge University Press, 1911), 111, emphasis added.
3. Christopher Eames, "Uncovering the Bible's Buried Civilizations: The Philistines," Armstrong Institute of Biblical Archaeology, March 26, 2017, https://armstronginstitute.org/30-uncovering-the-bibles-buried-civilizations-the-philistines, emphasis added.
4. Byron Chesney, "Jeremiah 47:1–7—Oracle Against the Philistines," Bible Outlines, accessed May 28, 2024, https://www.bibleoutlines.com/jeremiah-471-7-oracle-against-the-philistines/.
5. *Interactive Encyclopedia of the Palestine Question*, s.v. "Battle of al-Karama, 1968," accessed May 14, 2024, https://www.palquest.org/en/highlight/165/battle-al-karama-1968.
6. "Release: Bipartisan Group of 50 to Administration: Negotiate an End to Martyr Payments to Terrorists," Office of Rep. Josh Gottheimer, July 18, 2023, https://gottheimer.house.gov/posts/release-bipartisan-group-of-50-to-administration-negotiate-an-end-to-martyr-payments-to-terrorists.
7. "Palestinian Public Opinion Polls: Attitudes About Terrorism (2002–2023)," Jewish Virtual Library, accessed May 10, 2024, https://www.jewishvirtuallibrary.org/palestinians-attitudes-about-terrorism.
8. Ezekiel 25:15, HCSB, emphasis added.
9. "Ezekiel 25: Matthew Poole's Commentary," Bible Hub, accessed May 28, 2024, https://biblehub.com/commentaries/poole/ezekiel/25.htm, emphasis added.
10. "Ezekiel 25," Bible Hub.
11. John Gill, "Exposition on Ezekiel 25," Bible Hub, accessed May 28, 2024, https://biblehub.com/commentaries/gill/ezekiel/25.htm, emphasis added.
12. Carl Friedrich Keil and Franz Delitzsch, "Ezekiel 25," Bible Hub, accessed June 11, 2024, https://biblehub.com/commentaries/kad/ezekiel/25.htm.

Chapter 18

1. 1 Samuel 17:33, emphasis added.
2. Itamar Marcus, "The Palestinian Authority's Child Soldier Strategy Against Israel—Opinion," *Jerusalem Post*, February 3, 2022, https://www.jpost.com/opinion/article-695445.
3. "Hamas and Islamic Jihad Summer Camps in Gaza: A Framework for Jihadi Indoctrination, Military Training," Middle East Media Research Institute, June 28, 2021, https://www.memri.org/reports/hamas-and-islamic-jihad-summer-camps-gaza-framework-jihadi-indoctrination-military-training.
4. Joe Truzman, "Islamic Jihad Begins Military Summer Camp for Palestinian Youth," Foundation for Defense of Democracies, accessed May 28, 2024, https://www.fdd.org/

analysis/2023/06/13/islamic-jihad-begins-military-summer-camp-for-palestinian-youth; "Fatah Summer Campers in the Nablus District Undergo Military Training," Meir Amit Intelligence and Terrorism Information Center, July 31, 2022, https://www.terrorism-info. org.il/en/fatah-summer-campers-in-the-nablus-district-undergo-military-training/.

5. Nan Jacques Zilberdik, "The PA Summer Camps for Terror and Martyrdom," Palestinian Media Watch, August 3, 2023, https://palwatch.org/page/34418.

6. "Hamas' Indoctrination of Children to Jihad, Martyrdom, Hatred of Jews," MEMRI, November 3, 2023, https://www.memri.org/reports/hamas-indoctrination-children-jihad-martyrdom-hatred-jews; Bethania Palma, "Did Gaza Preschoolers Perform a Mock Execution of an Israeli Soldier?," Snopes, June 6, 2018, https://www.snopes.com/news/2018/06/06/gaza-preschoolers-mock-execution-israeli-soldier/; Steve Israel, "The Roots of Hamas' Terror Attack Can Be Found in Gaza's Schools," *Forward*, October 25, 2023, https://forward.com/opinion/566841/hamas-schools-indoctrination-antisemitic-textbooks-gaza/.

7. Itamar Marcus and Nan Jacques Zilberdik, "Are Palestinian Mothers Genuinely Joyous Over the Deaths of Their Children as 'Martyrs' or Are They Just Keeping Up Appearances?," MEMRI, September 22, 2021, https://palwatch.org/page/29176; "Palestinian Authority Media Glorifies Murderers," Meir Amit Intelligence and Terrorism Information Center, accessed May 28, 2024, https://www.terrorism-info.org.il/en/17793/.

8. Alan Rowe, "The Temples of Dagon and Ashtoreth at Beth-Shan," *Museum Journal* 17, no. 3 (September 1926): 295–304, https://www.penn.museum/sites/journal/1392/; "Did the Canaanites Really Sacrifice Their Children?," Bible Reading Archeology, May 13, 2016, https://biblereadingarcheology.com/2016/05/13/did-the-canaanites-sacrifice-their-children/.

Chapter 19

1. Aren M. Maeir and Joe Uziel, eds., *Tell es-Safi/Gath II Excavations and Studies* (Munster, Germany: Zaphon, 2020), 24.

2. 1 Samuel 31:1–3, emphasis added.

3. James Moyer, "The Bible: Weapons and Warfare in Ancient Israel," Grace Communion International, accessed May 11, 2024, https://archive.gci.org/articles/weapons-and-warfare-in-ancient-israel/.

4. Alan Johnson, *Israel and the Palestinians: A Guide to the Debate* (n.p.: We Believe in Israel, 2020), 24; "Rocket Threat From the Gaza Strip, 2000–2007," Intelligence and Terrorism Information Center at the Israel Intelligence Heritage & Commemoration Center, December 2007, https://web.archive.org/web/20110813152324/http://www.terrorism-info.org.il/malam_multimedia/English/eng_n/html/rocket_threat_e.htm; Wikipedia, s.v. "Palestinian Rocket Attacks on Israel," modified April 24, 2024, 14:50, https://en.wikipedia.org/wiki/Palestinian_rocket_attacks_on_Israel.

5. *Oxford Languages*, s.v. "missile," accessed May 11, 2024, https://www.google.com/search?q=missile.

6. *Merriam-Webster*, s.v. "arrow," accessed May 11, 2024, https://www.merriam-webster.com/dictionary/arrow, emphasis added.

7. Daniel Whedon, "Bible Commentaries—1 Samuel 31: Whedon's Commentary on the Bible," StudyLight.org, accessed May 28, 2024, https://www.studylight.org/commentaries/eng/whe/1-samuel-31.html, emphasis added.

8. Peter Pett, "Bible Commentaries—1 Samuel 31: Pett's Commentary on the Bible," StudyLight.org, accessed May 28, 2024, https://www.studylight.org/commentaries/eng/pet/1-samuel-31.html, emphasis added.

Chapter 20

1. 1 Samuel 17:50.

2. Blue Letter Bible, s.v. "*qela'*," accessed May 28, 2024, https://www.blueletterbible.org/lexicon/h7050/nkjv/wlc/0-1/.

3. "The First Intifada Against Israel," Al Jazeera, accessed May 12, 2024, www.aljazeera.com/gallery/2023/12/8/history-illustrated-the-first-intifada-against-israel; "The First Intifada," Yplus, accessed May 12, 2024, https://yplus.ps/2023/12/26/the-first-intifada-2/; Joe Stork, "The Significance of Stones," *Middle East Report,* September/October 1988, https://merip.

org/1988/09/the-significance-of-stones/; Brian Whitaker, "Intifada 2000 Dwarfs the Original," *The Guardian,* October 26, 2000, https://www.theguardian.com/world/2000/oct/27/israel1.

4. 1 Samuel 17:51.
5. Benny Morris, *Righteous Victims* (New York: Vintage Books, 2001), emphasis added.
6. Moslih Kanaaneh et al., eds., *Palestinian Music and Song: Expression and Resistance Since 1900* (Bloomington, IN: Indiana University Press, 2013), 152, emphasis added.

Chapter 21

1. *Encyclopaedia Judaica*, 2nd ed., s.v. "Philistines," accessed May 28, 2024, https://ketab3.wordpress.com/wp-content/uploads/2014/11/encyclopaedia-judaica-v-16-pes-qu.pdf.
2. 1 Samuel 13:19.
3. Moyer, "The Bible."
4. Linah Alsaafin and Ashraf Amra, "Gaza Recycles Rubble as Israel Upholds Ban on Construction Goods," Al Jazeera, June 17, 2021, https://www.aljazeera.com/news/2021/6/17/gaza-recycles-rubble-as-israel-upholds-ban-on-construction-goods.
5. Marc Español, "Hamas Weaponry: Made in Gaza," *El Pais,* February 3, 2024, https://english.elpais.com/international/2024-02-03/hamas-weaponry-made-in-gaza.html; Brad Lendon, "How Does Hamas Get Its Weapons? A Mix of Improvisation, Resourcefulness and a Key Overseas Benefactor," CNN, October 12, 2023, https://www.cnn.com/2023/10/11/middleeast/hamas-weaponry-gaza-israel-palestine-unrest-intl-hnk-ml/index.html; Michael Biesecker, "Hamas Fights With a Patchwork of Weapons Built by Iran, China, Russia and North Korea," Associated Press, January 15, 2024, https://apnews.com/article/israel-hamas-war-guns-weapons-missiles-smuggling-adae9dae4c48059d2a3c8e5d565daa30; Daniel Sonnenfeld, "Made in Gaza: Hamas Rockets the Product of Foreign Aid and Smuggled Material," *Media Line*, December 30, 2021, https://themedialine.org/top-stories/made-in-gaza-hamas-rockets-the-product-of-foreign-aid-and-smuggled-material/.
6. "Iron Dome Family," Rafael Advanced Defense Systems, accessed May 11, 2024, https://www.rafael.co.il/iron-dome/.
7. Vasudevan Sridharan, "'Iron Spade'—Israel's New Weapon Against Hamas Terror Tunnels," *International Business Times*, August 17, 2014, https://www.ibtimes.co.uk/iron-spade-israels-new-weapon-against-hamas-terror-tunnels-1461480.
8. "Israel Completes 'Iron Wall' Underground Gaza Barrier," Al Jazeera, December 7, 2021, https://www.aljazeera.com/news/2021/12/7/israel-announces-completion-of-underground-gaza-border-barrier.
9. Yuval Azulay, "Beam Me Up: Israel's New Laser System Is a Security Game Changer," CTech, April 30, 2023, https://www.calcalistech.com/ctechnews/article/t7ac5asht.
10. "David's Sling," Rafael Advanced Defense System, accessed May 11, 2024, https://www.rafael.co.il/system/medium-long-range-defense-davids-sling/.

Chapter 23

1. Revelation 20:2, TLB, emphasis added.
2. 1 Peter 5:8, emphasis added.
3. Revelation 12:9, emphasis added.
4. Will Timmons, "Wolves in Sheep's Clothing 4: Their Paternity," Bible by Day, May 25, 2023, https://biblebyday.com/blog/wolves-in-sheeps-clothing-paternity.

Chapter 24

1. Becky Sullivan, "What Is a Kibbutz? The Roots of Israel's Communal Villages Where Violence Raged," NPR, October 12, 2023, https://www.npr.org/2023/10/12/1205284601/what-is-a-kibbutz-the-roots-of-israels-communal-villages-where-violence-raged; Liam Hoare, "Left in the Dust," *Slate*, March 17, 2015, https://slate.com/news-and-politics/2015/03/meretz-may-cease-to-exist-after-the-israeli-election-the-campaign-to-oust-benjamin-netanyahu-may-cause-chaos-on-the-israeli-left.html; Annick Cojean, "Israel, the Weissmann Family's Pioneer Dream," *Le Monde*, December 1, 2023, https://www.lemonde.fr/en/international/article/2023/12/01/israel-the-weissmanns-pioneering-dream_6305191_4.html; Chris McCullough, "Israeli Dairy Farmers Slaughtered by

Hamas as They Milked Their Cows," *Tri-State Livestock News*, October 13, 2023, https://www.tsln.com/news/israeli-dairy-farmers-slaughtered-by-hamas-as-they-milked-their-cows/; Tamar Mor Sela, "'I Moved to Israel Driven by a Strong Love for the Country. But the State Has Left Us to Fend for Ourselves,'" Times of Israel, December 30, 2023, https://www.timesofisrael.com/uprooted-guido-cohen-24-from-kibbutz-ein-hashlosha-this-is-his-story/.

2. 2 Chronicles 11:11.

3. 2 Chronicles 11:10.

4. Mark Weiss, "Israel Completes Construction of 'Iron Wall' Around Gaza," *Irish Times*, December 8, 2021, https://www.irishtimes.com/news/world/middle-east/israel-completes-construction-of-iron-wall-around-gaza-1.4749888/.

5. Times of Israel and *Agence France-Presse* staff, "Years of Subterfuge, High-Tech Barrier Paralyzed: How Hamas Busted Israel's Defenses," Times of Israel, October 11, 2023, https://www.timesofisrael.com/years-of-subterfuge-high-tech-barrier-paralyzed-how-hamas-busted-israels-defenses/.

Chapter 25

1. "Sea Peoples (Bronze Age)," The History Files, accessed May 28, 2024, https://www.historyfiles.co.uk/KingListsMiddEast/AnatoliaSeaPeoples.htm.

2. 1 Samuel 7:13, NIV, emphasis added.

3. 2 Chronicles 21:16–17.

4. 2 Chronicles 28:16–18.

5. Patrick Reevell, "Reporter's Notebook: In Israeli Kibbutz Rampaged by Hamas, Volunteers Still Cleaning Blood From Homes," ABC News, November 15, 2023, https://abcnews.go.com/International/israeli-kibbutz-kfar-aza-volunteers-cleaning-blood/story?id=104848791.

6. Noga Tarnopolsky, Shira Rubin, and Miriam Berger, "'Humiliated and Defeated': Fear, Shock Grip Israel After Hamas Assault," *Washington Post*, October 7, 2023, https://www.washingtonpost.com/world/2023/10/07/israel-gaza-hamas-attack-netanyahu/.

Chapter 26

1. 2 Chronicles 28:18, emphasis added.

2. "Negev Desert," Tourist Israel, accessed May 28, 2024, https://www.touristisrael.com/negev/295/.

3. "Joshua 15," STEP Bible, accessed May 28, 2024, https://www.stepbible.org/?q=version=KD%7Creference=Jos.15.

4. "Bible Commentaries: Joshua 15," StudyLight.org, accessed May 28, 2024, https://www.studylight.org/commentaries/eng/bnb/joshua-15.html#verses-21.

5. Joshua 15:33, 46–47, author's translation, emphasis added.

6. Jacoba Urist, "Israeli Music Festival That Hamas Attacked on 7 October Is Re-Created in New York Exhibit," *Art Newspaper*, April 22, 2024, https://www.theartnewspaper.com/2024/04/22/nova-music-festival-israel-hamas-war-exhibition-new-york.

Chapter 27

1. 2 Chronicles 21:17, emphasis added.

2. 1 Samuel 30:3–4.

3. Joel 3:4, 6, emphasis added.

4. "Benson Commentary: Amos 1:6–8," Bible Hub, accessed May 23, 2024, https://biblehub.com/commentaries/amos/1-6.htm, emphasis added.

5. Josef Federman and Issam Adwan, "Hamas Surprise Attack Out of Gaza Stuns Israel and Leaves Hundreds Dead in Fighting, Retaliation," Associated Press, October 7, 2023, https://apnews.com/article/israel-palestinians-gaza-hamas-rockets-airstrikes-tel-aviv-11fb98655c256d54ecb5329284fc37d2.

6. "Hamas, Islamic Jihad: Holding Hostages Is a War Crime," Human Rights Watch, updated October 20, 2023, https://www.hrw.org/news/2023/10/19/hamas-islamic-jihad-holding-hostages-war-crime.

7. "Benson Commentary," Bible Hub, emphasis added.

8. "Benson Commentary," Bible Hub, emphasis added.

9. Newsnation Live, "Israeli Grandmother Held Hostage 'Won't Let Them Humiliate Her,'" YouTube, October 16, 2023, https://www.youtube.com/watch?v=xKKS0wv5-_0; Roni Caryn Rabin, "Families Fear for the Health of Ailing, Frail Israelis Held Hostage," *New York Times*, November 21, 2023, https://www.nytimes.com/2023/11/21/world/ middleeast/hamas-hostages-health.html; Raphaelle Bacqué, "A Hostage Freed by Hamas Campaigned All Her Life for Palestinian Rights," *Le Monde*, October 27, 2023, https://www.lemonde.fr/en/international/article/2023/10/27/a-hostage-freed-by-hamas-campaigned-all-her-life-for-palestinian-rights_6207124_4.html.

10. 1 Samuel 30:3.

11. Sue Surkes, "Kibbutz Kfar Aza, Devastated on October 7, Becomes a Grim Place of Pilgrimage," Times of Israel, January 5, 2024, https://www.timesofisrael.com/kibbutz-kfar-aza-devastated-on-october-7-becomes-a-grim-place-of-pilgrimage/.

12. "Now-Freed Hostage Seen in Video Fighting Against Her 7 Hamas Kidnappers on October 7," Times of Israel, December 5, 2023, https://www.timesofisrael.com/footage-shows-now-freed-hostage-fighting-against-hamas-kidnappers-on-october-7/; "Why Hamas Took So Many People Hostage—and How That Complicates Israel's Response," *Radio Canada International,* October 10, 2023, https://ici.radio-canada.ca/rci/en/ news/2016715/why-hamas-took-so-many-people-hostage-and-how-that-complicates-israels-response.

13. Rabin, "Families Fear for the Health of Ailing, Frail Israelis Held Hostage."

Chapter 28

1. Revelation 12:4.

Chapter 29

1. Ezekiel 32:23, emphasis added.

2. Ezekiel 32:24, emphasis added.

3. Ezekiel 32:26, emphasis added.

4. Ezekiel 32:30, emphasis added.

5. 1 Samuel 17:11, emphasis added.

6. Robert Bain, "Women, Fundamentalism and Terror: Echoes of Ancient Assyria," Heinrich Böll Stiftung, February 9, 2017, https://lb.boell.org/en/2017/02/09/women-fundamentalism-and-terror-echoes-ancient-assyria.

7. David Makovsky, "Death of a Symbol: Yasser Arafat Leaves Behind a Complicated Legacy of Nationalism and Terrorism," The Washington Institute for Near East Policy, November 11, 2004, https://www.washingtoninstitute.org/policy-analysis/death-symbol-yasser-arafat-leaves-behind-complicated-legacy-nationalism-and; David Holden, "Article 7," *New York Times*, March 23, 1975, https://www.nytimes.com/1975/03/23/archives/ article-7-no-title-arafat.html; Kali Robinson, "Who Governs the Palestinians?," Council on Foreign Relations, updated March 19, 2024, https://www.cfr.org/backgrounder/who-governs-palestinians.

8. Jewish Telegraph Agency, "Was Hamas's Attack on Saturday the Bloodiest Day for Jews Since the Holocaust?," Times of Israel, October 9, 2023, https://www.timesofisrael.com/ was-hamass-attack-on-saturday-the-bloodiest-day-for-jews-since-the-holocaust/; Avner Cohen et al., "Deadliest Day for Jews Since the Holocaust Shakes the Foundations of Israel as a Safe Homeland, Says Double Macarthur-Winning Historian," *Fortune*, October 15, 2023, https://fortune.com/2023/10/15/deadliest-day-for-jews-since-holocaust-shakes-zionism-israeli-historian-says/.

9. Ezekiel 32:2, emphasis added.

Chapter 30

1. Harriet Sherwood, "How the Hamas Attack on the Supernova Festival in Israel Unfolded," *The Guardian*, October 9, 2023, https://www.theguardian.com/world/2023/ oct/09/how-the-hamas-attack-on-the-supernova-festival-in-israel-unfolded; "The Nova Music Festival October 7," The Nova Music Festival Exhibition, accessed May 11, 2024, https://www.nova0629exhibition.com/aboutthenovafestival.

2. American Jewish Committee, "Tal Shimony Survived the Hamas Attack on the Nova Music Festival: Hear Her Story of Courage, Resilience, and Remembrance," February

1, 2024, in *People of the Pod*, podcast, https://www.ajc.org/news/podcast/tal-shimony-survived-the-hamas-attack-on-the-nova-music-festival-hear-her-story-of-courage; Sherwood, "How the Hamas Attack on the Supernova Festival in Israel Unfolded"; Loveday Morris et al., "How a Night of Dancing and Revelry in Israel Turned Into a Massacre," *Washington Post*, October 8, 2023, https://www.washingtonpost.com/world/2023/10/08/israel-festival-attack-gaza-militants/; "Survivors Confront Their Trauma at Site of Hamas Massacre of Music Festival," Times of Israel, April 14, 2024, https://www.timesofisrael.com/survivors-confront-their-trauma-at-site-of-hamas-massacre-of-music-festival/; Mustafa Abu Ganeyeh and Leonardo Benassatto, "'I Was Reborn' on Oct. 7 Says Survivor of Hamas Attack on Israeli Festival," Reuters, October 31, 2023, https://www.reuters.com/world/middle-east/i-was-reborn-oct-7-says-survivor-hamas-attack-israeli-festival-2023-10-31/; Renee Ghert-Zand, "Sheryl Sandberg's New Film Testifies to Hamas's Brutal Sexual Violence on October 7," Times of Israel, April 26, 2024, https://www.timesofisrael.com/sheryl-sandbergs-new-film-testifies-to-hamass-brutal-sexual-violence-on-october-7/; "Israeli Forensic Teams Describe Signs of Torture, Abuse," Reuters, October 15, 2023, https://www.reuters.com/world/middle-east/israeli-forensic-teams-describe-signs-torture-abuse-2023-10-15/.

3. Agence France-Presse, "Survivor Recalls Watching Israel Music Fest Massacre From Atop Tree," NDTV, November 11, 2023, https://www.ndtv.com/world-news/survivor-recalls-watching-israel-music-fest-massacre-from-atop-tree-4565949; The Independent, "Festival Goers Hide in Undergrowth During Deadly Hamas Attack," YouTube, accessed May 11, 2024, https://www.youtube.com/watch?v=8uPkD_JJx9w; David Browne, Nancy Dillon, and Kory Grow, "They Wanted to Dance in Peace. And They Got Slaughtered," *Rolling Stone*, October 15, 2023, https://www.rollingstone.com/music/music-features/hamas-israel-nova-music-festival-massacre-1234854306/; Sumanti Sen, "Exclusive: 'We Pretended to Be Dead, but They Found Us and Then...,' Israel Music Fest Survivor Recounts Horror," *Hindustan Times*, October 10, 2023, https://www.hindustantimes.com/world-news/exclusive-we-pretended-to-be-dead-but-they-found-us-and-then-israel-music-fest-survivor-recounts-horror-101696902733579.html; American Jewish Committee, "Tal Shimony Survived the Hamas Attack on the Nova Music Festival"; "Nova Music Festival," October7.org, accessed May 28, 2024, https://www.october7.org/nova-festival; Sinéad Baker, "Israeli Festival Attendees Played Dead for Hours to Try to Stay Alive During Hamas Attack," Business Insider, October 9, 2023, https://www.businessinsider.com/israel-festival-attendees-played-dead-for-hours-during-hamas-attack-2023-10.

4. 1 Samuel 13:6.

5. Robert Jamieson, A. R. Fausset, and David Brown, "1 Samuel 13:6," Bible Hub, accessed May 28, 2024, https://biblehub.com/commentaries/1_samuel/13-6.htm.

6. Jamieson, Fausset, and Brown, "1 Samuel 13:6."

7. Madhur Sharma, "Israel-Hamas War: How Hamas's Mass Murder Unfolded at Desert Music Festival, Survivors Recount Hours of Horrors," *Outlook*, updated October 10, 2023, https://www.outlookindia.com/international/israel-hamas-war-how-hamas-mass-murder-unfolded-at-desert-music-festival-survivors-recount-hours-of-horrors-news-323643, emphasis added.

8. John Gill, "1 Samuel 13:6," John Gill's Exposition of the Bible, Bible Study Tools, accessed May 28, 2024, https://www.biblestudytools.com/commentaries/gills-exposition-of-the-bible/1-samuel-13-6.html, emphasis added.

9. Deborah Danan, "'The Holocaust, All Over Again': The Supernova Festival Massacre, in Survivors' Words," Times of Israel, October 12, 2023, https://www.timesofisrael.com/the-holocaust-all-over-again-the-supernova-festival-massacre-in-survivors-words/, emphasis added.

10. Gill, "1 Samuel 13:6," emphasis added.

11. "Release of Two More Hostages Gives Some Hope to Families of Others Abducted in the Attack on Israel," Associated Press, updated October 23, 2023, https://apnews.com/article/hostages-israel-hamas-war-what-to-know-406920c384818fa4fe3525327adf3f50, emphasis added.

12. Eliza Mackintosh et al., "How a Rave Celebrating Life Turned Into a Frenzied Massacre," CNN, October 14, 2023, https://www.cnn.com/interactive/2023/10/middleeast/hamas-music-festival-attack-investigation-cmd-intl/, emphasis added.

13. David Guzik, "1 Samuel 14—Victory Over the Philistines," Enduring Word, 2022, https://enduringword.com/bible-commentary/1-samuel-14/, emphasis added.

14. "5 Hostages of Hamas Are Free, Offering Some Hope to Families of More Than 200 Still Captive," Arab News, November 4, 2023, https://www.arabnews.com/node/2402946/amp, emphasis added.

15. 1 Samuel 14:11, emphasis added.

16. "1 Samuel 14 Commentary," Precept Austin, accessed May 28, 2024, https://www.preceptaustin.org/1-samuel-14-commentary, emphasis added.

17. Joel B. Pollak, "Family of Russian-Israeli Hostage: He Escaped Hamas, Was Recaptured by Palestinian Civilians," Breitbart, November 27, 2023, https://www.breitbart.com/middle-east/2023/11/27/family-of-russian-israeli-hostage-he-escaped-hamas-was-recaptured-by-palestinian-civilians/, emphasis added.

18. Ganeyeh and Benassatto, "I Was Reborn," emphasis added.

19. Sam Mednick, "New Signs Emerge of 'Widespread' Sexual Crimes by Hamas, as Netanyahu Alleges Global Indifference," Associated Press, December 6, 2023, https://apnews.com/article/sexual-assault-hamas-oct-7-attack-rape-bb06b950bb6794affb8d468cd283bc51, emphasis added.

20. Alexi Demetriadi, "Sydney's Jewish Community: 'Me Too, Unless You're a Jew?,'" The Australian, December 17, 2023, https://www.theaustralian.com.au/nation/sydneys-jewish-community-me-too-unless-youre-a-jew/news-story/cca8e4e7f99971d053af1e9fac7b8b67, emphasis added.

21. Survived to Tell (@survived.to.tell), Survivor stories from Israel, Instagram, accessed May 28, 2024, https://www.instagram.com/p/CyPA8sRIsuu/, emphasis added.

22. Katie Bain, "Artist Manager Describes Israeli Rave Massacre: 'It Turned Into a Nightmare,'" Billboard, October 8, 2023, https://www.billboard.com/music/music-news/israel-music-festival-attack-artist-manager-account-massacre-1235436829/, emphasis added.

23. 1 Samuel 13:6, emphasis added.

Chapter 31

1. Isaiah 20:2.

2. Isaiah 20:3–4.

3. Liza Rozovsky, "15 Witnesses, Three Confessions, a Pattern of Naked Dead Bodies. All the Evidence of Hamas Rape on October 7," Haaretz, April 18, 2024, https://www.haaretz.com/israel-news/2024-04-18/ty-article-magazine/witnesses-confessions-naked-dead-bodies-all-the-evidence-of-hamas-rape-on-oct-7/0000018e-f114-d92e-abfe-f77f7e3f0000.

4. "Shani Louk, 22: German-Israeli Partygoer Had 'a Huge Heart,'" Times of Israel, November 3, 2023, https://www.timesofisrael.com/shani-louk-22-german-israelis-kidnap-video-seen-globally/.

5. Watson's Biblical and Theological Dictionary, s.v. "Captives," StudyLight.org, accessed May 28, 2024, https://www.studylight.org/dictionaries/eng/wtd/c/captives.html.

Chapter 32

1. 1 Samuel 31:8–10.

2. 1 Chronicles 10:9–10.

3. "Father of Fallen Soldier: Terrorist Decapitated My Son, Tried to Sell Head for $10,000," Times of Israel, January 18, 2024, https://www.timesofisrael.com/father-of-fallen-soldier-terrorist-decapitated-my-son-tried-to-sell-head-for-10000/; Qanta Ahmed, "I Saw the Children Hamas Beheaded With My Own Eyes. Shame on Queen Rania," Newsweek, December 27, 2023, https://www.newsweek.com/i-saw-children-hamas-beheaded-my-own-eyes-shame-queen-rania-opinion-1855472.

Chapter 33

1. Priyanka Chandani, "American Artist in Israel for a Wedding Cleared Dead Bodies After Hamas Attack: 'It Is Incredibly Hard to Narrate This, but I Will Try,'" *Orato*, November 27, 2023, https://orato.world/2023/11/27/american-artist-in-israel-for-a-wedding-cleared-dead-bodies-after-hamas-attack-it-is-incredibly-hard-to-narrate-this-but-i-will-try/; Aaron Poris, "Evidence on Display at Israel's Forensic Pathology Center Confirms Hamas' Atrocities," Medialine, November 6, 2023, https://themedialine.org/top-stories/evidence-on-display-at-israels-forensic-pathology-center-confirms-hamas-atrocities/; Jeffrey Gettleman, Anat Schwartz, and Adam Sella, "'Screams Without Words': How Hamas Weaponized Sexual Violence on Oct. 7," *New York Times*, updated March 25, 2024, https://www.nytimes.com/2023/12/28/world/middleeast/oct-7-attacks-hamas-israel-sexual-violence.html.
2. 2 Kings 8:12, emphasis added.
3. Grzegorz Rossoliński-Liebe, "Holocaust Amnesia: The Ukrainian Diaspora and the Genocide of the Jews," in *German Yearbook of Contemporary History*, vol. 1 (Berlin: De Gruyter Oldenburg, 2016), 107–143, https://muse.jhu.edu/article/846190/pdf.

Chapter 35

1. Judges 16:2.
2. Judges 16:12, 20.
3. Judges 16:21.
4. Guest Contributor, "Israel Shows Foreign Press Footage of Hamas Massacre," EU Reporter, October 25, 2023, https://www.eureporter.co/world/israel/palestinian-authority-pa/hamas/2023/10/25/israel-shows-foreign-press-footage-of-hamas-massacre/; Frank Hofmann, "Israel Shows Hamas Terror Videos to Document Horrific Attack," Deutsche Welle, November 4, 2023, https://www.dw.com/en/israel-shows-hamas-terror-videos-to-document-horrific-attack/a-67305110; Joe Barnes, "Israel Yet to Identify Baby Murdered by Hamas in Photograph That Shocked World," *The Telegraph*, October 13, 2023, https://www.telegraph.co.uk/world-news/2023/10/13/israel-still-trying-to-identify-baby-murdered-by-hamas/.
5. Amnon Sofrin, "The Intelligence Failure of October 7—Roots and Lessons," *Jerusalem Strategic Tribune*, November 2023, https://jstribune.com/sofrim-the-intelligence-failure-of-october-7-roots-and-lessons/, emphasis added.
6. Aric Toler, "How Hamas Attacked Israel's Communications Tower," *New York Times*, October 10, 2023, https://www.nytimes.com/2023/10/10/world/middleeast/hamas-israel-attack-gaza.html, emphasis added.
7. Shira Rubin and Loveday Morris, "How Hamas Broke Through Israel's Border Defenses During Oct. 7 Attack," *Washington Post*, October 27, 2023, https://www.washingtonpost.com/world/2023/10/27/hamas-attack-israel-october-7-hostages/, emphasis added.
8. Judges 16:21, HCSB.
9. Daniel Ben-David, "Sheryl Sandberg Film Details Horrific Sexual Crimes Committed by Hamas on October 7," *Jewish Chronicle*, April 26, 2024, https://www.thejc.com/news/israel/sheryl-sandberg-film-details-horrific-sexual-crimes-committed-by-hamas-on-october-7-gxmsu7bz.; Howard Goller, "Freed Israeli Hostages Tell Families of Beatings and Death Threats," Reuters, November 29, 2023, https://www.reuters.com/world/middle-east/freed-israeli-hostages-tell-families-beatings-death-threats-2023-11-29/.

Chapter 36

1. Judges 16:21, emphasis added.
2. Judges 16:21.
3. "Gaza Tunnels Stretch at Least 350 Miles, Far Longer Than Past Estimate—Report," Times of Israel, January 16, 2024, https://www.timesofisrael.com/gaza-tunnels-stretch-at-least-350-miles-far-longer-than-past-estimate-report/; Peter Saidel, Summer Said, and Anat Peled, "Hamas Took More Than 200 Hostages From Israel. Here's What We Know," *Wall Street Journal*, updated May 8, 2024, https://www.wsj.com/world/middle-east/hamas-hostages-israel-gaza-41432124.
4. Amos 1:6, emphasis added.

5. Amos 1:6, NIV, emphasis added.
6. Amos 1:6, NLT, emphasis added.
7. Charles John Ellicott, "Curse on Philistia," *Ellicott's Commentary for English Readers*, Bible Hub, accessed May 28, 2024, https://biblehub.com/commentaries/amos/1-6.htm, emphasis added.
8. Amos 1:6, AMP, emphasis added.

Chapter 37

1. Judges 16:23.
2. Judges 16:25.
3. Drew Harwell and Elizabeth Dwoskin, "Hamas Turns to Social Media to Get Its Message Out—and to Spread Fear," *Washington Post*, October 18, 2023, https://www.washingtonpost.com/technology/2023/10/18/hamas-social-media-terror/; Camilla Turner, "Israeli Hostage Paraded Through Gaza Like a 'Trophy,'" *The Telegraph*, March 13, 2024, https://www.telegraph.co.uk/world-news/2024/03/13/israeli-held-hostage-by-hamas-paraded-through-gaza-trophy/.
4. Isaiah 14:29, emphasis added.
5. Isaiah 14:29, KJV, emphasis added.
6. 2 Samuel 1:19–20, emphasis added.
7. Ezekiel 25:6, emphasis added.
8. Judges 16:24.
9. Aaron Feis, "Watch: Gazan Mob Swarms Hamas Hostages With Shouts of 'God Is Great,'" MSN, November 29, 2023, https://www.msn.com/en-us/news/world/watch-gaza-residents-swarm-israeli-hostages-shout-allahu-akbar-during-hamas-handover/ar-AA1kJR; Hadas Gold et al., "Hamas Captures Hostages as Israelis Share Photos of Those Missing," CNN, updated October 8, 2023, https://www.cnn.com/2023/10/07/middleeast/hostages-hamas-israel-gaza/index.html.
10. "Palestinians in Gaza and the West Bank Celebrate on October 7, Hand Out Sweets, Fire Guns in the Air, Following Hamas's Invasion and Massacre of Israeli Civilians in the Gaza Envelope," MEMRI TV, October 7, 2023, https://www.memri.org/tv/palestinians-gaza-west-bank-celebrate-october-seven-massacre-hand-out-sweets-fire-guns/.
11. "Education for Terrorism in Palestinian Schools: 2023 Israel-Hamas War," Impact-se, November 2023, https://www.impact-se.org/wp-content/uploads/Education-for-Terrorism-in-Palestinian-Schools.pdf.

Chapter 38

1. Judges 16:25–26.
2. Judges 16:27.
3. Judges 16:23.
4. Arieh Elad, "Pico, Hamas Terror Flipped the Switch on Happiest Holiday of the Year," Boiling Point, December 7, 2023, https://shalhevetboilingpoint.com/outside-news/2023/12/07/from-israel-to-pico-hamas-terror-flips-the-switch-on-happiest-holiday-of-the-year/.
5. Judges 16:23.
6. Judges 16:23, emphasis added.
7. "Stories That Teach: Shmini Atzeret," Orthodox Union, June 29, 2006, https://www.ou.org/holidays/stories_that_teach/.
8. Yoav Zitun, "New Estimate: About 3,000 Terrorists Infiltrated Israel on October 7," Ynetnews.com, November 1, 2023, https://www.ynetnews.com/article/hytrcje76.
9. Judges 16:27, emphasis added.

Chapter 39

1. Philip Mattar, *The Mufti of Jerusalem Al-Hajj Amin al-Husayni and the Palestinian National Movement*, rev. ed. (New York: Columbia University Press, 1988), 6, 10; *Holocaust Encyclopedia*, s.v. "Hajj Amin Al-Husayni: Arab Nationalist and Muslim Leader," United States Holocaust Memorial Museum, accessed May 12, 2024, https://encyclopedia.ushmm.org/content/en/article/hajj-amin-al-husayni-arab-nationalist-and-muslim-leader.

2. Oren Kessler, "Herbert Samuel's Secret 1937 Testimony on the Infamous Mufti of Jerusalem Revealed," Times of Israel, August 19, 2023, https://www.timesofisrael.com/uk-reveals-herbert-samuels-secret-1937-testimony-on-the-infamous-mufti-of-jerusalem/.

3. Nadav Shragai, "3. Father of the Lie: Haj Amin al-Husseini," Jerusalem Center for Public Affairs, accessed May 12, 2024, https://jcpa.org/al-aksa-is-in-danger-libel/al-aksa-libel-advocate-mufti-haj-amin-al-husseini/.

4. John Rosenthal, "The Mufti and the Holocaust," Hoover Institution, March 28, 2008, https://www.hoover.org/research/mufti-and-holocaust; Shragai, "Father of the Lie."

5. Bernard Lewis, *The Jews of Islam* (Princeton, NJ: Princeton University Press, 1984), 190; "Full Official Record: What the Mufti Said to Hitler," Times of Israel, October 21, 2015, https://www.timesofisrael.com/full-official-record-what-the-mufti-said-to-hitler/; Ben Cohen, "The Mufti and the Holocaust, Revisited," *Algemeiner*, October 23, 2015, https://www.algemeiner.com/2015/10/23/the-mufti-and-the-holocaust-revisited/.

6. Steven Wagner, "Unmasking Hajj Amin al-Husseini Through His Wartime Letters and Diaries," Brunel University London, December 10, 2023, https://www.brunel.ac.uk/research/projects/unmasking-hajj-amin-al-husseini-through-his-wartime-letters-and-diaries; *Holocaust Encyclopedia*, s.v. "Hajj Amin Al-Husayni: Wartime Propagandist," accessed May 28, 2024, https://encyclopedia.ushmm.org/content/en/article/hajj-amin-al-husayni-wartime-propagandist; Rosenthal, "The Mufti and the Holocaust"; Daniel Carpi, "The Rescue of Jews in the Italian Zone of Occupied Croatia," Shoah Resource Center, International School for Holocaust Studies, accessed May 14, 2024, https://www.yadvashem.org/odot_pdf/Microsoft%20Word%20-%204803.pdf.

7. Jeffrey Herf, "Haj Amin al-Husseini, the Nazis and the Holocaust: The Origins, Nature and Aftereffects of Collaboration," Jerusalem Center for Public Affairs, January 5, 2016, https://jcpa.org/article/haj-amin-al-husseini-the-nazis-and-the-holocaust-the-origins-nature-and-aftereffects-of-collaboration/; Shaul Shay, *Islamic Terror and the Balkans* (New Brunswick, NJ: Transaction, December 31, 2011), 33; David G. Dalin and John F. Rothman, *Icon of Evil: Hitler's Mufti and the Rise of Radical Islam* (New York: Random House, 2008), 60; George Lepre, *Himmler's Bosnian Division: The Waffen-SS Handschar Division, 1943–1945* (Atglen, PA: Schiffer Military History, June 10, 2008), 32.

8. Wolfgang G. Schwanitz, "Amin al-Husaini and the Holocaust. What Did the Grand Mufti Know?," *World Politics Review*, May 8, 2008, https://www.worldpoliticsreview.com/amin-al-husaini-and-the-holocaust-what-did-the-grand-mufti-know/.

9. Norman A. Stillman, "Frenchmen, Jews, or Arabs? Jews of the Arab World Between European Colonialism, Zionism, and Arab Nationalism," in *Judaism and Islam: Boundaries, Communications, and Interaction: Essays in Honor of William M. Brinner* (Brill: August 4, 2021), 134, emphasis added.

10. Jeffrey Herf, "Nazi Antisemitism & Islamist Hate," *Tablet*, July 5, 2022, https://www.tabletmag.com/sections/history/articles/the-nazi-roots-of-islamist-hate; "Backgrounder: Hajj Amin al-Husseini," Middle East Forum, October 30, 2015, https://www.meforum.org/5597/backgrounder-hajj-amin-husseini; Matthias Küntzel, "The 1948 Arab War Against Israel: An Aftershock of World War II?," *Fathom*, June 2023, https://fathomjournal.org/the-1948-arab-war-against-israel-an-aftershock-of-world-war-ii/.

11. Ben Sales, "Who Was Haj Amin al-Husseini, the Grand Mufti of Jerusalem?," *Haaretz*, October 22, 2015, https://www.haaretz.com/israel-news/2015-10-22/ty-article/who-exactly-was-the-grand-mufti-of-jerusalem/0000017f-dc83-db5a-a57f-dcebf3770000.

12. "Arabs Pick Mufti to Head Assembly; Delegates at Gaza Gathering Give a Confidence Vote to Provisional Government," *New York Times*, October 2, 1948, https://www.nytimes.com/1948/10/02/archives/arabs-pick-mufti-to-head-assembly-delegates-at-gaza-gathering-give.html.

13. That leader was Hassan al-Banna. (Herf, "Haj Amin al-Husseini.")

14. Danny Rubinstein, "Yasser Arafat, 1929-2004: Father of the Palestinian Nation," *Haaretz*, November 9, 2004, https://www.haaretz.com/2004-11-09/ty-article/yasser-arafat-1929-2004-father-of-the-palestinian-nation/0000017f-e0c0-d568-ad7f-f3eb69e00000.

15. Wolfgang G. Schwanitz, "Twofold Germans and Islamism in the Cold War," *Outremers* 98, no. 372–373 (2011): 63–94, https://www.persee.fr/doc/outre_1631-0438_2011_num_98_372_4571.

16. David G. Dalin, "Hitler's Mufti," *First Things*, August 2005, https://www.firstthings.com/article/2005/08/hitlers-mufti.

Chapter 40

1. *Oxford Bibliographies*, s.v. "Hasan al-Banna," December 14, 2009, https://www.oxfordbibliographies.com/display/document/obo-9780195390155/obo-9780195390155-0006.xml.

2. Gudrun Kramer, "Hasan al-Banna," in *Makers of the Muslim World* (Oneworld: 2013), 19, 35, 40–43, 48; "History of the Muslim Brotherhood in Egypt," Ikhwanweb (The Muslim Brotherhood's Official English website), accessed May 12, 2024, https://ikhwanweb.com/history-of-the-muslim-brotherh/; *Encyclopaedia Britannica*, s.v. "Muslim Brotherhood," April 11, 2024, https://www.britannica.com/topic/Muslim-Brotherhood.

3. *Holocaust Encyclopedia*, s.v. "The Nazi Party," accessed May 28, 2024, https://encyclopedia.ushmm.org/content/en/article/the-nazi-party-1; "Hassan al-Banna Praises Hitler as a Model for Attaining Fortune, Influence and Success," Point de Bascule Canada, February 4, 2014, https://pointdebasculecanada.ca/hassan-al-banna-praises-hitler-as-a-model-for-attaining-fortune-influence-and-success/; John Loftus, "The Muslim Brotherhood, Nazis and Al-Qaeda," *Jewish Community News*, April 10, 2006, https://www.ocnus.net/artman2/publish/Dark_Side_4/The-Muslim-Brotherhood-Nazis-and-Al-Qaeda.shtml.

4. David Patterson, "Islamic Jihad and the Holocaust: From Hitler to Hamas," SHERM 4, no. 1 (Summer 2022): 65, https://www.shermjournal.org/vol-4-no-1; "The Qatari Regime, Hamas and the Muslim Brotherhood: The Globalisation of Antisemitism and Anti Democracy," The Institute for the Study of Global Antisemitism and Policy, 2023, https://isgap.org/wp-content/uploads/2023/11/QATAR-REGIME_HAMAS_MB_FINAL.pdf; Amir Darwish, "Fascistic Tendencies in the Muslim Brotherhood," *Fair Observer*, November 18, 2022, https://www.fairobserver.com/politics/fascistic-tendencies-in-the-muslim-brotherhood/#; David Patterson, "The Muslim Brotherhood and the Evolution of Jihadist Antisemitism," Flashpoint, January 17, 2018, https://isgap.org/flashpoint/the-muslim-brotherhood-and-the-evolution-of-jihadist-antisemitism/; Matthias Küntzel, "National Socialism and Anti-Semitism in the Arab World," *Jewish Political Studies Review* 17, no. 1/2 (Spring 2005), https://jcpa.org/article/national-socialism-and-anti-semitism-in-the-arab-world/; Amichai Chikli (@AmichaiChikli), "This Amazing document from the British archive reveals, Hassan al-Banna, the founder of the Muslim Brotherhood, served as a spy for Nazi Germany," X, May 6, 2024, 11:07 a.m., https://twitter.com/AmichaiChikli/status/1787514542248866234; "Saudi Arabia Escalates the Conflict With the Muslim Brotherhood (MB): Saudi Government Daily Claims MB Founder Hassan Al-Bana Worked for the Nazis," MEMRI, February 18, 2020, https://www.memri.org/reports/saudi-arabia-escalates-conflict-muslim-brotherhood-mb-saudi-government-daily-claims-mb; John C Zimmerman, "Book Review of Martyn Frampton, The Muslim Brotherhood and the West: A History of Enmity and Engagement," *Current Research Journal of Social Sciences and Humanities* 7, no. 1 (2024), https://bit.ly/49Pwww5.

5. Evin Ismail, "The Antisemitic Origins of Islamist Violence: A Study of the Muslim Brotherhood and the Islamic State," doctoral thesis, Uppsala (Sweden) University, 2022, 14–15, 227, https://uu.diva-portal.org/smash/get/diva2:1650054/FULLTEXT01.pdf; "Nazi Antisemitism & Islamist Hate"; Markos Zografos, "Genocidal Antisemitism: A Core Ideology of the Muslim Brotherhood," *Occasional Paper Series* (Institute for the Study of Global Antisemitism and Policy) 4 (2021): 9, 18–19, https://isgap.org/wp-content/uploads/2021/06/GenocidalAntisemitism-Markos-Zografos.pdf.

6. Joseph S. Spoerl, "Parallels Between Nazi and Islamist Anti-Semitism," *Jewish Political Studies Review* 31, no. 1/2 (2020): 214, https://www.jstor.org/stable/26870795.

7. *Counter Terrorism Guide*, s.v. "Hamas," Office of the Director of National Intelligence, accessed May 12, 2024, https://www.dni.gov/nctc/ftos/hamas_fto.html.

8. *Counter Terrorism Guide*, "Hamas."

Chapter 41

1. Samia Nakhoul, "How Hamas Secretly Built a 'Mini-Army' to Fight Israel," Reuters, October 16, 2023, https://www.reuters.com/world/middle-east/how-hamas-secretly-built-mini-army-fight-israel-2023-10-13/.
2. Jodi Rudoren, "In Jerusalem Unrest, Signs of a 'Run-Over Intifada' for the 21st Century," *New York Times,* Nov. 6, 2014, https://www.nytimes.com/2014/11/07/world/middleeast/israel-palestinians-jerusalem-unrest-al-aqsa.html.
3. "Hamas Covenant 1988: The Covenant of the Islamic Resistance Movement," Lillian Goldman Law Library, Yale Law School, accessed May 28, 2024, https://avalon.law.yale.edu/20th_century/hamas.asp, emphasis added.
4. "The Charter of Allah: The Platform of the Islamic Resistance Movement (Hamas)," Federation of American Scientists, accessed May 12, 2024, https://irp.fas.org/world/para/docs/880818.htm, emphasis added.
5. "Hamas Covenant 1988," Lillian Goldman Law Library, emphasis added.
6. "Hamas Covenant 1988," Lillian Goldman Law Library, emphasis added.
7. "Hamas Covenant 1988," Lillian Goldman Law Library, emphasis added.
8. "Hamas Covenant 1988," Lillian Goldman Law Library, emphasis added. ("Ye shall be overcome, and thrown together into hell" is credited in the charter to Al-Imran, verse 12, in the Koran.)
9. "The Charter of Allah," Federation of American Scientists, emphasis added. (The charter credits this line to two famed medieval Islamic scholars who compiled *hadiths*, Al-Bukhari and Imam Muslim.)
10. J. Fitz-Gibbon, "Arabic Copy of Adolf Hitler's 'Mein Kampf' Found Inside Child's Room in Gaza," *New York Post*, November 12, 2023, https://nypost.com/2023/11/12/news/arabic-copy-of-adolf-hitlers-mein-kampf-found-inside-childs-room-in-gaza.

Chapter 42

1. *Encyclopaedia Britannica,* s.v. "Hamas: Definition, History, Ideology, & Facts," updated May 10, 2024, https://www.britannica.com/topic/Hamas.
2. *Encyclopaedia Britannica*, s.v. "Hamas"; Muhammad Maqdsi, "Charter of the Islamic Resistance Movement (Hamas) of Palestine," *Journal of Palestine Studies* 22, no. 4 (summer 1993), 127, https://www.palestine-studies.org/sites/default/files/attachments/jps-articles/2538093.pdf; Said Khatib, "Hamas Run Palestinian Youth Military Camp in Gaza," photographs, *Daily Telegraph*, January 31, 2015, https://www.telegraph.co.uk/news/picturegalleries/worldnews/11380165/In-pictures-Hamas-run-Palestinian-youth-military-camp-in-Gaza.html.
3. Psalm 140:1, People's Edition (C.A. Bartlett, 1843).
4. Obadiah 10, author's translation, emphasis added.
5. Adolfo Arranz et al., "Inside the Tunnels of Gaza," Reuters, December 31, 2023, https://www.reuters.com/graphics/ISRAEL-PALESTINIANS/GAZA-TUNNELS/gkvldmzorvb/.
6. Psalm 74:20, author's translation, emphasis added.
7. Ezekiel 7:11, author's translation, emphasis added.
8. Ezekiel 7:23, author's translation, emphasis added.
9. Jeremiah 51:35, author's translation, emphasis added.
10. Isaiah 60:18, author's translation, emphasis added.

Chapter 43

1. Amos 1:6–7, NIV, emphasis added.
2. Amos 1:7, emphasis added.
3. Silvie Zamazalová, "Before the Assyrian Conquest in 671 B.C.E.: Relations Between Egypt, Kush and Assyria," paper from master's dissertation, University College London, 2009, https://www.ucl.ac.uk/sargon/downloads/zamazalova_crossroads.pdf; Hussein Bassir, "The Egyptian Expansion in the Near East in the Saite Period," *Journal of Historical Archaeology and Anthropological Sciences* 3, no. 2 (March 16, 2018), https://medcraveonline.com/JHAAS/the-egyptian-expansion-in-the-near-east-in-the-saite-period.html.
4. 2 Chronicles 26:6, NIV.

5. 2 Kings 18:8, ERV, emphasis added.

6. Emanuel Fabian et al., "Footage Shows Hostages Being Rescued From Hamas Captivity in Daring Rafah Operation," Times of Israel, February 12, 2024, https://www.timesofisrael.com/footage-shows-hostages-being-rescued-from-hamas-captivity-in-daring-rafah-operation/; Michelle Nichols, "Israel Warns Half of Gaza's Population to Move South, UN Says," Reuters, October 12, 2023, https://www.reuters.com/world/un-says-israeli-military-warns-11-mln-gazans-relocate-south-2023-10-13/.

Chapter 44

1. Yuval Azulay, "Elbit CEO: 'We Recruited Hundreds of Employees and Brought Back Retirees Due to Demand and War,'" Calcalist, November 28, 2023, https://www.calcalistech.com/ctechnews/article/dyvahswpj.

2. 1 Samuel 13:19, ERV, emphasis added.

3. "Operation Swords of Iron," Jerusalem Post, accessed May 12, 2024, https://www.jpost.com/tags/operation-swords-of-iron.

Chapter 45

1. Revelation 12:15, emphasis added.

2. Isaiah 59:19.

3. Brandon Friedman and Joshua Krasna, "Between Swords of Iron and the Al Aqsa Deluge: The Regional Politics of the Israel-Hamas War," Foreign Policy Research Institute, November 1, 2023, https://www.fpri.org/article/2023/11/between-swords-of-iron-and-the-al-aqsa-deluge-the-regional-politics-of-the-israel-hamas-war/.

Chapter 47

1. Genesis 2:1–3.

2. Exodus 20:8.

3. "Shabbat 101," My Jewish Learning, accessed May 12, 2024, https://www.myjewishlearning.com/article/shabbat-101/.

4. Patrick Anidjar, "Opening the Gates of Hell: How Hamas Carnage Unfolded on Israel's 'Black Shabbat,'" Times of Israel, October 27, 2023, https://www.timesofisrael.com/opening-the-gates-of-hell-how-hamas-carnage-unfolded-on-israels-black-shabbat/.

Chapter 48

1. Leviticus 23:36.

2. "Shemini Atzeret and Simchat Torah," Judaism 101, accessed May 13, 2024, https://www.jewfaq.org/shemini_atzeret.

3. "Shemini Atzeret-Simchat Torah: FAQ," Tablet, October 9, 2009, https://www.tabletmag.com/sections/belief/articles/simchat-torah-faq.

4. "Palestinians in Gaza and the West Bank Celebrate on October 7," MEMRI TV, emphasis added.

5. "Simchat Torah: About," Sephardic U, accessed May 13, 2024, https://sephardicu.com/holidays/simchat-torah/.

6. "Palestinians in Gaza and the West Bank Celebrate on October 7," MEMRI TV.

7. AFT and TOI staff, "Arab Support for Palestinians Swelled by Euphoria Over Hamas Blow to Israel," Times of Israel, October 10, 2023, https://www.timesofisrael.com/arab-support-for-palestinians-swelled-by-euphoria-over-hamas-blow-to-israel/; Mataeo Smith, "US and Israel Flags Burned Across World as Terrifying Scenes Show Tensions Explode," Mirror US, October 8, 2023, https://www.themirror.com/news/world-news/israel-flags-burned-across-world-133663.

8. "Religious Services Ministry to Distribute 100,000s of Shekels Worth of Sweets to Children," Jerusalem Post, September 28, 2023, https://www.jpost.com/breaking-news/article-760904.

9. "Palestinians in Gaza and the West Bank Celebrate on October 7," MEMRI TV, emphasis added.

10. AFT and TOI staff, "Arab Support for Palestinians Swelled by Euphoria Over Hamas Blow to Israel," emphasis added.

11. AFT and TOI staff, "Arab Support for Palestinians Swelled by Euphoria Over Hamas Blow to Israel," emphasis added.

Chapter 49

1. Leviticus 25:10.
2. Nimrod Luz, "The Holy Land From the Mamluk Sultanate to the Ottoman Empire: (1260–1799)," in *Oxford History of the Holy Land*, abstract, accessed May 13, 2024, https://academic.oup.com/book/45676/chapter-abstract/398062280; Ahmed H. Ibrahim, "Viewing the Tanzimat From Tulkarm," *Jerusalem Quarterly* 70 (September 19, 2017): 132, https://www.palestine-studies.org/sites/default/files/jq-articles/Pages_from_JQ_70_-_Ibrahim_0.pdf.
3. Arthur Penrhyn Stanley, in Charles William Wilson, *The Recovery of Jerusalem: A Narrative of Exploration and Discovery in the City and the Holy Land* (New York: D. Appleton, 1871).
4. "Immigration to Israel: The First Aliyah (1882–1903)," Jewish Virtual Library, accessed May 14, 2024, https://www.jewishvirtuallibrary.org/the-first-aliyah-1882-1903.
5. "Palestine Campaign," New Zealand History, accessed May 13, 2024, https://nzhistory.govt.nz/war/palestine-campaign/overview; Tom Segev, "View With Favor," *New York Times*, August 20, 2010, https://www.nytimes.com/2010/08/22/books/review/Segev-t.html.
6. Gerald Steinberg, "Remembering the Jordanian Occupation of Jerusalem," *Mosaic*, May 26, 2020, https://mosaicmagazine.com/picks/israel-zionism/2020/05/remembering-the-jordanian-occupation-of-jerusalem/.
7. "Arab Threats Against Israel," Committee for Accuracy in Middle East Reporting and Analysis, accessed May 13, 2024, https://www.sixdaywar.org/precursors-to-war/arab-threats-against-israel/; "The Six-Day War: The Liberation of the Temple Mount and Western Wall," Jewish Virtual Library.
8. "S.Res.176—A Resolution Commemorating the 50th Anniversary of the Reunification of Jerusalem," Congress.gov, accessed May 13, 2024, https://www.congress.gov/bill/115th-congress/senate-resolution/176/text.
9. "Presidential Proclamation Recognizing Jerusalem as the Capital of the State of Israel and Relocating the United States Embassy to Israel to Jerusalem," Trump White House Archives, December 6, 2017, https://trumpwhitehouse.archives.gov/presidential-actions/presidential-proclamation-recognizing-jerusalem-capital-state-israel-relocating-united-states-embassy-israel-jerusalem/.

Chapter 50

1. Olivia B. Waxman, "How the Yom Kippur War Changed Israel," *Time*, October 11, 2023, https://time.com/6322802/yom-kippur-war-israel-history/.
2. "Mrs. Meir Was Close to Suicide at Early Stages of the Yom Kippur War," *Jewish Telegraph Agency*, December 14, 1979, https://www.jta.org/archive/mrs-meir-was-close-to-suicide-at-early-stages-of-the-yom-kippur-war; Waxman, "How the Yom Kippur War Changed Israel."
3. Waxman, "How the Yom Kippur War Changed Israel"; Lorris Beverelli, "The Importance of the Tactical Level: The Arab-Israeli War of 1973," The Strategy Bridge, November 19, 2019, https://thestrategybridge.org/the-bridge/2019/11/19/the-importance-of-the-tactical-level-the-arab-israeli-war-of-1973; Steven Simon, "The Israel That Fought the Yom Kippur War No Longer Exists," *Responsible Statecraft*, October 6, 2023, https://responsiblestatecraft.org/yom-kippur-war-50th-anniversary/.
4. Adam Goldman et al., "Where Was the Israeli Military?," *New York Times*, updated January 3, 2024, https://www.nytimes.com/2023/12/30/world/middleeast/israeli-military-hamas-failures.html.
5. Isabel Kershner, "Hamas Attack Has Haunting Echoes of the 1973 Yom Kippur War," *New York Times*, October 7, 2023, https://www.nytimes.com/2023/10/07/world/middleeast/for-many-israelis-the-attacks-have-haunting-echoes-of-the-1973-yom-kippur-war.html.
6. Kershner, "Hamas Attack Has Haunting Echoes of the 1973 Yom Kippur War."

Chapter 51

1. Kershner, "Hamas Attack Has Haunting Echoes of the 1973 Yom Kippur War."

2. *Encyclopaedia Britannica*, s.v. "Six-Day War," updated May 5, 2024, https://www. britannica.com/event/Six-Day-War.

Chapter 52

1. Deuteronomy 4:30, author's translation, emphasis added.
2. Matthew 24:12.

Chapter 53

1. Revelation 6:2.
2. Revelation 6:4.
3. Revelation 6:5–6.
4. Revelation 6:8.
5. Revelation 6:8.
6. *Encyclopaedia Britannica*, s.v. "Flag of Palestine Liberation Organization," accessed May 13, 2024, https://www.britannica.com/topic/flag-of-Palestine-Liberation-Organization; Elie Podeh, "The Symbolism of the Arab Flag in Modern Arab States: Between Commonality and Uniqueness," *Nations and Nationalism* 17, no. 2 (January 2011): 423–4, https://www.researchgate.net/publication/230308624_The_symbolism_of_the_Arab_flag_in_modern_Arab_states_Between_commonality_and_uniqueness.
7. Revelation 6:2, emphasis added.
8. Revelation 6:4, emphasis added.
9. Revelation 6:5, emphasis added.
10. Revelation 6:8, author's translation, emphasis added.

Chapter 54

1. Revelation 16:13, author's translation.
2. Revelation 16:14.
3. Amr Hamzawy, "Pay Attention to the Arab Public Response to the Israel-Hamas War," *Emissary*, November 1, 2023, https://carnegieendowment.org/2023/11/01/pay-attention-to-arab-public-response-to-israel-hamas-war-pub-90893; "Germany Announces Complete Ban of Hamas Activities," Al Jazeera, November 2, 2023, https://www.aljazeera.com/news/2023/11/2/germany-announces-complete-ban-of-hamas-activities; Yash Bajaj, "London: People, With Palestine Flags, Celebrate Hamas' Attack on Israel," *Times Now*, October 8, 2023, https://www.timesnownews.com/world/london-people-with-palestine-flags-celebrate-hamas-attack-on-israel-video-article-104248832; Mauricio Casillas, "Crowds Rally in DC to Stand in Solidarity, Pressure US After Hamas Attack on Israel," NBC4 Washington, October 9, 2023, https://www.nbcwashington.com/news/local/crowds-rally-in-dc-to-stand-in-solidarity-pressure-us-after-hamas-attack-on-israel/3439583/.
4. "Jewish Man and Woman Attacked in Ypres," *Brussels Times*, October 12, 2023, https://www.brusselstimes.com/735385/jewish-man-and-woman-attacked-in-ypres; Etan Smallman, "Jews Are Not Safe on Britain's Campuses," UnHerd, November 9, 2023, https://unherd.com/2023/11/jews-are-no-longer-safe-on-britains-campuses/?=refinnar; Kelsey Osgood, "Orthodox Jews Aren't Safe in New York," UnHerd, November 15, 2023, https://unherd.com/2023/11/orthodox-jews-arent-safe-in-new-york/; "ADL Records Dramatic Increase in U.S. Antisemitic Incidents Following Oct. 7 Hamas Massacre," Anti-Defamation League, October 24, 2023, https://www.adl.org/resources/press-release/adl-records-dramatic-increase-us-antisemitic-incidents-following-oct-7.
5. Ariel Zilber, "Coca-Cola Has Quietly Scrubbed References to Hamas-Supporting BLM From Its Website," *New York Post*, October 23, 2023, https://nypost.com/2023/10/23/business/coca-cola-quietly-removed-references-to-hamas-supporting-blm-from-website/; Patrick Staveley, "Australian Jewish Community Argues NSW Police's Claims Pro-Palestine Protesters Chanted Where's the Jews' Is No Better," *SkyNews*, February 2, 2024, https://www.skynews.com.au/australia-news/mob-of-thugs-executive-council-of-australian-jewry-shut-down-police-revelation-of-what-propalestinian-protesters-really-shouted-at-opera-house/news-story/98faca7992cdec9f4b1b4700eb43ddb3; Dara Horn, "Why the Most Educated People in America Fall for Anti-Semitic Lies," *The Atlantic*, February 15, 2024, https://www.theatlantic.com/ideas/archive/2024/02/

jewish-anti-semitism-harvard-claudine-gay-zionism/677454/; Luke Tress, "Pair of Swastikas Spotted at Pro-Palestinian Rally at NYC Christmas Tree Lighting," Times of Israel, November 30, 2023, https://www.timesofisrael.com/pair-of-swastikas-spotted-at-pro-palestinian-rally-at-nyc-christmas-tree-lighting/; TOI Staff, "Antisemitic Cartoons Proliferate in Mideast Amid Israel-Hamas War, ADL Report Finds," Times of Israel, December 21, 2023, https://www.timesofisrael.com/antisemitic-cartoons-proliferate-in-mideast-amid-israel-hamas-war-adl-report-finds/.

6. Ryan Chatelain, "Harvard President Faces Backlash Over Response to Hamas Attacks on Israel," Spectrum News NY1, October 11, 2023, https://ny1.com/nyc/all-boroughs/education/2023/10/11/harvard-president-faces-backlash-over-response-to-hamas-attacks-on-israel.

Chapter 55

1. Ezekiel 38:8, emphasis added.

2. Don Stewart, "What Is the Age/Day Theory?," Blue Letter Bible, accessed May 12, 2024, https://www.blueletterbible.org/faq/don_stewart/don_stewart_657.cfm.

3. Ezekiel 38:11–12.

4. Ezekiel 38:15–23.

5. Ezekiel 27:10; 36:8; 38:2, 5.

6. *Encyclopaedia Britannica*, "Sudan: History, Map, Area, Population, Religion, & Facts," May 11, 2024, https://www.britannica.com/place/Sudan/The-kingdom-of-Kush#ref245867; "Room 65, Sudan, Egypt and Nubia: Prehistory—AD 1000s," British Museum, accessed May 12, 2024, https://www.britishmuseum.org/collection/galleries/sudan-egypt-and-nubia#; "Representing Cush in the Hebrew Bible—Biblical Archaeology Society," Biblical Archaeology Society, accessed May 12, 2024, https://www.biblicalarchaeology.org/magazine/representing-cush-in-the-hebrew-bible/.

7. Nakhoul, "How Hamas Secretly Built a 'Mini-Army' to Fight Israel," emphasis added.

8. "Wikileaks: Iranian Weapons Pass Through Sudan to Hamas," *Sudan Tribune*, December 19, 2010, https://sudantribune.com/article37017/, emphasis added.

9. Marwa Awad, "Egypt's Bedouin Smugglers Ply Arms Trade to Gaza," Reuters, December 15, 2010, https://www.reuters.com/world/middle-east/how-hamas-secretly-built-mini-army-fight-israel-2023-10-13/, emphasis added.

10. "Sudan Blames Israel for Khartoum Arms Factory Blast," BBC News, October 24, 2012, https://www.bbc.com/news/world-africa-20050781; Khalid Abdelaziz, Nafisa Eltahir, and John Irish, "After Fall of Bashir, Sudan Closes Door on Support for Hamas," Reuters, September 23, 2021, https://www.reuters.com/world/africa/after-fall-bashir-sudan-closes-door-support-hamas-2021-09-23/.

11. Abdelaziz et al., "After Fall of Bashir."

12. Nahum 3:9.

13. Rick Wadholm Jr., "Gog, Magog, and Premillennialism," *W.onderful W.orld of W.adholms*, July 18, 2014, https://rickwadholmjr.wordpress.com/2014/07/18/gog-magog-and-premillennialism/.

14. Flavius Josephus, *The Antiquities of the Jews*, trans. William Whiston (Project Gutenberg), chap. 6, 1, accessed May 12, 2024, https://www.gutenberg.org/files/2848/2848-h/2848-h.htm.

15. Samer Al-Atrush Tunis, "Marwan alAshqar: Hamas Envoy to Libya Attempted to Smuggle Missiles Into Gaza," *Times* (London), accessed May 12, 2024, https://www.thetimes.co.uk/article/marwan-alashqar-hamas-envoy-to-libya-attempted-to-smuggle-missiles-into-gaza-thclb0t68, emphasis added.

16. Ido Levy, "How Iran Fuels Hamas Terrorism," Washington Institute for Near East Policy, June 1, 2021, https://www.washingtoninstitute.org/policy-analysis/how-iran-fuels-hamas-terrorism, emphasis added.

17. Levy, "How Iran Fuels Hamas Terrorism," emphasis added

18. J. Richardson, "The Nations of Gog and Magog," *The New Moody Atlas of the Bible*, accessed May 12, 2024, https://joelstrumpet.com/wp-content/uploads/2018/04/The-Location-of-Magog-Meshech-and-Tubal-1.pdf; Seton H. F. Lloyd et al., "Anatolia:

Definition, History, Map, People, & Facts," *Encyclopedia Britannica*, March 28, 2024, https://www.britannica.com/place/Anatolia.

19. Jo Becker and Justin Scheck, "Israel Found the Hamas Money Machine Years Ago. Nobody Turned It Off," *New York Times*, updated December 28, 2023, https://www.nytimes.com/2023/12/16/world/europe/israel-hamas-money-finance-turkey-intelligence-attacks.html, emphasis added.

20. Jonathan Spicer, "U.S. Presses Sceptical Turkey to Curb Hamas Fundraising," Reuters, November 30, 2023, https://www.reuters.com/world/us-presses-sceptical-turkey-curb-hamas-fund-raising-2023-11-30/, emphasis added.

21. Abdullah Bozkurt, "Turkish-Backed Group in Libya Smuggling Arms to Hamas," *Nordic Monitor*, January 17, 2024, https://nordicmonitor.com/2024/01/turkish-intelligence-suspected-to-have-a-hand-in-arms-transfer-to-libya-in-a-breach-of-the-un-sanctions/, emphasis added.

22. *Online Etymology Dictionary*, s.v. "Persia," accessed May 12, 2024, https://www.etymonline.com/word/Persia.

23. Becker and Scheck, "Israel Found the Hamas Money Machine Years Ago," emphasis added

24. Kenneth Katzman, "Iran's Foreign and Defense Policies (R44017)," Congressional Research Service, January 30, 2020, https://www.google.com/url?q=https://crsreports.congress.gov/product/pdf/R/R44017/75&sa=D&source=docs&ust=1715561521522284&usg=AOvVaw00sBBuBVpRiIRt-6M4P2NF, emphasis added.

25. Michael Biesecker, "Who Builds the Weapons That Hamas Fighters Use," AP News, January 15, 2024, https://apnews.com/article/israel-hamas-war-guns-weapons-missiles-smuggling-adae9dae4c48059d2a3c8e5d565daa30, emphasis added.

26. Ido Levy, "How Hamas Built an Army," Washington Institute for Near East Policy, January 2, 2024, https://www.washingtoninstitute.org/policy-analysis/how-hamas-built-army, emphasis added.

27. Levy, "How Hamas Built an Army," emphasis added.

28. *Encyclopaedia Britannica*, "Ezekiel: Hebrew Prophet & Biblical Visionary," April 12, 2024, https://www.britannica.com/biography/Ezekiel-Hebrew-prophet; "Judaea: Ancient Region, Middle East History & Culture," *Encyclopaedia Britannica*, May 27, 1999, https://www.britannica.com/place/Judaea.

29. Ezekiel 38:9, emphasis added.

Chapter 56

1. Revelation 12:7, emphasis added.
2. Daniel 1:1–6.
3. Daniel 10:4–5.
4. Daniel 10:12–13, emphasis added.
5. "Persian Empire," History, May 30, 2023, https://www.history.com/topics/ancient-middle-east/persian-empire.
6. Daniel 10:14.
7. "From Friends to Foes: How Iranian-Israeli Relations Transformed Over 70 Years," *The New Arab*, October 23, 2023, https://www.newarab.com/news/how-iran-and-israel-went-being-allies-bitter-foes; Behnam Ben Taleblu, "When Iran Says 'Death to Israel,' It Means It," *Atlantic*, July 15, 2022, https://www.dailyalert.org/rss/Mainissues.php?id=84381.
8. "Country Reports on Terrorism 2021: Iran," US Bureau of Counterterrorism, accessed May 13, 2024, https://www.state.gov/reports/country-reports-on-terrorism-2021/iran/.
9. "Country Reports on Terrorism 2021," US Bureau of Counterterrorism.
10. Efraim Inbar, "Iran and Israel: The Inevitable War?," Abstract, *SIRIUS—Zeitschrift für Strategische Analysen*, 4, no. 4 (2020), De Gruyter, November 27, 2020, https://https://doi.org/10.1515/sirius-2020-4007.
11. Daniel 10:13.
12. Daniel 12:1, HNV, emphasis added.
13. Revelation 12:7, author's translation, emphasis added.

Chapter 57

1. Maziar Motamedi, "Who Was Mohammad Reza Zahedi, an Iranian General Killed by Israel in Syria?," Al Jazeera, April 2, 2024, https://www.aljazeera.com/news/2024/4/2/who-was-mohammad-reza-zahedi-the-iranian-general-assassinated-by-israel; "Counter Terrorism Designations; IRGC Foreign Terrorist Organization Designation," US Department of the Treasury, April 15, 2019, https://ofac.treasury.gov/recent-actions/20190415_33; "Spotlight on Terrorism: Hezbollah, Lebanon and Syria (April 8–15, 2024)," The Meir Amit Intelligence and Terrorism Information Center, April 16, 2024, https://www.terrorism-info.org.il/en/spotlight-on-terrorism-hezbollah-lebanon-and-syria-april-8-15-2024/.

2. "Hezbollah Barrages Deal Heavy Damage in Northern Israel," Agence France-Presse, May 24, 2024, https://www.france24.com/en/live-news/20240524-hezbollah-barrages-deal-heavy-damage-in-northern-israel.

3. Motamedi, "Who Was Mohammad Reza Zahedi?"

4. "Coalition Council of Islamic Revolution Forces: Zahedi 'Played a Strategic Role' in 'the Planning and Execution of Al-Aqsa Flood,'" MEMRI, April 9, 2024, https://www.memri.org/reports/close-associate-iranian-supreme-leader-khamenei-irgc-qods-force-commander-syria-and-lebanon.

5. Maziar Motamedi, "'True Promise': Why and How Did Iran Launch a Historic Attack on Israel?," Al Jazeera, April 14, 2024, https://www.aljazeera.com/news/2024/4/14/true-promise-why-and-how-did-iran-launch-a-historic-attack-on-israel.

6. Ben Aris, "Iran's Attempt at a 'Goldilocks Retaliation' Strike on Israel Was Designed to Fail, but Tensions Remain High," *bne IntelliNews*, April 14, 2024, https://www.intellinews.com/iran-s-attempt-at-a-goldilocks-retaliation-strike-on-israel-was-designed-to-fail-but-tensions-remain-high-320918/.

7. Aris, "Iran's Attempt at a 'Goldilocks Retaliation' Strike on Israel Was Designed to Fail."

8. John Jeffay, "15 Things You Don't Know About Israel's Air Defense Systems," Israel21c, April 22, 2024, https://www.israel21c.org/15-things-you-dont-know-about-israels-air-defense-systems/; Mark Vitner and Saul Vitner, "Israel Responds With a Precise, Limited Strike," Piedmont Crescent Capital, April 23, 2024, https://piedmontcrescentcapital.com/israel-responds-with-a-precise-limited-strike/.

9. 1 Chronicles 27:34, emphasis added.

Chapter 58

1. Jon Gambrell, "Iran's President and Foreign Minister Die in Helicopter Crash at Moment of High Tensions in Mideast," Associated Press, May 20, 2024, https://apnews.com/article/iran-president-ebrahim-raisi-426c6f4ae2dd1f0801c73875bb696f48.

2. Doha Madani, "Iranian President Ebrahim Raisi, Known for Brutal Crackdowns Against Political Opposition, Dies at 63," NBC News, May 20, 2024, https://www.nbcnews.com/news/world/iranian-president-ebrahim-raisi-dead-63-helicopter-cras-rcna152967.

3. Madani, "Iranian President Ebrahim Raisi"; Gambrell, "Iran's President and Foreign Minister Die in Helicopter Crash at Moment of High Tensions in Mideast."

4. Genesis 12:3.

5. Zechariah 2:8.

6. Reuters and TOI staff, "Iranian President Threatens Israel's Annihilation If Major Attack Occurs," Times of Israel, April 23, 2024, https://www.timesofisrael.com/iranian-president-threatens-israels-annihilation-if-major-attack-occurs/.

7. TOI staff and Agencies, "'Nothing Will Be Left of Israel' If It Attacks Us, Iranian Commander Threatens," Times of Israel, September 28, 2019, https://www.timesofisrael.com/nothing-will-be-left-of-israel-if-it-attacks-iranian-commander-threatens/.

8. "Nothing Will Remain of Israeli Regime If It Attacks Iran: Raisi," Islamic Republic News Agency, April 23, 2024, https://en.irna.ir/news/85454609/Nothing-will-remain-of-Israeli-regime-if-it-attacks-Iran-Raisi.

9. "Former Iran President Threatens Israel in Final Public Speech," *Middle East Monitor*, May 20, 2024, https://www.middleeastmonitor.com/20240520-former-iran-president-threatens-israel-in-final-public-speech/.

10. Ezekiel 39:2–4.

11. "Nothing Will Remain of Israeli Regime if It Attacks Iran," Islamic Republic News Agency.
12. Leviticus 24:16.
13. Leviticus 24:16.
14. Leviticus 24:23.

Chapter 59

1. Revelation 13:1–2, author's translation.
2. 2 Thessalonians 2:3–4, ESV, emphasis added.
3. 2 Thessalonians 2:4.
4. Revelation 13:6.
5. Daniel 7:25, LEB.
6. 2 Thessalonians 2:4, author's translation.
7. 1 John 4:3.

Chapter 61

1. Revelation 16:14, 16.

Chapter 62

1. Revelation 12:13–14, author's translation, emphasis added.
2. Daniel 12:7, emphasis added.
3. Daniel 7:25, author's translation, emphasis added.
4. Revelation 13:5, emphasis added.
5. Revelation 12:6, emphasis added.
6. Revelation 11:2, emphasis added.
7. Daniel 9:27, emphasis added.
8. Daniel 9:27.

Chapter 63

1. Isaiah 2:2.
2. "Ben Gvir Reportedly Makes It a Ministry Policy to Change Temple Mount Status Quo," Times of Israel, April 17, 2024, https://www.timesofisrael.com/ben-gvir-reportedly-makes-it-a-ministry-policy-to-change-temple-mount-status-quo/.
3. Nidal Al-Mughrabi and Sinan Abu Mayzer, "Violence Erupts Again at Jerusalem's Al-Aqsa Mosque," Reuters, April 5, 2023, https://www.reuters.com/world/middle-east/cross-border-fire-gaza-after-israeli-police-raid-al-aqsa-mosque-2023-04-05/.
4. Richard Allen Greene et al., "Attacks in West Bank, Tel Aviv as Tensions Remain High Following Israeli Strikes," CNN, April 8, 2023, https://www.cnn.com/2023/04/06/middleeast/lebanon-rockets-israel-intl/index.html.
5. "Resistance Groups Warn Israel Against 'Playing With Fire' After Al-Aqsa Mosque Incursion," PressTV, April 26, 2023, https://www.presstv.ir/Detail/2023/04/26/702244/Palestinian-groups-warn-Israel-against-%E2%80%98playing-with-fire%E2%80%99-after-incursion-into-Aqsa-Mosque-prayer-space.
6. "Haniyeh Outlines Context and Objectives of Hamas Operation Al-Aqsa Flood," Middle East Monitor, October 9, 2023, https://www.middleeastmonitor.com/20231009-haniyeh-outlines-context-and-objectives-of-hamas-operation-al-aqsa-flood/, emphasis added.
7. "Haniyeh Outlines Context and Objectives of Hamas Operation Al-Aqsa Flood," Middle East Monitor, emphasis added.
8. "Haniyeh Outlines Context and Objectives of Hamas Operation Al-Aqsa Flood," Middle East Monitor, emphasis added.
9. Nan Jacques Zilberdik, "Fatah: Hamas Massacre Brought 'a Morning of Victory, Joy, [and] Pride,'" Palestinian Media Watch, October 8, 2023, https://palwatch.org/page/34628, emphasis added.
10. Giulia Carbonaro, "Osama Bin Laden's Letter to America: Transcript in Full," Newsweek, November 18, 2023, https://www.newsweek.com/osama-bin-laden-letter-america-transcript-full-1844662, emphasis added.
11. "Haniyeh Outlines Context and Objectives of Hamas Operation Al-Aqsa Flood," Middle East Monitor, emphasis added.

12. "Resistance Strikes Will Increase in Coming Days—Abu Obeida's Speech on the 100th Day of War," *Palestine Chronicle*, January 14, 2024, https://www.palestinechronicle.com/resistance-strikes-will-increase-in-coming-days-abu-obeidas-speech-on-the-100th-day-of-war/, emphasis added.

13. "Resistance Strikes Will Increase in Coming Days," *Palestine Chronicle*, emphasis added.

14. Matthew Tostevin, "Holy War: Red Cows, Gaza and the End of the World," *Newsweek*, April 5, 2024, https://www.newsweek.com/israel-gaza-hamas-temple-mount-islam-jews-jerusalem-red-heifers-jerusalem-religion-1886787.

15. Tostevin, "Holy War."

16. Abdennour Toumi, "Al-Aqsa Flood Operation: Reactions in the Maghreb," NATO Defense College Foundation, March 13, 2024, https://www.natofoundation.org/food/al-aqsa-flood-operation-reactions-in-the-maghreb/.

Chapter 64

1. Leviticus 23:5.

2. "Gaza, Temple Mount, and the Passover Lamb: A Story of Holiday Conflict," *Israel Today*, April 5, 2023, https://www.israeltoday.co.il/read/gaza-temple-mount-and-the-passover-lamb-a-story-of-holiday-conflict/.

3. "Haniyeh Outlines Context and Objectives of Hamas Operation Al-Aqsa Flood," *Middle East Monitor*, emphasis added.

Chapter 65

1. 1 Kings 8:54–55.

2. 1 Kings 8:63.

3. 1 Kings 8:65.

4. 1 Kings 8:66.

5. Yitzi Hurwitz, "The Dedication of the Holy Temple," Chabad-Lubavitch Media Center, October 16, 2017, https://www.chabad.org/library/article_cdo/aid/3816050/jewish/The-Dedication-of-the-Holy-Temple.htm#.

Chapter 66

1. Revelation 12:17, author's translation, emphasis added.

2. Revelation 13:7, author's translation, emphasis added.

3. Daniel 7:25, HCSB, emphasis added.

4. 2 Thessalonians 2:3, emphasis added.

Chapter 69

1. Ephesians 2:12, 19, HCSB, emphasis added.

2. Ezekiel 37:10, emphasis added.

3. Aaron Leibel, "The Unknown Story of Smuggling Weapons to Help Win Israel's Independence," *Jerusalem Post*, June 4, 2020, https://www.jpost.com/israel-news/the-unknown-story-of-smuggling-weapons-to-help-win-israels-independence-630300.

4. Jeremiah 30:10; 46:27, ESV.

5. Eric Black, "An Oath and a Chant," *Frontline*, accessed May 13, 2024, https://www.pbs.org/wgbh/pages/frontline/shows/oslo/parallel/13.html.

Chapter 70

1. Revelation 12:4, author's translation.

2. Luke 19:41–42.

Chapter 71

1. 1 John 3:8, author's translation.

Chapter 72

1. Revelation 12:11.

2. Revelation 12:12, author's translation, emphasis added.

3. Christian Goeschel, *Suicide in Nazi Germany* (Oxford University Press, 2009).

4. Psalm 136, NIV.

5. Shushma Malik and Caillan Davenport, "Mythbusting Ancient Rome—Throwing Christians to the Lions," University of Queensland, November 22, 2016, https://hpi.

uq.edu.au/article/2016/11/mythbusting-ancient-rome-%E2%80%93-throwing-christians-lions.

6. Lyubov Soskovets, Sergei Krasilnikov, and Dina Mymrina, "Persecution of Believers as a Systemic Feature of the Soviet Regime," *Semantic Scholar* (2016), https://doi.org/10.1051/shsconf/20162801098.

Chapter 73

1. Jeremiah 31:35–36, author's translation, emphasis added.

Chapter 75

1. 1 Corinthians 2:9.

ABOUT JONATHAN CAHN

Jonathan Cahn caused a worldwide stir with the release of the *New York Times* best seller *The Harbinger* and his subsequent *New York Times* best sellers. He was named, along with Billy Graham, as one of the top forty spiritual leaders of the last forty years "who radically changed our world." He has addressed members of Congress and spoken at the United Nations. He is known as a prophetic voice for our times and for the opening up of the deep mysteries of God. His teachings and prophetic messages on his YouTube channel have over one hundred million views.

Jonathan leads Hope of the World, a ministry of bringing the Word of God to the world and sponsoring projects of compassion to the world's most needy—and Beth Israel/the Jerusalem Center, his ministry base and worship center in Wayne, New Jersey, just outside New York City. He ministers and speaks throughout America and the world.

To get in touch, to receive prophetic updates, to receive free gifts from his ministry (special messages and much more), to find out about his over two thousand messages and mysteries, for more information, to contact him, or to have a part in the Great Commission, use the following contacts.

Go to: Or write direct to:
HopeoftheWorld.org   Hope of the World
                                                Box 1111
                                                Lodi, NJ 07644 USA

*To be kept up to date and see some of Jonathan's latest words and messages, go to:

Facebook: Jonathan Cahn (Official Site)
YouTube: Jonathan Cahn Official
X (formerly Twitter):   @Jonathan_Cahn
Instagram: jonathan.cahn
Email: contact@hopeoftheworld.org

*To find out how you can go to the Holy Land with Jonathan** on one of his upcoming **Israel Super Tours** go to **JonathanCahnIsraelTours.com** or email at contact@hopeoftheworld.org.

OUR <u>FREE</u> GIFT TO YOU

Dear Reader,

We sincerely hope that *The Dragon's Prophecy* was as awe-inspiring and mind-blowing as Jonathan Cahn's previous *New York Times* bestselling masterpieces.

If you can't wait to read more explosive books from Jonathan Cahn, you're in luck! We have a **FREE GIFT** for you.

SCAN THIS CODE

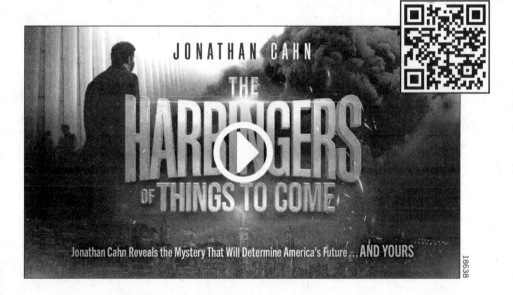

Scan the code above to get this **FREE GIFT**, or go to:

BooksByJonathanCahn.com/freebie2024

May the Lord be with you in the times to come and forevermore!

—Publishers of FrontLine books

FRONT LINE